THE SECRET LETTERS OF
PRESIDENT DONALD J. TRUMP, AGED 73

VOLUMES ONE AND TWO
(From March 2018 – June 2019)

Praises for The Secret Letters of President Donald Trump, Age 72 1/6.

"Rudolf Hess should be arrested and locked up for breaking into president Donald Trump's brain. How he came out alive is something that I'm sure the Russians are investigating."
—*New York Daily Apple*

"Don't pick this book up unless you are willing to let reason, your reason, crumble as soon as laughter tickles it."
—*Miami Bell*

"Rudolf t.g. Hess must have been dropped on a hard floor when he was a toddler. There is no other way to explain his unique madness."
—*Washington Ghostwriters*

"You must not read this fucking book if you do not want to be offended. LOL. I'm not kidding." —*London Daily Chips*

"If you do not find yourself screaming at some of these letters, then you are a conscientious objector carried away by your chuckles."
—*Publishers' Slush Pile*

"For making me spill my coffee on my pants, sorry, groin, I say fuck eight generations of your ancestors."
—*Moscow Golden Shower Times*

"Be ready for your conscience to lose its virginity before you open this book. You will not come out the same way you went in, even if you were President Donald Trump."
—*European Rags of Paris*

"Rudolf t.g. Hess has sprinkled lies into non-fiction the same way Bill Cosby sprinkled drugs into women's drinks, with the same effect."
—*Philadelphia Evening Answers*

"This Trump is smarter than the one in the White House."
Grace Upbeat, the author of *My Nuclear Button Is Bigger than Yours*.

"For spending this much time inside Trump's head, I hope Rudolf t.g. Hess is forced to pay rent." – Tony Bacharach, DC Attorney.

"I don't care who you are, this Trump will surprise you in some pleasant ways as you read these letters. Sometimes, against his best interest, he is really really pee your pant funny." - Jasper Bush, Rock Musician.

"Finally, I understood Donald Trump's mind. Thank you, Mr. Hess." – Michael York, Homeless New Yorker.

THE SECRET LETTERS OF
PRESIDENT DONALD J. TRUMP, AGED 73

Yours truly,
Donald J. Trump
(45th President of the United States of America)

VOLUMES ONE AND TWO
(From March 2018 – June 2019)

Rudolf t.g. Hess

Irokopost
Books

Winepress
by **NOIRLEDGE**

Jointly published by
Noirledge Limited, under its Winepress Publishing imprint
and Irokopost Media Group Inc., Rosedale, NY 11422

Noirledge Limited
Suite 223, Ogun-Osun River Basin Development Authority,
Adjacent Palms Shopping Mall, Ring-Road, Ibadan
Tel: +234 809 816 4359 | +234 805 316 4359
Email: winepress@noirledge.com | www.noirledge.com
twitter.com/noirledge | facebook.com/noirledge | instagram.com/noirledge

ISBN: 978-1-9499110-0-8
A catalogue record for this book is available from the National Library of Nigeria.

Cover Design: Stephen Adakole
Book Design: Servio Gbadamosi
Typesetting: www.noirledge.com

Dedication

To
Edna, my wife
For the decorations you brought to my life.
There is no better book to dedicate to you than this one.

There is a fat worm in these waters
In these lands a predatory worm:
He ate the Island's flag
Hoisting up his overseer's banner,
He was nourished from the captive blood
Of the poor buried patriots.

—Muños Marín by Pablo Neruda

Contents

You've read his tweets, but have you read his letters? If his tweets were that bombastic, how would his secret letters be? Welcome in.

Donald Trump's Letters to:
Volume I:

Donald Trump's Letters to:
Volume II:

Renunciation

Because in today's world we have to warn customers to eat the bread and not the plastic wrap and to drink very hot coffee slowly and not in one go, it is necessary to state here that this book is a work of satire.

You know, the way a short story is fiction. Yeah! But these days, you need to make it clear, else someone calls it fake news.

So, let me make it abundantly clear. Some names in this book are real names. What is not real is the name of the author. Some events depicted in this book actually happened. What did not actually happen is what the author of the letters thinks about these events. Okay, we don't know if it happened. It could have. Considering...

Believe me, we do not need authorization to break into the brain of anyone and take up residence. After all, every night when we dream, people, imaginary and real, break into our subconscious minds to interact with us.

That is all that I have done here.

Any character that feels a little defamed should take a second look at the fame this work bestowed upon him or her. Anyone who feels a little bit libeled should consider that by making an appearance here, his or her place in high-end literature is secured.

I'm sorry that I have to say all these at the end of the book. (My God, I hope they did not trick me and put this at the beginning of the book despite my protest.) I just don't want to deface the book's opening pages by putting what is so obvious at the front.

I hope you will not demand a refund of your money—Amazon takes 55 percent, just so you know. And I'm sure it is part of their First Amendment rights.

Now, please close the book gently. I didn't say you should flip it on the desk. Close gently.

Thank you.

Now think deeply about what you have read—no, not this renunciation. I mean, the whole book. I bet you, it will soon begin to make sense. Yeah, it is that kind of a book.

As you do so, stay tuned for more works from the Wiseguy Satire Series. And thank you for taking this ride with me.

How I Got Possession of Donald Trump's Secret Letters

On the day Rachel Maddow of MSNBC got ahold of the exclusive story that two pages of president Donald Trump's 2005 tax papers were in the hands of a journalist, David Cay Johnston, I was one of the four million people who were glued to the TV watching and waiting for her to reveal the contents of the tax papers.

I made popcorn and lemonade, took off my shoes, and sat on the couch with my legs propped up. I set my cell phone on vibrate to escape the ringing of friends who would want to discuss the matter before the presentation was finished.

As Rachel dragged it on and on, milking it for ratings purposes, I flipped through other channels and back to her. At one point, I decided to write a comment on her show's MSNBC website.

"Get on with it, Rachel. Stop having an orgasm on live TV over Donald Trump's 2005 tax papers. You liberals are easily fooled. What if the tax papers were not sent to the journalist by a whistleblower? What if they were sent to him by Donald Trump himself?"

I posted the comment and waited. After about five minutes, I deleted the comment. I was getting paranoid over American liberals. I did not want anyone to come after me.

But it was too late.

I watched Mr. Johnston reveal that Trump paid a 25 percent effective tax rate. The total amount was $38 million. The 25 percent rate, which is respectable for American billionaires, always eager to avoid paying taxes, strengthened my suspicion that Trump could have released the tax papers himself to distract the country from the ongoing Russian investigation.

I was glad I deleted my post.

As a relatively unknown journalist, I was slightly jealous of Mr. Johnston. His possession of Trump's 2005 tax returns had once again brought him national limelight, especially for those who were not of age when he won the 2001 Pulitzer Prize for Beat Reporting. I was sure even if he did not want it to, the exposure would increase the sale for his best-selling book on taxes. It was the kind of break I needed. In these challenging days of journalism, any opportunity that a reporter gets must be maximized before the gig economy swallows us all.

I thought about Johnston's story and how he got the tax papers. According to him, he got a call from home that some documents came in the mail that he needed to see. He left his assignment post and returned home. When he opened the package, it was Donald Trump's tax papers.

He did not satisfactorily answer the question, "Why him?" He had known Trump for decades and was an investigative reporter who had written several books on taxes and how the American tax system favors the rich at the expense of the poor. But he was not the only one who had such a reputation.

One year after, I had forgotten about Rachael Maddow's not-so-big-revelation. Like many Americans, I had endured another unrealized expectation, as the tax revelation did nothing to move the needle of public opinion anywhere close to making president Donald Trump see the need for himself to release his tax returns.

And that was when the email came.

I could not identify the email address Wiseguysatire@gmail.com. I almost deleted it because of the title: "Today is your lucky day."

My hunch was that it must be one of those Nigerian scams or Eastern European phishing emails. I was sure it would talk about a fortune of a prince or president in Africa that I would get a share of if I helped move some money abroad. Or it could be a random lottery I had won without ever submitting my name. Knowing the endless creativity of these scammers, it could be someone selling Viagra over the Internet.

Just because I had never seen this particular title, I opened the email:

> Hey Rudi,
>
> Today is your lucky day. We saw what you wrote on the MSNBC website and we think that you are the right man to receive "The Secret Letters of Donald Trump" and share them with the world. Are you interested? If you are, just click reply.

The first question that came to my mind was, what did I write on the MSNBC website? I could not recall at that point. Like I said, it had been over a year ago.

But because I had no penchant for writing comments on websites, I flashed back and could recall what I wrote. But I had deleted it almost immediately.

Some years back, I had played along with one of the scammers who wanted help to move money from Senegal after his father died. I not only enjoyed my conversation with him, but I also was able to extract an article out of it. Remembering that, I decided to play along with this group.

I replied with a request to be reminded of what I wrote on MSNBC.

I soon got an email back that simply pasted the exact comment that I wrote—word for word.

Sweat seeped through the pores of my skin as I read. It did not make sense. Even if I did not delete the comment, just considering the number of comments made on the website on that day, why me? And how did they get my email address? I did not register on the website with my real name or my real email address. But the email they sent came to my real email address.

What else did they know about me? I had numerous questions. Just while I was still composing an email full of questions for them, I got another email. This one was brief.

"Are you in or out?"

At this point, my journalistic instinct kicked in. I wrote back that I was in.

"Great! We know your questions. We have no time to answer them. We will send you the letters as we capture them. If you like them, get them published and your career will be great again. If you don't like them, delete them and you will never hear from us. But if you choose to publish them, do not alter them. Publish as they are."

I desperately wanted to ask just one question, but they shut me down. It wasn't about how they got the letters or who owns the copyrights. It wasn't about how I would be able to prove to the world that they were authentic.

I consoled myself by just remembering that these were the same questions David Cay Johnston confronted when he got Donald Trump's 2015 tax returns in the mail.

As I prepared the letters for publication, more of them came in. It appears as if the people sending these letters were getting them as President Trump was writing them. Maybe they have control of his computer screen or the screen of whatever tool he was using to write the letters.

I guess with their publication, Trump will know his letters have been leaking out. So here are the secret letters of President Donald Trump.

THE SECRET LETTERS OF
PRESIDENT DONALD J. TRUMP, AGED 73

VOLUME ONE

Donald Trump's Letter to His Son's Teacher

Tuesday, March 20, 2018

Dear Teacher,

Today is the birthday of my son, Barron. I write you today because I need your help to teach my amazing son, Barron, some universal truths that I subscribe to and highly recommend for any young man who wants to be a success in America. I'm living proof that you don't need to fight in Vietnam or Iraq or Afghanistan to be a success. Believe me, those days are gone.

My son is a fantastic kid, just like his father. I would have taught him myself, but I am very busy running the country, making our America great again. It is a super tremendous responsibility, and I am sure that you appreciate my wholesome dedication to the task. I'm bigly kicking butts and giving the enemies of America hell. Dear teacher, don't teach him that Cold War era nonsense that I was taught at the Wharton School about Russia being an enemy of America.

No one really knows, but I suspect that my son is watching the filth that the fake news media are peddling about me. Stormy Daniels. Karen McDougal. Nasty people. Terrible! I'm talking about all the salacious and bigoted lies they tell about a magnificent person like me. Very sad! How could more people have watched that disgrace of an interview that Stormy Daniels had with CNN's Anderson Cooper, than my classy *60 Minutes* interview? The pit of hell that is the Internet is full of those types. Dear teacher, we need to do something about it. Please, steer my son toward the very few sophisticated and right channels left in American media, like Fox News and Breitbart news site. Do it, and half of the job will be done.

He is a good guy, my son. I'm sure he will listen to you more than he listens to Melania or myself. He resists, even though deep inside him, I know that I'm the greatest superhero he knows. I see it in the way he looks at me in awe when it is raining and I hold up the umbrella and he follows behind. If you doubt me, ask him to name his greatest hero and watch him gush about me and the great feats that I am accomplishing for America each blessed day to the astonishment of our enemies both foreign and domestic. Wonderful job I'm doing. Even the fake news CNN agrees that it is hugely unprecedented.

I write this letter not because Abraham Lincoln wrote one. I'm sure you know about it. By the way, mine is more terrific. Senator Orrin Hatch already said that I am smarter than Abraham Lincoln and George Washington put together. If you like, throw in Barack Obama. So, there is no contest here. I write this letter because of something very, very important to me. I don't want all these women coming on TV and talking trash about me to affect my boy and his relationship with women. Quite unfair! As I look at him, I'm worried that he is picking up the softness of his mother. That will be a total disaster. I want him to, instead, pick up the sternness of my beloved, Ivanka—my perpetual Miss Universe. She is a tough cookie, like her father. She is a maestro in the art of the deal.

I want my boy to be crazy enough to believe in himself and the possibilities of everything his mind conjures. That is 100 percent true. Did I mention that he is destined to be a winner? I would hate to see him toe the lines of those lightweight "monkey see, monkey do" types that are common with lazy African-American people. I want him to be as smooth as a real estate salesman, a successful one at that, not the heavily indebted Jared Kushner types. Let the failures amongst his peers waste the low energy they have (just like Mitt Romney and Jeb Bush) talking about him while he soars to great heights that his father has carved out for him from nothing. Believe me, the $1 million loan from my father in 1975 is nothing compared to the billions and billions that I have today. Teach him that humility is totally overrated. Once he knows that, it is all he needs to be unstoppable. Not even ten Robert Muellers can stop him.

I want him to grow up looking at my face on Mount Rushmore and all the luxurious monuments created in my name and admire them with pride. Teach him to measure success by how freaking tall and large his houses are, and how marvelously beautiful his women are. When all is said and done, those are the only things that matter. Frankly, the rest of human postulations, like the spirit behind the Paris Agreement, are mere superstitions. Trust me, a kiss is a more tangible commodity than a soul. Build a great wall inside him to separate him from those out-of-control simpletons who think otherwise. I bet you, he will figure out how to make those simpletons pay for the wall.

Teach him not to aim for the stars, but to be the star, the brightest that God ever created. He may be twelve now, but soon, he will know the difference. Those dumb morons who aim for the stars get burnt, but those who become a star, like reality stars—how do I say this mildly—have women throwing panties at them on stage. That is where I want my son to be—in the same orbit with Princess Diana. When it comes to women, remind him of that great quote of mine: "If you need Viagra, you're probably with the wrong girls." Believe me, an orgasm is the closest anyone has been to heaven.

Teach him the rules of the good life. They are incredibly important. The weak serve the strong, the cowards take orders from the brave, and the victims soak the field of the heroes with their tears. Let my boy know that for him to be in the big league, it pays to be the menace. The best scenario is always the one that makes him come out on top. By the way, let him know that the only battle lost is the one fought with empathy. Let those with sickle cell help those with seizure disorders. We the good breeds are preordained to have a perfect life. It may be shocking to people, but he should not apologize for being perfect. It is not our fault.

My whole life is about drama subdued. Teach him to be at home with drama. Let drama energize him and trigger his antennas to stay alert. There is no higher order. It is in that sphere, like on a golf course, that he will find a lot of people. Teach him to sieve the fake and bad people in the heat of the drama. Let him not cry for those who must be fired. He must learn that regret and apology are disgraceful habits. Tell him that there is always another option even after the final answer.

When it comes to his obligation to America, teach him to hold close to his heart America first. Teach him not to be lured by the antics of people from some exotic lands. Let me tell you, those crooked and dangerous types have zero American homegrown skills. Their values are incompatible with our great American values. Teach him that it is not true that any way people worship God is valid. Okay? If that were true, I wouldn't have divorced Ivana and Maria, my first two wives. Some gods demand specific and rigorous catechism. And some other gods like their women as meek as Melania.

Let my son understand why I said that those exotic people in our country should go back home. To be honest with you, teach him that I'm trying to help them pay a debt they owe to the roads. In the words of *This American Life Sef*'s writer, "Every sojourner owes a debt/To the roads, the rivers/And the spirits that pilot the stars. /But the debt that lives in whispers/Is the debt of return…" You see, it is one of their own that said it, not me. My noble goal is to help them pay the debt of return.

Above all, teach my son to love himself. There is nobody bigger and better in loving himself than me, his father. Everybody likes me because of that. If he fails to love himself because of what people may say, he will end up a loser. And I don't want my son to be a loser, like Crooked Hillary Clinton, Weak Mitt Romney, and Lying James Comey. It will be totally embarrassing if it should happen to my son. The Trumps are the best in the world.

People are telling me that my son has got my great brain, so he is as smart as his father. Your job is to pull out of him the things that make him come alive. The rest will be easy. For I know, and you know, that he is not like all those stupid lads that you teach. He will answer his father's name—Trump the Great.

Dear teacher, do this for me, and I will give you the greatest deal of your life—a blanket pardon for past, present, and future infractions. Believe me, Paul Manafort would die for this.

Yours truly,
Donald J. Trump
The 45th President of the United States of America

Donald Trump's Letter to Hillary Clinton

Saturday, March 24, 2018

Hi Hillary,

I know that you will be surprised to receive this letter from me. I am that generous, you know. Despite what the liberal media wants the world to think of me, I am a practical Queens, New York kid who made good on his promise to his father. That is what it is all about for us from our part of town. Nothing personal. In our pursuit of success, we treat anyone in our way as an enemy combatant.

I've attained the pinnacle of self-actualization. You may not understand the feeling because it is somewhere you will never get to. I can imagine the bitterness you must feel having aimed for the glass ceiling with a sledgehammer. Your swing at it and your failure to shatter it must have left you scarred for life. Sad!

I recognize that. And I have resolved to do something to reduce the pain. Won't that be marvelous?

We used to be cool, Hillary. Remember that I used to donate to your political campaigns. You and Bill came to some of my weddings—I don't remember which ones. What really happened? Where did things fall apart?

I guess it is politics. In my quiet moments, I wonder how we ended up where we are now. Deep inside me, that I call you

"Crooked Hillary" does not make me feel good. I want to make that clear. Even though your history is full of crooked things you and Bill did, who doesn't have such a dark history?

Bill has Monica Lewinsky. I have Stormy Daniels. Bill has Gennifer Flowers. I have Karen McDougal. Frankly, there is nothing new about any of this stuff.

Here is my plan: after I win the re-election, I want to change things. I want to return to that jolly good fellow that you used to run after for campaign money. Melania said that I have become a monster. And that made me feel sad. Though, personally, I do not think that I have changed. I think that now she has the opportunity to follow my activities, including words that I say. Before she was just interested in fashion, shoes, leggings, makeup, and hats.

But, then, even Ivanka is beginning to despise some of my recent decisions. And that is unacceptable to me. You know how I feel about Ivanka. Isn't she classy?

As part of my plan, I will invite you and Bill to the White House. I can even throw in Barack and Michelle Obama. Who knows? It depends on how I feel that day. I mean, we can have a happy White House reunion. If Jimmy Carter is still alive then, even though I doubt it, I will invite him too. And maybe George W. Bush too. Why not? There must be a place for failed presidents.

To be honest with you, it sometimes feels lonely here. Nobody around here understands the extent of the burden that I bear. All that I have around me are people who think I am a moron and an idiot. Meanwhile, the people who have been here, like you and Bill, people who really understand what I am going through, are not talking to me. It sucks.

By the time we have the meeting, I must have done all the things that my native constituents demand of me. You know them very well. The people you and Obama aptly described as bitter, Bible-clinging, gun-carrying baskets of deplorables. Once I build the wall for them and imprison them in their miserable world of yesterday, like Native Americans, we will go ahead and move the nation forward.

That will be a great time to unify the country. I will be up for healings of any kind. If need be, I will smoke a cigar with your husband, Bill. I will give you a shoulder massage if that will help. It is going to be better than the weak massage Joe Biden gives. I'm talking about healing, full healing for us all. I will be born again.

At that point, I will stop talking about Mueller investigating your ties with Russia. I will also stop demanding that you should be locked up for your email scandal. But until then, you will remain my reliable bogeyman. I will keep calling you "Crooked Hillary."

But lest be assured that it will come to an end one day.

Until then, I'm your president.

Yours truly,
Donald J. Trump
The 45th President of the United States

Donald Trump's Letter to Chris Matthews

Saturday, March 24, 2018

Hi Chris,

How is reality looking from the very bottom of the mainstream fake news media where you are gasping for air? Truth be told, I have been a lifeline for all you low-ratings shows. In another one year of watching every step that I take, I am sure you will experience a different kind of thrill going up your lightweight leg.

I will give it to you – at least you are not sleepy like that Todd Chuck, or is it Chuck Todd? I do flip through your show some days to see if spits have started hanging down your lips.

I write just to let you in on a big scoop. Oh yeah. This one will blow your mind. Piers Morgan has just nominated me for the 2018 Nobel Prize for Peace. It is happening, baby. Just in case you have not figured it out – it is for my work in unifying the Korean peninsula, and also for solving a problem that no American president in the last sixty years could solve, which is to end the Korean War and denuclearize the Korean peninsula.

Please tell me what is left for me to do to impress you mainstream media types. In less than one and half years in power, I solved what Obama called the most difficult problem I would face as president. The rest, like Mueller and Melania, are minor league.

I have ordered the National Parks Department to begin work on putting the face of Donald J. Trump on Mount Rushmore. I hope you will support the move when it is leaked to the media. Even if you don't, it is going up anyway. I have given the order. Your support is irrelevant. By the time you all get to hear about it and begin your usual kick at the blue sky, I will be in Oslo, Norway, accepting the Nobel Peace Prize. Who knows, I may decide to come back from Norway with some good journalists to replace some of you fake news people. I'm unstoppable.

So, your darling Bill Cosby has been convicted. The original nigga will spend the rest of his life in prison. I wonder why we cannot send one of you journalists to prison, just like Bill Cosby, as an example of what could happen to fake news peddlers? I want to start with one of your people at MSNBC. I don't remember his name, but he tweeted, "Cosby convicted, heading to prison. Finally, there is hope for Donald Trump." For a tweet like this, that man should be locked up for life. How dare he compare me with Cosby?

Cosby is such a weak, and I must say, foolish man. How could you have the level of success and fame that he had and still resort to sprinkling drugs in women's drinks? I don't get it. Like I told Billy Bush, I am a man's man. I know my worth. I know that women want me. And I know how to go after them aggressively when I need to. I don't need the aid of any substance to make my move. That was so dumb of Cosby. He is a Philadelphia guy like you. I hope you are not into that kind of lifestyle.

So, I have seen you talk about Stormy Daniels as if you don't have your own Stormy Daniels. Why are all you liberals like this? Your CNBC people even paid hush money of about $40,000 to your accuser. And that is for making inappropriate jokes and comments. Imagine if I have to pay for such jokes and comments. It would be in billions of dollars. So, I actually got a great deal for my $130,000 payout to that woman. The bottom line is that I did not have any abnormal relationship with that woman.

Look at how Matt Lauer crumbled. Shameful! I knew that guy was plastic. I could see beyond his facade. He looked like the type that would sprinkle drugs into women's drinks. But when the lights were on, he sounded holier than thou. I wasn't surprised. Well, his lamps are dimmed forever.

Look at how Charlie Rose was destroyed. The old man of sleepy PBS TV was creepy to begin with. I was not surprised that he was groping small girls. The guy did not even respect his age. I could understand if he was dealing with mature and professional women, but interns? And for him to be walking around naked, that's disgusting. He deserved more than a spanking.

Look at Glenn Thrush, Mark Halperin, Lockhart Steele, Michael Oreskes, and so many others. Now they are coming after Tom Brokaw. These are people that you see in suits pontificating as if they are beyond reproach. You lived in Africa, so you must have heard this saying Omarosa told me. It says that there is no anus that you will dig your finger into without touching shit. Men will always be men. I like my men to be men enough to stand their ground.

Do you know why I survived while all these people folded up like pieces of newspapers? Because I am real. I am not fake. I do not present myself as a Pope of some sort. If Bill O'Reilly and Roger Ailes had listened to me, they still would have been around doing what they know how to do best. You don't ever want to appear weak. If you do, they pounce at you. That is the modus operandi of your tribe of condoners of evil.

I am sure that in your quiet moments you see my close similarity with John F. Kennedy, your hero. Like Kennedy, I have refused to accept the world that I have found. I am working hard to change it, from Iran to India. I am busting norms and rearranging alliances. I am shaking things up. You are a nice enough guy to acknowledge that when all your mischievous friends are not around. If you watch me carefully, you will see that over time, I will make politics work again in America. I am scrambling things as a prerequisite to rearranging them. Damn! That was a good one. You can use that expression to describe me. I don't need the credit.

In no time, I will cease to be elusive to your likes. You will then begin to see the hero in me. At that time, I will bring you closer as a token Democrat. I know that you like hanging around the staircase of power. If you like, I can tactically help you accomplish your life goal of becoming a US Senator. If you begin to treat me well, I may even consider having you as my biographer. Best opportunity that you will ever have. You can do for me what you did for Kennedy, Tipper O'Neil, and Reagan. You can be sure that any book with my image and name on the cover is a success. More success than you ever knew.

As someone who has proved beyond any reasonable doubt that I know how the game of politics is played, I can teach you a thing or two. I will tell you what I really think beyond the things I say when I call into *Fox and Friends*. You may become the luckiest member of your despicable class to get the first insight into how I plan to reshape America for the next one thousand years. Really smart ideas.

Write back and let me know what you think about this proposal.

Yours truly,
Donald J. Trump
The 45th President of the United States of America

Donald Trump's Letter to Pope Francis

Sunday, March 25, 2018

Dear Pope Francis,

Your Holiness, how are you doing? The last time we met, your face was gloomy until I stood up to leave. I hope this letter meets you in a better mood. I have forgiven you for spending only twenty-nine minutes with me when you spent over one hour with Obama in 2014. I have asked God to forgive you, for you did not know what you were doing.

Just so you know, after you asked my wife if she fed me their popular Slovenian cake, she ordered one from Uber Eats. Not my kind of cake. I'm perfectly okay with MacDonald's.

You know that I am not your kind of Christian and I do not need anything from your God. But I do think we can work together on a few things. So, stop checking out my Christian credentials. Check out my business credentials and my gut feeling. They are in excellent shape. My trinity is made of me, myself, and I. I cannot be wrong when my conscience is right. On my conscience are etched my ten commandments.

I know you were mad that I pulled out of the climate change agreement. Believe me, it is a hoax. I will get my scientists to reveal the secrets of the fake climate science when you visit me. As for the migrants, we've had enough of those Mexicans. Do you know that they have brought down the average height of Americans? Preposterous. If you like, let Rome take in more Muslims than there are Christians in Italy. When Muslims surround the Vatican and they start bidding to turn Peter's tomb into a mosque, you will understand why I'm fighting for you today.

Like so many men of the cloth like you, I know you do not understand me. I am not fretting about it either. Just like you leave some matters to your God in heaven, I leave some matters to my God, which is history books.

People like you think I'm going too far. As president of the greatest nation in the history of mankind, with the greatest army ever assembled by man, I know there is nothing like going too far. I am the "too far" they are talking about. I decide what is far enough and what is too far. The same way I decide what is classified and what is not.

In simple terms, I don't do sentiments. Believe me, nobody can manipulate me by appealing to my sentimentality. Not me. I see things the way they are, and my first instinct about things has always turned out to be right. It is true, even for projects that I have gone into that failed. Not so many of such, I must say. Even at that, the failure was never my fault.

I'm very tough. I don't bend to extortion by people who think I owe them. I don't owe anyone. I fly with my wings. I don't do favors either, because I don't need favors from people. I only need people to do the right things—half of which is being loyal. And if they fail to do the right thing, I get rid of them.

I don't need men or stones to rise up and praise me. The unprecedented crowd that came to the Washington, DC, Mall at my inauguration can disappear. It won't move me an inch. Unlike losers out there, I don't do this to hear their chants. I do these things because I can hear the chant of yet unwritten history.

I am entitled to one thing and one thing alone—my own stand from which I will try to move the world, just like anybody else. That I am moving the world the farthest of any other president in history is a tribute to my ingenuity. Believe me, the template of my success will be embraced by the generations yet unborn.

If I allow myself to be emotional like all of you, I will cease to be effective. I will join the rest of you in bending over and exposing my backside to those who specialized in drilling into the body to excavate the soul. Pathetic!

It is easy to betray the climate, the angels who escort rain into the clouds and the God who holds the sky in place. What is not easy to betray is our conscience. I will take the knife from friends and enemies, in the front and at the back, but I will never compromise the very thing that makes me, me. You can take that to the bank.

I have a quick question for you. I would have sent it as a tweet, but I know I don't want it to leak out to the press. I will write you a comprehensive letter at a later time.

Since they will not allow me to write "Trump" on the beams of the White House, I need to establish new norms and traditions that will live on when I'm gone. I'm thinking of building a new chimney at the White House when I am reelected president. I'm thinking of gathering the Electoral College people in a room that night for them to cast the vote. Can I please send an aide to come to the Vatican City to understudy the history and tradition of the chimney at the Vatican where smoke gushes out with the election of a new pope?

I am seriously thinking of my next inauguration. I want ten million Americans at the Mall. I want our greatest military in the world to have a parade and display our nuclear weapons for the world to see – and for the world to know not to mess with me. I want the parade to be like the Eucharist of our politics. If you could convince your feeble-minded followers for two thousand years that the Eucharist is the body and blood of that Jewish guy, I can convince Americans that the parade is the artery of our nation.

I had this dream where I was in a toga, like a Roman emperor with a crown on my head. As I was inspecting a parade, Mike Pence stabbed me in the back and ran into the White House. Pope, pray for Pence. Remind him that I am not as naïve as Caesar and he is not as smart as Brutus.

My whole life I have always believed that if one must think, why not think big? If you allow me to send an aide to study your smoke chimney, I can use that opportunity to send Michael Cohen out of the country on a special assignment to the Vatican.

If you do this for me, I will ask my wife's parents to cook *potica*, your favorite Slovenian dessert, for you.

I await your discreet response.

Yours truly,
Donald J. Trump
The 45th President of the United States

Donald Trump's Letter to God

Thursday, April 5, 2018

Dear God,

I'm Donald J. Trump. I guess you know already, but just in case you do not know, I am the 45th president of the United States of America. Okay, I'm just messing around. I know that you are fully aware of who I am. After all, all TV channels in heaven are talking about me just the same way they are doing on Earth. Humongous, isn't it? I am a ratings bonanza for them here on Earth. And I believe it must be the same thing there in heaven.

Come to think of it, maybe I should ask the Pew people to conduct a poll. I bet you, I will come out more popular than you, at least here on Earth. When I get there, I will also give you a run for your money. Terrific run! Mind you, I am not in any rush to get there. So, don't start getting any ideas, buddy.

I would have preferred to send you a tweet, but you don't have a verified Twitter account. Let me tell you, for a man of your status, that is a total disgrace, if you ask me. How do you clap back at your enemies, the Nancy Pelosis, the Obamas, and the Clintons, without a Twitter account? How? I don't get it. Very disappointing!

Anyway, that is not why I am writing you today. God, I have never asked you for anything. Have I? I have never asked you for forgiveness. I don't apologize for anything. So, you should be excited that I am coming to you today with the best deal ever.

My friend pastor John Hagee said that if I moved the US Embassy in Israel from Tel Aviv to Jerusalem that you would do anything I ask you to do. I didn't believe it at first. Then, the other night, you appeared in my dream and asked me to ask for anything, that you would grant it. It told me you were ready to strike a deal. I will now lay out for you the deal.

I am sure you saw me going to church on Easter day. You know I wasn't there to show reverence to you or to your son, Jesus. Forget about his mother—I place all women where they belong—on a different floor from mine. My people said the optics of me going to church was good politics, so I did that. It keeps my poorly educated followers very happy. Just like your followers who are deplorable. I mean, it is the only thing that I agree on with Crooked Hillary Clinton, even though I must not say so in public.

I write to you because the other day, upon my request, my generals showed me what our nuclear arsenals could do. You would not believe this. Do you know that I have the power to wipe out your prized creation, Earth, in just thirty seconds? All I need to do is to wait for the absence of General Kelly, maybe when he is in the toilet. Then I will grab the box containing the nuclear codes. Once I press some buttons (I have them written on my thighs), voilà! North Korea, China, and Russia are off the map of the world. Wait, did I say Russia? That was a mistake.

Last time I checked, I do not have a Trump Tower that I built with my own money in any of those countries. This power to destroy the world is very intoxicating. I wonder how you feel knowing that you have similar powers as I do. I guess the difference is that unlike me, you don't have Congress to explain your actions to. You don't have those unpatriotic knucklehead Democrats flexing their filibuster threat.

My question for you is this: if you had not destroyed the world in Noah's time, do you think that people would have this respect that they have for you now? I don't think so. That is why I am thinking of wiping two or three countries off the face of this earth, and right there I would be ranked higher than any other American president ever. Ever! Ever! Ever!

Learning from your action in Lot's country, Sodom and Gomorrah, all that I need to do is to make a case for the attack of those countries. Maybe I should say that they were taking gold showers in those countries on a Sunday morning. I can pull off an easy case against Iran and North Korea. I know Americans will want me to add Russia, their archenemy, to that list, but that is not happening. Putin and I will dominate the world the way Hitler and Mussolini dreamt of. Of course, I won't acknowledge this publicly, or some of those liberal types would lose their minds. If Hitler and Mussolini had won, the whole of the Western world would have become like Germany without those two million Muslims that Angela Merkel allowed in. Total disaster.

While I have your attention, let me ask you... can you reverse time and make me look the way I did when I was in the US Military Academy in New York. Remember? I mean, you should be able to do so, if you truly are the all-powerful God. Do it slowly so that you won't scare Americans. Instead of letting me grow older in the next seven years of my presidency, make me grow younger and younger until I stabilize as that dashing young man women were dying to date. If you do that transformation, I am sure that the American people would be so impressed that they would suspend their constitution and ask me to keep ruling as their president forever.

After all, the Chinese just did that for Xi Jinping, and the Russians just did the same for Vladimir Putin. America would need a strong man like me in power to keep up with those two. Frankly, I can take care of figuring out how to manipulate public opinion to get what I want. My good friend Putin has promised to help. Good guy! The only thing that can stop me is this age thing and growing old. Americans like their presidents young. I am sure you can do it. Whatever you want me to do for you to raise your profile, I will gladly do so. To be honest with you, if you want me to renovate your throne in heaven, I will send my Mexican workers over to take care of that for you.

While you think about my request, can you make that fucking Robert Mueller disappear? He is the worst person that you ever created. I know you can do it. After all, you made the Titanic sink. You can get one of those alien ships that are on America's skyline every night to come down and pick him up and take him to Jupiter where he belongs. I will ask our air force to hold fire until the operation has been successfully completed. Nobody gets hurt. Please drop him in the same Arabian Sea where Obama dropped Osama. Let the same whale that ate Osama eat him. Like I said, nobody gets hurt. If you do that, I promise to name that sea "Trump Sea." Why not? By the way, why is there no sea named after Trump? Long overdue, if you ask me.

I need to enjoy my presidency, you know. I need to put my legs up on the center table and relax. I need to enjoy the Oval Office the same way Bill Clinton did. I am sure Bill was not having fun when Kenneth Starr was all up in his business. Obama wouldn't have brought Stevie Wonder and that thug, Common, to perform in the White House if he had a Mueller after his black ass over his birth certificate or for smoking weed at Columbia University. Believe me, I have held up fine under intense pressure that no president in the history of America has endured. Don't tell me about Nixon. Nixon was a crook; I am sure you know that. Me, I only sell my name to buildings and most probably, my soul to women. Not bad… considering how rich I am. But you are used to that. King David did worse things and you still struck a deal with him and his household that the Jews could have the Star of David on their flag. I want the Star of Trump on the American flag. If I need to make a sacrifice to redeem myself, I am willing to sacrifice any of my children, with the exception of Ivanka.

I don't want to be selfish, my guy. If you need me to take care of anything for you here on Earth, just say so. You know what? You and I can form a partnership. You take care of some things from over there while I take care of some other things over here for you. Trust me, it can help fix your damaged reputation. I can absorb some blame from you while you do the same for me. The stupid amendments to the US Constitution won't let me do some things that I want to do. Bigly frustrating!

Oh, one more thing – about Ivanka. Is there any chance that you can make an exception to the rule? You know the rule that I am talking about. After all, Cain and Abel did something with their siblings or mother or daughter or alien to keep your creation going. My White House doctor, rear admiral Ronny Jackson, told me that genetic sexual attraction (GSA) is a real medical condition. So I am sure that you understand perfectly what I'm going through.

Don't think that I am crazy for raising these issues. You are the one that is considered bipolar or at least schizophrenic. Based on how destructive you are and quick-tempered, I think I am mild in comparison.

My proposal would be a win-win for us. Anyway, I have to go. General Kelly is bringing Melania over to see me.

Yours truly,
Donald J. Trump
The 45th President of the United States of America.

Donald Trump's Letter to Stormy Daniels

Thursday, April 5, 2018

Dear Stormy Daniels,

My name is Donald J. Trump. By the way, I am the 45th president of the United States of America.

I write just to say, fuck you.
Fuck you.
Fuck you.
Fuck you.
Excuse me! Oops, I've done that already.

In case you are wondering why—fuck you for making me look bad. In 2006, you looked okay. Maybe I should say, you looked decent enough then. But now, I don't think so. You look like a horseface. A sad horseface.

After thirty, you should've just checked your fat self out, quietly. But you didn't. So, I fired you the same way I fired that Miss Universe from Venezuela.

Fuck you for not making that distinction. For giving people the impression that I would ever touch a woman like you. Even if I had married you, by the time you had gotten this old with horrible wrinkles all over your face, I would have divorced you. That would be the smart thing to do. If you doubt me, ask my ex-wives, Maria and Ivana. I cannot deal with old layers like you hanging around me. Trust me on that.

Fuck you for putting an image in the minds of my fans that being with you meant that I have technically been with thirteen million other women. I may be bad in math, but I know that calculation too well. You sleep with about sixty men a month. Those sixty men, being in your industry, also sleep with sixty other women in a month. And those sixty other women had also slept with sixty other men. In essence, if you multiply those, 60 x 60 x 60 x 60 x 60, I essentially slept with over thirteen million women by sleeping with you without a condom. What an inordinate amount of diseases that I exposed myself to. Dangerous!

Fuck you for stealing $130,000 from me. Go and ask Mexican workers who work for me, I don't part with such an amount of money for that kind of shitty job you did. My whole life is about making sure I'm not cheated. It's only that I was running for president and I did not want any BS from you. Otherwise, I wouldn't have asked my lawyer, Michael, to pay you a penny. You don't even know how to spank a man – a basic requirement of your career. Such a disgrace! If you want to learn, go to Russia and learn from the best.

Nonsense!

I knew you were a Democrat. Pornography is to Democrats what Sunday Mass is to the family-friendly Republicans. I'm sure Schumer and Pelosi put you up to this. It is another plot by the deep state to impeach a president they do not like.

Fuck you for bastardizing my "Make America Great Again" slogan to "Make America Horny Again." Big-league theft!

Fuck you.

Fuck you.

Fuck you.

Excuse me! Oops, I did that already.

Yours truly,
Donald J. Trump
The 45th President of the United States

Donald Trump's Letter to Dr. Martin Luther King Jr.

Friday, April 6, 2018

Dear Dr. Martin Luther King Jr.,

How are you, man? Bored with channel flipping, I went on YouTube and saw this old clip of yours. I just finished watching the old footage of an interview you had with Fake NBC news. In the interview, you were talking of black folks having a disadvantage because they were given nothing after slavery. You were ranting about how white folks were given American land in the Midwest and in the West. You talked as if we did not know what happened when Robert Mugabe of Zimbabwe gave black folks land that he stole from white farmers. We knew what happened. They did not know what to do with the land. They let it go to waste. Unbelievable. So why do you think it would have been any different if America had given land to black folks?

What are we even talking about? We have tried it. Look at the historical black colleges. We gave them to you guys to run. What happened? You ran them into the ground. Losers! And you people turned around and came to the White House with hats in hand begging for handouts. Meanwhile, when I try to get them to answer, "Who is your daddy?" they are too pompous to say, "Donald J. Trump."

Even to find one of your fine women and give her to me, they won't. I am sure you know that I won't mind having one of your luscious ladies—not the second-class poorly endowed type like Lupita Nyong'o. When I was free to hunt, they kept saying no, even with my money. They do not want my kind of white man. As if there was not a time that I looked like George Clooney. Have you seen my New York Military Academy pictures?

Wasn't it in *The Wolf of Wall Street* that a character said that black women taste sexually different? If I remember correctly, it said black women taste like Jamaican sugar. I used to crave for such, but not anymore. Seeing me around them would destroy my reputation with the owners of this country. Have you tasted white women? Did you ask her while you were doing it if she had a dream that one day she would be moaning beneath a black man?

I feel we would have gotten along considering that you liked women just like me. But you were just too poor to come near my circle. But you eventually did well for yourself. Knowing where you came from, your achievement was huge. People say what happened to you was horrible. But I don't think so. You have a holiday named after you. So far, I don't see Democrats doing that for me. I have Mitch McConnell in my armpit. I could make his wife Secretary of Happiness and he would carve out a holiday in my name. The only obstacle in my path is the stupid filibuster rule in the Senate.

Another way to look at it is that, if you were still alive, you would have become like an older version of Jesse Jackson or Al Sharpton. Have you seen Al of late? He looks like those beef jerky sticks from Jamaica or the dry meats from Africa. As for Jesse Jackson, I think he has diabetes, or is it Parkinson's disease? Maybe you would have caught HIV or AIDS. Granted, the great American health system that Obama wanted to destroy with his Obamacare would have kept you alive just like it kept Magic Johnson alive. But who wants to live that kind of life, popping pills day and night? I have left instructions with my doctors: any day that my health is no longer tremendously excellent, 100 percent, they should quietly end it. My will has been written. Everything is all set. Don Jr. is up for the surprise of his life.

By the way, did you hear that I have brought black unemployment to its lowest level since recorded history? Did you hear that? I didn't do it by giving out food stamps and other handouts to your people in the inner cities. I did it by being a role model for them. You talked of America demanding that black people pull themselves up by their bootstraps. Why not? Your excuse is that America is asking people who had no boots to pull themselves up by the straps.

In case you have forgotten, my grandfather came here with nothing. He worked his ass off to establish the little things my father built on. With nothing but sheer genius, I have built on that little beginning to the place where I am on top of the world's most historical individuals. I am no longer in a fight with the rich guys on who is richer. I have since left that to them and *Forbes* magazine. The only question left unanswered now is whether my image should be carved on Mount Rushmore with the great presidents or whether a new gigantic one should be carved on a brand-new mountain. One of my people said I should consider a new mountain that emerged on Virginia Beach called Mount Trashmore. I will go and check it out as soon as I am done with this Mueller nonsense and I set my mind on building the Donald Trump Presidential Library. It would be sited at the original campus of Trump University. Rudy Giuliani is working on those tiny details. My job is to come and cut the red tape.

I am sure that I have taken a lot of your time. But before I go, I want to let you know that I had the privilege of looking at your FBI files the other day. That is one perk of being president and having your own handpicked FBI guys, not those leftover Obama moles. Anyway, so you were quite a stud, my friend. Without money, you got the church going, Bible-carrying women to fight for space on your bed. And by the way, I saw the white women too. Nice taste you had, I must say. How did you do that? You should have written a best-selling book on that topic, if not that, unfortunately, you got shot.

By now, I know that your wound must have healed, but the wound of this nation has not. Even after my white folks elected one of your people president, black folks are not yet satisfied. I don't know what more your people want. I was the only one screaming that the guy was born in Kenya, but your folks did not support me. Eight years after, he was disgraced out of office as I kicked him and his handpicked successor out. Now black people knew the man did nothing for them. Knowing how sneaky he was, he probably did more for his home country of Kenya than the inner city of Chicago where five hundred young black men are killed each year.

It may interest you to know my solution to that horrific killing field called Chicago. I said that every child old enough to hold his or her mother's breast should be taught how to shoot a gun. Bad gunmen thrive simply because good kids are not armed. Give every black kid on the street of Chicago a gun, and the bad guys will know that they do not have a monopoly of violence anymore. And they will chill. That is exactly what I do to bullies, using my Twitter account. I knock them to size and to the shape that I want. If you doubt me, ask Jeff Sessions. I am sure he was a senator when you were making your "I Have a Dream" speech.

Trust me, Mississippi is no longer burning. It is now a hub for alternative facts.

Let me tell you what some of your overpaid brothers whose sole job was to entertain us on the football field did recently. They followed that crazy boy Colin Kaepernick to disrespect our national anthem. They said they were protesting the killing of black thugs by the police. Disgusting waste of brain. But trust me, I got the job done. I went on my bully pulpit. I told my fellow rich white people who owned the sports teams to fire those sons of bitches. Knowing that they would go broke in less than one year after leaving their professional leagues, nobody told them to shape up quickly.

As you can see, I am taking care of my white nationalists who discovered this country, own it and built it. I know what you are thinking now. That it is the sweat of black folks that built this country. Wrong! It is the brain that designed the structure that truly built it. Not the ordinary labor that machines and animals could do. Do you understand? If you guys were the ones who built this country, why haven't your people transformed the inner cities? Why? Who is stopping you from building a replica of the White House in Harlem? Answer me.

I am not very sure that you know me. I am the billionaire whose life is the model of that '80s movie *Pretty Woman*, remember? Trust me, you are not my first choice of a leader. You are kind of a sissy. Malcolm X is my kind of leader. He is fierce and not intimidated. He was also not interested in the direction the wind blows. But during your time, you overshadowed him. Not anymore. This is Trump's time. Hm. I need to get Ivanka to trademark Trump's Time for me.

One last thing – did you hear that my "America First" speech now has more views than your "I Have a Dream" speech?

I just thought you would like to know that. All the best. When I win a Nobel Prize for Peace, I will write you again.

Yours truly,
Donald J. Trump
The 45th President of the United States of America

Donald Trump's Letter to Vladimir Putin

Friday, April 13, 2018

My buddy Putin,

Thank you for giving me the permission to mention your name in my tweet. It was clear proof that our back channel is working. Is my Jewish in-law, Jared, a genius or what? It fooled a lot of them. One called me to say that it was good to see the Donald getting his balls back. I have always had my balls. They might have been spanked here and there, splashed with golden shower mixed with holy water by daughters of Eve, but all and all, they are intact all the time and ever ready to spring into action when needed.

You know, we should do more of this. You give me the free hand to do some of those things that American presidents do to feel presidential. Things that do not make sense. Like firing a few Tomahawk missiles here and there, call you names while at the same time nothing changes fundamentally. I love that. One day, though, I hope someone will explain to me why we look away when hundreds of thousands of people die but make all the noise when sixty people die from a chemical weapon.

What we do is similar to what my grandmother and grandfather did during the days of their secret love affairs. My mother used to tell me of how my grandmother was a member of a church choir and her boyfriend, my grandfather, was a choirmaster. Each time my grandmother was late for choir practice, my grandfather would punish her severely for coming late. That way he covered up their love affair. Genius!

If you ask me, you can even shoot down one or two of our missiles over Syria. It only costs $2 million apiece. We have a stockpile of over 3,500 Tomahawk missiles looking for a war to deploy them. Do you know that we keep increasing our military budget each year, buying equipment that even our military is telling us that they don't need anymore just to keep our vast military-industrial complex going?

In your own case, I guess you are the Russian industrial complex yourself. You and your friends and family determine what to build and who to build it. You don't answer to any senator or useless FBI people. Imagine! My own Justice Department ordering a search of my attorney's offices without giving me a heads-up. Why did I appoint them? Why do I pay them? Can you believe it? Do I need to do an intervention in my Justice Department before they protect my interest? Do I have to do to them what you are doing in Ukraine? Or do I have to go the whole way and annex the unpatriotic bunch of people the way you annexed Crimea? I know why government sucks. I know why – nobody knows what they should be doing much less how they should do it. This kind of nonsense does not happen in the Trump Organization. Never!

So, my buddy, when are you going to visit me in Mar-a-Lago, Florida? I have a very nice place there. Though it is not as nice as your posh $1B secret hideout in Praskoveevka off the coast of the Black Sea. The CIA showed me pictures. I could not believe that you have your own casino in that place and four heliports. What I don't understand is why you also need a church inside the place. Come on! Didn't you hear that the pope recently confirmed what I have always believed—that there is no hell? You have quite good taste, I must say. But if you let me visit, I can show you a few finishing touches that you can add to it that would make it all the more exquisite. Trust me.

Oh, I have a small request to make. Would it be possible for you to announce that Russian women don't pee on themselves for others to watch? It would help Melania to calm down a bit. She thinks there is a 1 percent chance that such a thing happens in Russia. Such a rumor destroys the reputation of all the beautiful girls that Russia is endowed with. As someone who has been privileged to be in the midst of these heavenly beauties, it hurts me to know that some scrupulous hypocritical people have these images of Russian women in their dirty minds. It would be a PR win for Russia if you come out and deny the possibility of such in Moscow, where you don't even let gay people display their disgusting lifestyle. You and I are in locked steps about that one. It is just that the liberals in America have gone so far with their madness that I cannot put the genie back into the box. Otherwise…

Don't worry about the part about hookers in my hotel. Every country has its hookers. And sometimes, you never know who a hooker is, you know. Some smart men, with a single look, turn decent women into hookers. I think it was Dominique Strauss-Kahn, a lawyer who once said, "I defy you to tell the difference between a nude prostitute and a nude classy woman." Some hookers don't even know that they are hookers. Even if someone finally shows the world a picture of the Donald and some loose women in Moscow, I can explain it away. After all, we all have been around women that we had no idea were hookers.

Let me ask you, how do you handle people who do not abide by agreements not to disclose things? It is an epidemic here in America. People's words do not mean a thing anymore. Not even threats to have them pay $1million. I fear that the American society will collapse if there is no way to keep people from spilling all they know. I know you have mastered that act. Wonderful job you did in Britain. Please, when you reply to my letter, could you shed more light onto how you sealed the mouths of despicable slimeballs in Russia? Maybe my last letter to you wasn't detailed enough, or maybe something was lost in translation.

I don't even want to talk about loyalty. That tested ancient value is dead in America. People just open their mouths and say anything without consequences. In public, I condemned what you did to those untruthful former KGB slime balls of yours in England, but you know that I understand. Our whole Western society will collapse if things that happened at the Moscow Ritz-Carlton cannot stay at Moscow Ritz-Carlton. If every conversation that took place in Air Force One or the White House is made public, we might as well turn off the lights and shut down the republic. I don't know why all these weak-minded people in my country could not get it. I wished I were president in the '60s when John F. Kennedy could bring Marilyn Monroe to the White House and everyone would look the other way. These days, there are so many fake news people hanging around. You put them in their place so well in Russia that I want you to share some of your secrets with me. Please, when you have the time, do that for me, or else I may snap one day. You may hear that I walked into that White House briefing room, opened my zipper, and peed on all of them so that they really would have something to write about.

If for any reason I leave office before you, please assure me that no matter what the next president of the United States does for you, you will never reveal what happened between us. For the sake of my Ivanka, my Ivanka, please seal it for another seventy years after my death. I know you vowed that you are going to your grave with them, but you know how old age often makes someone start to rethink certain things. As for me, you have nothing to fear from my end.

How is our November midterm election looking like from your end? I am counting on you. The polls here do not look good. But I am sure that if you won reelection by 76 percent, you could make my party at least retain control of the House of Representatives. It is the only way I can avoid impeachment.

You know, sometimes I wish I did not marry again after my second divorce. I wish I could be like you, free and outgoing without anyone looking at me the way my vice president often looks at me when I am shaking the hands of beautiful women. All these church people have a way of making someone feel guilty. Maybe I should get a cross and wear it around my neck all the time, like you do, so that Mike Pence will stop looking at me with suspicion.

Or maybe I should get a dog. What do you think? Maybe it will soften my image and make these liberals get off me a bit. It is just that those animals stink. Also, I always feel that they are for low-class people. I have expensive carpets, and those animals pee all over the place, even those that are well-groomed. But I think it has done you some good in softening your image. Maybe we should arrange for you to give me a dog when I visit Moscow in the near future. That would be a symbol of a new relationship between our two great countries. Who knows, it may rub off on me some of your great leadership skills that I greatly admire.

Until next time.

Your friend,
Donald J. Trump
The 45th President of the United States of America

Donald Trump's Letter to Allah

Wednesday, April 19, 2018

Dear Allah,

I swear to God, I don't know if you are God or not. My gut tells me that you are something else… like a kind of substitute God. I am just being honest with you. And as you can imagine, that is one hell of a difficult thing for me to be.

Are you God that answers to another name? Why do I even care? It doesn't matter so much. I would have written your son, Muhammad, sorry, I mean, your prophet, but his worshippers, sorry, I mean, his followers, get angry so quickly at the slightest mention of his name. They particularly get mad if anyone mentions his name without putting "peace be unto him." I don't get it. But what business is it of mine?

Do you ever talk to the Christian God? Do you guys ever have a meeting of the Gods? How do you do this job? How do you decide where to intervene and where not to? Do you think of the poverty that is perpetuated by those who fervently carry your book, the Koran, and the book of the Christian God, the Bible?

I understand that unlike the Christian God, you don't have a son. Which makes perfect sense, because if you have a son, it follows that you have a wife, or at least a baby mama. The first means that you have some annoying in-laws while the later means you have to deal with your baby mama's obnoxious girlfriends who tell her all that is wrong with you and how to put you in your place. I have been there. That was why I decided to hire Michael Cohen to fix such inconveniences for me. I asked him to spend as much as a cool million dollars if necessary.

I don't care who you are, even as a billionaire, I still have to deal with those annoying matters. I think it is the same thing with all you gods. So, it is a smart move on your part not to have a son. If you ask me, whenever you want to have a baby, go for a daughter. They are easier to raise, and they have greater loyalty to their father than sons.

I think if you want to surpass the Christian God in a jiffy, you should have a daughter as soon as possible. A daughter as tall and beautiful as my classy Ivanka will do you good. When you have her, send her to Pakistan or India. Let her be persecuted and killed like Benazir Bhutto. She was a piece of ass when she was young. If Malala Yousafzai was given the Nobel Peace Prize for being shot, women would worship your daughter at this point in history.

But then again, you need a son to inherit your name. Daughters, you can love them to pieces, but they can still end up marrying Jews. Imagine if Muhammad had a daughter that he loved and she decided that she would marry a Jew. How would Muhammad feel about that? Despite my wisdom, I wouldn't have stomached it if not for the fact that my son-in-law is rich, in real estate, and understands the back channels of New York City business.

Forget all these preliminary talks. Let me go straight to why I am writing. You see, your worshippers are one nuclear bomb away from destroying the world. I don't know how long we have before they get it. They are already calling the bomb in Pakistan, Allah's own bomb. Who knows how long we can keep one of those from the hands of your bad children determined to kill us all? During dinner one day, Stephen Miller told me that another Saudi prince could go rogue again. But this time, instead of carrying his wealth into the mountains of Afghanistan, he may just use it to buy the bomb from Pakistan or a crazy country like North Korea. If that happens, we are screwed.

I write to let you know that it is not necessary. Please tell your worshippers that it is not. They have won. Anything drastic from them would be just overkill. Without firing one shot, your worshippers have taken over Europe from Britain to France. The fate of Europe was finally sealed when Germany let in two million Muslims from Syria, Iraq, and Afghanistan. In another two hundred years from now, the Emir of London and the Emir of Rome will be taking the wealth of Europe to Mecca. Stephen said that was how Mansa Musa liquidated Africa.

Out in public, I won't accept this, but I can confide in you that it is a hopeless situation for us. It is similar to the fight I'm having with those Mexicans. Even if I build a wall and don't let any one of them come into America anymore, we are already screwed. The number that are in already are having babies like rabbits, such that in another one hundred years, they will have taken over the land we took from them in wars, without firing a shot. Even if Europe does not let another Muslim in, those in, like our Mexicans and other Latinos, are already having enough babies to take over.

So you might as well tell your foot soldiers to chill. There is no need to burn down the London Bridge when they can mount the crescent on top of it in a short while without any opposition. The same goes for the Eiffel Tower in Paris. It is all theirs if only they have patience. The way they are taking over churches from Europeans who do not go to church anymore and turning them into mosques is the same way they will take over all the monuments therein. In as little as two hundred years from now, the Vatican may become the official residence of the Sultan of Rome. The grave of St. Peter will be turned into another pit where Muslim's faithful, too old to go to Medina, will go and stone the devil.

While you communicate with them, Allah please, you need to pick someone amongst them who will lead a reform within Islam. You know the way Martin Luther reformed Christianity. The way the Bible's Old Testament has in it enough provisions to chop off heads, but modern Christians pretend that it does not exist.

Though I wish I could chop off the heads of some fake news peddlers. Without moderation, Islam will destroy itself. And because Christianity is already packing up, we need to have a reformed Islam just in case it is the only religion we on Earth are left with. So, think about updating the Koran. It has been a while since someone looked at it.

All the best handling those monsters that you have unleashed on the world. But I will tell you what Pompeo told me. He said, "Muslims' silence in the face of extremism coming from the best-funded Islamic advocacy organizations and many mosques across America is absolutely deafening. It casts doubt upon the commitment to peace among adherents of the Muslim faith." He also said, "It has made these Islamic leaders across America potentially complicit in these acts of terrorism." The guy is a smart man. When he is not bullshitting just for political purposes, he thinks just like me. I love him.

If any Islamic terrorism act happens again in America, I will make all Muslims prove that they are good Muslims by not criticizing America. If they do, I won't think twice before I lock them up, all Muslims. So, you better warn your folks. My national security advisor, John Bolton, said that the virus of Wahhabism has infiltrated my America. And that was how some of our white boys learned how to shoot kids studying in school. They learned it from your boys. Our white boys learned terrorism from your boys since the days of Yasser Arafat. That is a total disaster.

It is up to you do something about this.

It will surprise you to know that I am reading a book on how the Spanish expelled Muslims from their land in the seventeenth century. I don't remember the book's title now, but I am getting hints. It is never too late. We can reverse this trend. Insha Allah.

Yours truly,
Donald J. Trump
The 45th President of the United States of America

Donald Trump's Letter to Michael Cohen

Thursday, April 19, 2018

To Michael Cohen:

Micoo, you fucked up, big time. You really fucked up. This is not *The Sopranos*. This is for real. Moron! Damn!

How could you not know that they could raid your law office and your hotel room? What kind of law school did you go to? So much for Jewish lawyers being the best there is. I should have known when you were driving a Porsche in college that you were not paying attention to what you were being taught. Stupid! Next time, I'm getting a lawyer who went to Harvard.

If I did not ask you of the possibilities of that happening, I would not be this mad. But you assured me that it would not happen. You said that these documents would never be made public. And I trusted you. You said that the US Constitution protected and guaranteed lawyer-client privilege. So, what happened? Were you reading your own constitution upside down?

How could you not know there were exceptions? You screwed up. You screwed yourself up. You want to make me look bad, but I won't let you. It so happens that even New York City taxi drivers driving with your medallions know this about the limits of lawyer-client privilege.

I should have known that you are not that smart when you used the email of my Trump Organization to negotiate the nondisclosure agreement with that woman. Also, I made you a millionaire, yet you had the effrontery to go about complaining to low-lives that you hang out with that I had not reimbursed you the $130,000 that you gave that woman. Imagine! You were collecting dirty dollar bills from taxi drivers when I picked you up from that gutter and made you a millionaire.

That aside, I'm disappointed that when the crooked FBI boys came to your doorstep, you folded up. What kind of a pit bull does something like that? Whatever happened to your often-quoted pledge of eternal loyalty? "If somebody does something Mr. Trump doesn't like, I do everything in my power to resolve it to Mr. Trump's benefit. If you do something wrong, I'm going to come at you, grab you by the neck, and I'm not going to let you go until I'm finished."

What happened? You just saw a few FBI officers and you peed in your pants. Disgusting! All you needed to do was to pick up the phone and call me. You did not do that. That is really fucked up.

I could have rumpled the search warrant and thrown it into the trash can. I could have sent the CIA to storm your hotel room and law offices and have them disarm the FBI. I could have sent the NIA to storm in immediately afterward and disarm the CIA. I could have sent the MIA to storm in next and disarm the NIA. By the end of the day, nobody ever would know who had the documents.

You really messed up. But I won't let you mess me up. If your intention is to inflict emotional distress on me, it won't work. Never!

What happened in New York City won't happen in Putin's Moscow. What happened in Manhattan won't happen in Xi Jinping's Beijing. Why, then, should it happen in Trump's America?

It is all your fault!

America, in our own eyes, is becoming a shithole country. Under this condition, who wants to be the commander-in-chief of the armed forces? Fuck that.

I want to be the commander-in-chief of the New York City police. I want to be the commander-in-chief of the FBI.

When this is all over, I will demand those additional titles to that of the commander-in-chief of the armed forces. If I have to give up being the commander-in-chief of the coast guard to get command of the FBI, I will do so in a heartbeat. Fuck the coast guard.

Micco, I'm good at this. I will persevere. I thrive under pressure. You will see. America will soon have a reason to proclaim the categorical recognition of my genius. It is long overdue. It will blow all the naysayers away.

All that I ask you is not to crumble under pressure. There is no boundary to the options in front of me. People talk of pardoning you; that is the simplest option I have. But I did not make my name by doing simple things, going after low-hanging fruits. I made my name by tackling the big things, blowing up paths where bushes were before. I will use this case as another terrific teaching moment for Americans.

I hear those lazy talking heads talk about how I break the American norms. Tremendous knuckleheads they must be. By the time I am done with America, it will have become clear to them that I am the norms they were talking about.

So, my friend, do not fear. How did Kendrick Lamar say it? I am the butterfly that does not need pimping.

Stay strong. I will write you again.

I won't call you for a while because I have been told that you could be wearing a wire to record me confessing to crimes of some sort. You know that I am not stupid. When they approach you for that with a promise of a reduced sentence, tell them that my nuclear button and my pardon button are bigger than theirs.

My buddy, you really fucked up. But don't worry, big daddy will clean it up. I will not let any personal injury happen to you.

Yours truly,
Donald J. Trump (a.k.a. David Dennison)
The 45th President of the United States of America

Donald Trump's Letter to Nelson Mandela

Monday, April 16, 2018

Hello Mr. Mandela,

Sorry on the death of your ex-wife, Winnie Mandela. If I had wanted to be presidential, I would have said that Melania and I have your family in our thoughts and prayers. But that would give an impression that Melania's thoughts and my thoughts are anywhere close. Also, some people may assume that we are one of those traditional American families that sit at one dinner table to eat or kneel down to pray before going to bed. Wrong! We don't do things like that. If there is any kind of supplication going on, it is coming from Melania toward me. Believe me, the bigger truth is that we don't give a hoot what happens to you guys in that Dark Continent.

I once said in one of those candid moments at the White House that you all are from shithole countries. Your people and your liberal allies, who do not like to hear the truth, went ballistic. Huge hullabaloo erupted. I didn't get it. Please explain to me—where in that continent is there a glimmer of light? Is it the big-for-nothing giant, Nigeria? Is it the Islamist infested Egypt? Or it is the Portuguese colony of Angola? Just tell me. Even the midlevel countries like Kenya and Uganda cannot tell their right from their left after fifty years of independence. Which tells me that the footing of these nations is faulty.

In fact, I think the premise that you Africans are mature enough to govern yourself is up for debate. Sad! I know people like you may not like to hear straight talk like this, but it is the truth. Look at Zimbabwe. It was doing very well when white people were running the country. Mugabe and his group of thugs said they were the majority and that the majority should rule. Thirty years after, Zimbabwe went to the dogs. The same thing is happening to your beloved South Africa. If not for your people getting rid of Jacob Zuma, South Africa was less than a dozen years away from becoming another Zimbabwe.

Until your wife died, I could not figure out what was wrong with you all. Now I know. Africa lacks people like me. It is incredible. You people lack smart men of integrity who are willing to put Africa first. That was where you sucked. You were too accommodating, like American Democrats. It is always leading to total disaster. You keep giving and keep giving to make everyone feel good, until you turn a nation of men into a formless mash of weak-hearted individuals that stand on nothing.

Believe me, you don't treat white men with kids' gloves. It doesn't work. I don't acknowledge something like this in public, but I can say it in this secret letter. If we start developing soft bleeding hearts like you did in prison, we will one day call back what remains of Native Americans and hand Manhattan back to them. But we have them confined to whatever reservations they are in, build casinos for them, make sure there are sufficient alcohol and drugs for them. That way, we don't have to worry about them waking up to ask how they lost their country. Instead, they wake up to inject themselves with insulin, take 40 milligrams of Prozac, and pray to what remains of their mountains and their rivers just to see tomorrow. Those who do not get the answer they want either commit suicide or contract tuberculosis just for the fun of getting the United States government's assistance.

It is the same thing with your cousins here—African Americans. If we start having pity for them, acknowledging that they really did the manual labor that built America, it would embolden them. Losers. You will hear them scream that they need reparations for slavery and all that. You can see what we tell them when they raise matters like that. We say, hey, your fore-parents lived rent-free and were fed at the cost of the slave masters. The slave masters even provided security for them. That way, we shut them up.

The point that I am making is that if you had put South African blacks first, you would have given economic empowerment to them. But you didn't. I just did not have Africa on my radar then. Otherwise, I would have come down there and helped you guys build some high-rise buildings to get your black folks out of shanty towns into modern buildings with toilets and bathrooms. As a result, your country went on a total free fall.

Winnie wanted to do that, including giving them land to farm. I don't know about giving them land though. Your people in Uganda and Zimbabwe who received and occupied white-owned lands didn't know what to do with them. Instead of giving them land, I would build sports facilities for them, put in music studios in their neighborhoods. I think your people can do well singing and dancing, running around a field pursuing any kind of ball the white man throws out there. Big deal! You guys are good at entertaining the rich white folks like me, so you might as well have what you need to excel in that inconsequential aspect of life.

So let me ask you again, why don't you people allow the likes of your ex-wife to lead? You need people that would put Africa first. Whoever is stopping that from happening is not your friend. Some of my people in the White House told me you had someone like that in the person of Patrice Lumumba in Congo. What happened to him? Whoever stopped him from accomplishing his mission is the real enemy of the African people. I know what I am saying. The same kinds of losers are trying to stop me from accomplishing the work that I am determined to do for America.

I was told that while you were in Robben Prison worrying about wearing shorts instead of long pants, Winnie was in the battlefield of South Africa attending funerals of your dead activists and comrades. You can see why you came out soft while she remained strong and committed to the cause till the end. This is what I honestly believe: you cannot have mission accomplished if you are not ready to accomplish it by any means necessary. That was how I won the US presidential election that nobody believed that I would win, not even Melania. I did it all by myself and in my own way.

Anyway, I am thinking that after winning my second term in office, I should establish a Truth and Reconciliation Commission to look into Clinton's Vincent Forster, Obama's Birth Certificate, Crooked Hillary's Benghazi, and Slime James Comey's high crimes. I want them tried for sedition in a Rivona kind of dramatic way if they do not come to the commission to confess their sins. I want to personally assign James Comey his prison number. I have already made up my mind on what it would be. In a satirical way, I have decided to order the prison chief to give him your 46664 prison number. He is the kind of man that brought apartheid to your beautiful country. Just take a look at him. Doesn't he look like P. W. Botha?

I have seen women from your country: Charlize Theron, Sasha Pieterse, and Lesley-Ann Brandt in Hollywood. I'm very much impressed! I think there may be more of their type where they came from. Maybe when I retire from the presidency in 2028, I will visit South Africa. My only fear is the HIV/AIDs that you guys have over there. I hope by then your HIV/AIDS epidemic is under control. I don't want to take any risk, you know. If what happened at the penthouse of Moscow's Ritz-Carlton happens in Johannesburg's Ritz-Carlton, your countryman, Trevor Noah, would have an orgasm on air.

Okay, I have to go. This place sucks sometimes. John Kelly is knocking at the door. Who knows, it may be time to fire someone again.

Yours truly,
Donald J. Trump
The 45th President of the United States

Donald Trump's Letter to Barack Obama

Sunday, April 22, 2018

Dear Barack,

I saw you making my wife laugh out loud at Barbara Bush's funeral. I did not like it at all. She has not laughed out loud with me since she took in with our son, Barron. In all of my quarrels with you, I have never taken it out on your chimpanzee lookalike wife. I actually drafted a tweet to send out, tagging you, but I changed my mind. I knew you would not be courageous enough to respond. At best, you would run to your Hollywood comedy friends to give you something to say as a clapback.

I write to ask you to desist from going near my wife. No matter the temptation, do not try to talk to her when next you see her. If she talks to you, just ignore her. She is used to that. I do that all the time. If you fail to follow this simple rule, I may be forced to reveal the things I found in your FBI files. So, don't try me. Believe me, I won't say this again.

Imagine the cold shoulders I got from her because of you. I don't know what silly idea you put into her little brain that she came back acting puffed up. Maybe it is one of those little silly things you tell your Kool-Aid drinking crowd of simple-minded people. I worked hard to get her where I wanted her to be—a place where she knows very little but feels that she knows a lot. Do not mess it up for me.

I even heard that you recommended a book to her. And she actually bought the book and started to read it. What does she look like to you? A bimbo from Las Vegas or Novo Mesto? Mind your own business. You won't be happy if I recommend a plastic surgeon to Michelle. Or don't you think that her arms need to be trimmed to make her look like a woman? Don't get me started. You don't want to find out what extremes I will take if you stay on this current path.

Anyway, this is not why I am writing you today. As you can see, I have solved what you said would be the biggest challenge of my presidency, without raising a finger. I just used my incredible bully pulpit. It is something that was available to you, but you failed to use it. Shame, shame, shame. I hope you will be honest enough to call a world press conference and tell the world that I am the greatest president that ever existed in the 242-year history of these United States.

I am not holding my breath. If the Nobel Prize were like the Grammy Awards, I would have loved to see you come on stage and hand me the 2018 Nobel Prize for Peace. But to think of it, you giving that honor to me would be cheapening it. Yours was a token affirmative action kind of Nobel Prize. Even you acknowledged that you did not deserve it. If you had any iota of integrity in you, you should have returned it to the Nobel Committee after eight years as the president of the United States without making an inch of improvement in world peace. You failed in the Middle East. You failed in Libya. You failed even in your home country, Kenya. Unbelievable!

You couldn't even issue a green card to your uncle. This was a man whose house you squatted while you attended Harvard. You watched him get deported like your sick auntie. Pathetic. And you were supposed to be a lawyer. How smart were you, dear affirmative action lawyer? I got a green card for my ungrateful Melania and her parents. Nothing difficult there.

I singlehandedly unified North and South Korea without firing any weapon. I did not even sit down at a summit to accomplish it. I just showed my big nuclear buttons and my large thumbnail ready to press the button, and the Rocket Man knew that his game was up. While you were busy trying to appear presidential, I simply did it the way we do business in the New York real estate world. If you had any honor left in you, you should be screaming to the hearing of anyone in the world that I am a genius. You should be tweeting that nobody has done this job of being the president of the United States of America better than me.

It is good that we have not talked since you handed power over to me. And I want it to remain that way. In any case, there is nothing to talk about with a featherweight like you. When I am done wiping out your toxic footprints from the landscape of America, then I will declare to my fellow Americans that our nightmare is finally over. Maybe then I will consider pardoning you for the series of cons you perpetuated on our United States of America.

If questions about who you were forced you to consume alcohol, smoke marijuana, and do cocaine in your teenage years, I wonder what you will smoke when I reveal all the cons you have perpetuated in America, starting from your immaculate conception to your birth in a manger in Nyang'oma Kogelo, Kenya. Don't think I don't know. Maybe you will embrace opioids then.

I also know what you did when you visited Pakistan and India in 1981. And guess what? I know things that you did in the '80s with your little live-in Asian girlfriend, Sheila—things that your ever-trusting Michelle does not even know. As for Rev. Jeremiah Wright, your pastor that you threw under the bus for your vain presidential ambition, I am in possession of some stories. I have news for you. I know some terrible things about you and him that you do not want the world to know. So, don't even get me started.

By the way, despite the thorough cleaning we gave the White House before moving in, we still get this whiff of stinking smell around here. My butler says the stinking smell is from what your dog, Bo, left behind. I disagree. I think the smell is human in origin

– most likely, of a man high on shishi. Another reason why we should not have allowed someone like you anywhere near the White House. You were bad for America. We are going to take care of all the damages you caused.

I am sure that you are monitoring my poll numbers. But just in case you have given up out of frustration, my poll numbers are better than yours at this point in your presidency despite all the stupid norms that I have busted to the annoyance of your establishment type. You will have to deal with having me in the White House for another six and a half years. By the end of which, when anybody says, "Barack Obama," the response will be, "Who?"

That is when I'll know my job is done. It doesn't matter what happens when I am gone. It may interest you to know that I have written my epitaph. It is very simple: "The greatest of all time."

To recap, stay away from my wife, or else…

Yours truly,
Donald J. Trump
The 45th President of the United States of America

Donald Trump's Letter to Mark Cuban

Sunday, April 22, 2018

Hey Mark,

What's up with you? I know you are surprised to receive this letter from me considering our history. But you shouldn't be. Where I am, I have a close-up look at history, and what I see is disgusting. Excuse my French, but history is full of shit. The other day, I spoke with my last divorce lawyer. I might as well reach out to you. There are some things about this place that only billionaires like you will understand.

I know you have mulled the thought of running for president. I want to tell you in all honesty that it is not worth it. Believe me, you have the best life as a private billionaire in America. This office is nothing but a prison. Gene Fowler said, "A fool and his money can go places." But not in the White House. Maybe for poor people like Obama and Clinton who had no plane of their own, it may mean the world. But I can confidently tell you that my life before I came in here was a lot better.

I could do anything I wanted as a private citizen. Now all I deal with are a bunch of people trying to control me. This bullshit place is a prison. Ask Melania. She is having a tough time with menopause, according to Kellyanne. You know that thirty-five years is women's check-out time. I don't know why I'm still married to her at forty-nine. I can't wrap my mind around that number. It is a huge number. It is more like our trade deficit with China.

That you are the strongest man in the world is mere consolation for the prison that you are in. If I am the strongest man in the world, why can't I stop this Mueller witch hunt going on in Washington? Disgraceful. You saw the day Melania slapped my hand down. I could not even put her in her place. Think about it: she couldn't do that when I was not president. Shame.

I am the strongest man in the world, yet reporters like *The New York Times'* Maggie Headshot, or whatever her last name is, are writing rubbish about me, and I am not able to do anything to her. I cannot even get her to sleep in jail for a night. Oh, listen to the greatest bullshit of them all: despite her obnoxious nature, I must still let her into the building where my office is. Can you imagine that? Can you imagine being told that you must allow a stupid sports reporter talking nonsense about you into your Dallas Mavericks arena?

I tell you, I have had it up to here with all these people moving around me, saying, "Sir, sir, sir," yet searching for an adult in the room. What do they mean by that, anyway?

Mark, this is not the game that you and I are used to. There are so many cooks in the kitchen here and so many of them are terrible cooks, especially those Democrats. Believe me, anyone could be president, but not everyone should be. This place is highly overrated.

All around me, there is a sense of history. But the hunt for a place in that book of history is a lot harder than you think. Imagine. I am president, but my pronouncements do not mean much. A Mexican judge could just annul your declaration and executive order in one sentence. What kind of crooked structure is that? At Trump's Organization, I do not need to say a word for things to start happening. Someone like Michael Cohen was trained to read my body language and execute my desires appropriately.

I brought some billionaires in my cabinet hoping that they would be bold and come up with revolutionary changes. But most of them have failed me. If I owned a Dairy Queen, I wouldn't even let them manage it. They make me question how they made their money. Unlike you and I, who worked hard for our money, these people that I have around me obviously inherited their money. Look at that dumb woman that I made Secretary of Education. She doesn't even know her right from left. I would have loved to kick her out and get someone like you who would shake things up and tell me the truth without fear. But somehow, Kelly tells me there have been too many changes of recent and that I should wait for a few more weeks.

Let me make a confession here. Steve Bannon once suggested that I bring you into my administration, but I dismissed the idea. Kellyanne is again suggesting that I should get you into my cabinet a few weeks before the midterm elections. She said it would show the nation that I am grown up, now willing to get a cabinet of equals or something like that. I think that would be huge.

So please write me back and let me know if you would like to join my cabinet. I like your risk-taking persona, and I will give you any cabinet post you want. I think having you out there making things happen will be good for my presidency. And for America too.

I may not have shaved my hair, I may not have trimmed my ego, but goddamit, this place has given me an irritable bowel movement. It is something that I never had before. Disgusting! Very much.

Yours truly,
Donald J. Trump
The 45th President of the United States of America

Donald Trump's Letter to Gen. Michael Flynn

Monday, April 23, 2018

Hi Gen. Flynn,

I hope you are enjoying your laughter. I can assure you, it won't be the last laugh. You bet! This whole bullshit started with you. It was my effort to save your white ass that placed me in this shithole that I am in. If I had known, I would have allowed Comey to roast your behind. I went to bat for you and this is how you pay me back? Very unfair!

No problem. Loyalty, fidelity, courage are all hallmarks of a general. Oh, so much for being a general from the greatest military in the world. Crybaby. So, when you were on the campaign podium with me screaming, "Lock her up, lock her up," you were just a sissy afraid of being locked up. It is very unfortunate. Nasty, nasty character!

A small investigation and you crumbled like a pancake? What kind of man does something like that? What kind of general leaves his troops on the battlefront just to save his behind? Was that how you performed in the military for thirty-three years? How do you become an army lieutenant general that way?

You are worse than a deserter. Do you know what the military does to people like you on the battlefield? They get shot in the head. No need for court-martialing. Goddamn it, Flynn! America

75

is a battlefield.

I thought that the first principle to any soldier in any battle is to endure. I thought the second principle is to save your brother-in-arms. I thought that the third principle is not leaving any fallen soldier in the field. I don't get it. Even as you fell, I did not want to leave you in the field. I was preparing to evacuate you, whatever it took.

You were in Operation Urgent Fury, Operation Uphold Democracy, Operation Enduring Freedom, and yet, a small backdoor channel with the Russians was very hard for you to defend. Remember, that was your primary assignment. Nothing more. You were expected to walk up and down that Underground Railroad and wipe away your footprints. That was it. How hard could that be?

You spent a lot of time in the intelligence and counterterrorism areas of the military. Are you saying that you have never encountered situations where you had to take a bullet for the team? I have lost a lot of people who did that for me. I appreciate their sacrifices. I make sure I take care of their families for eternity. If you doubt me, watch how I will take care of Michael Cohen's family.

Even if you didn't want to do it for me, what do you think your cowardice means for the fate of your Flynn Intel Group? Even the Turks won't touch your company with a long pole. Just for $530,000 dollars from the Turks, you flipped sides. From clapping for Turkish exiled cleric Fethullah Gülen and the coup plotters, you quickly switched to the other side, even attending meetings where plans to kidnap Fethullah Gülen were discussed. I wish I knew this about you before. That I even considered you for the position of Vice President was absurd. During the campaign, you were all fired up and saying you were doing everything for the country. Little did I know it was all about you. For a man from the small town of Rhode Island, I expected more loyalty from you.

You were once a good guy. You could be one again. You were damn right about Hillary Clinton's Pizzagate that they now call a conspiracy theory. You did well by pushing it during the campaign at home and abroad. You saved me from being the face of that effective campaign attack. It worked. And I was proud of you. But I cannot say that about your recent moves. Nobody has ever made me contemplate saying for a brief second that Obama was right about anything. But you did. Obama warned me not to hire you as a national security advisor. For that nigga never to think he could tell me what to do and what not to do, I did it.

I do miss your counsel when it comes to issues of Islam. Like I told you, I agree with you that there is no good Muslim as long as Islam remains a political ideology tied to their lifestyle. It is a cancer that must be prevented from further metastasizing, you said. I never forgot that. That was the smart Flynn that I loved. That is why it pains me that you messed up and left me with people who are afraid to defend our position that there is nothing irrational about anyone's fear of Muslims. Nothing.

Because of the choices you made, you have gone from being the national advisor to the greatest president of the United States, to a felon. I bet you will need me to pardon you in the near future. Not looking good at this time!

You lied to Vice President Pence. Big deal! I do that every day. If you had asked me the best way to manipulate Pence into silence, I would have told you. What kind of national security advisor would not carry the president along with him? I know the former Russian ambassador Sergey Kislyak very well. He was helpful when I went to Russia. Very helpful, I must say. No, very, very helpful. If you had told me, he could have corroborated any story you wanted him to. In any case, the Logan Act is an archaic law that I am getting rid of anyway. It is the same with the emolument clause. As soon as I get all these Mueller matters behind me, I will go after all those encumbrances one after the other.

You lied to the FBI. Don't you know there is a limit to where you can be loose with facts? I made time to look at your FBI files recently. I discovered that you have a long history of making up your own facts and believing in them. Your people in the army even called it "Flynn facts." I didn't know that about you when I brought you near me. I am a man who insists on telling the truth. I embrace only verifiable facts, and I like people who work with me to follow the same line – case in point, Kellyanne Conway. How I missed that character flaw in you was a surprise to me.

Greed is not just bad. It is corrosive. That is what happened to you. When you came to me, you should have known that I would make you rich beyond your wildest dreams. Why were you still messing with the Russians and the Turks about money? Ask Michael Cohen. He met me and he had no need to drive taxis anymore. I was going to make you very rich after we were done doing our service to the United States of America. It would have been good. But you did not let it take off. You marred what would have been a great ride from the very beginning.

Even as things stand, if you were loyal to me, I would have protected you still. I always do. If you doubt me, ask my people in New York City. But you panicked because you had no faith.

Your reputation is damaged as it is. And because you are working with that evil man Mueller, I cannot help you. You will spend a long time in purgatory. More importantly, Hope Hicks said that you are fucking up eight generations of your ancestors.

Today is still early. You can still recant. You can still flip back to where you flipped up.

Call Rudy Giuliani if it is something that you are interested in.

Yours truly,
Donald J. Trump
The 45th President of the United States of America

Donald Trump's Letter to Rosie O'Donnell

Thursday, April 26, 2018

Hi Rosie,

You know that I have totally forgotten about you. Very sad! I was just searching for a website where I could buy flowers for Melania to mark her birthday, when I saw your name. Someone at Google should know that the last thing a man wants to see while looking for roses for his wife or girlfriend is your picture. Disgusting image!

How are you doing? Just a few months ago, when I was telling you how inconsequential you were, you did not believe me. See! From where I am, you have never looked so little to me. To imagine that there was a time I was wasting my energy sparing with you on Twitter makes me want to puke. I should have known that you were not worth the time.

As you must see every blessed day, I now dine with the likes of Justin Trudeau of Canada and Emmanuel Macron of France. Terrific guys! With one phone call, I can get any of the 195 presidents of any country in the world to come for dinner in the White House. They love me. Everyone loves me.

How do you spend your days these days? I heard that your most recent girlfriend – is it girlfriend or boyfriend? I don't know anymore and I don't care. I heard that she has dumped your ass and moved on. Who blames her? Who wants to hang around a lousy person like you? Slob! You have gotten two divorces in your bag, just like me, but your fame is waning. Every TV show you get onto, you are fired. Do I need to tell you now that people regret hiring you as soon as you walk into the office? Look at me; I am on the biggest TV show in the world. Kids from Kabul to Kilimanjaro want to be like the Donald. I am the most famous person in the world today. But go to the street of Commack, New York, and ask kids, "Who is Rosie O'Donnell?" They won't have a clue.

I pity those five kids you adopted. I hope you and your cheap nannies don't breed them to be like you. That would be a disaster. What am I saying? With you smoking weed at home, it is absolutely an inevitable end for those poor souls. I am not looking forward to seeing one of them join our military and become decorated like my White House doctor, rear admiral Ronny Jackson. A good man that your liberal type is destroying with unsubstantiated innuendos.

Having reached this pinnacle of life, what I feared most about your kind has been downgraded. I used to fear that gays like you would overwhelm America by breeding your type all over the place. Now I fear those Mexicans and the Muslims. The way they breed all over the suburbs of America is the greatest challenge America faces in the next century. It is not North Korea or Iran. You can see that I am handling those two very well. Things your darling Obama and Hillary could not handle. Weak, weak, weak.

You can be sure that I will solve the Muslim and Mexican problems. John Bolton, that guy is smart, recommended a book to me the other day. He said it is a New York Times bestseller. It is called *Suicide of the West: How the Rebirth of Tribalism, Populism, Nationalism, and Identity Politics Is Destroying American Democracy* by Jonah Goldberg. I told John that I have no time to read books. He summarized it for me. The book says that if I don't do the things I am doing for America at this point, America and the rest of Western Europe will collapse. It made me more resolute in my pursuit.

John said that people will mock me and condemn me but that two hundred years from now, I will be held as a hero across the West. An ordained savior, he said. John said my picture will be on the future $1,000 bill. I have already chosen the picture that will be used for the bill. I want it to be a perfect picture of me in my prime, playing golf.

As you can see, I am very busy for your kind. When you see the likes of Bill Maher and all his liberal friends, tell them that I am determined to undo all the regulations and fake climate laws that their darling Obama put in place. Scott Pruitt is doing a tremendous job. There is nothing the lying *New York Times* and *Washington Post* can do about it. If they like, let them bring out a video of Scott killing the last great white rhino left on Earth; he remains my man. Anyone that pisses off the likes of Barbara Streisand and Bette Midler is someone in whom I am well pleased. As for you grumbling about guns, it is now that more sophisticated guns are coming into the market. We will replace apple pie with guns as a symbol of America. If you don't like it, move to Canada.

By the way, I truly thought that some of you would have finished your move to Canada by now. Why are you still hanging around the United States? I don't remember who it was – one of your ultra-liberal kind – that was asked why he had not left. The foolish man said he was waiting to watch my extraordinary fall from power. I think it was Michael Moore; I am not sure.

For those of you Hollywood types waiting, just know that you all are waiting in vain. In no time, I will come around in Air Force One for reelection fundraising in Los Angeles. I am your liberal nightmare, and I am not going away any time soon. So tell your friends to brace up.

Like I told you in the past, what is holding you back are the things you missed when you dropped out of college to become a comedian. It is not too late to return to school and learn a skill. If it is too late for you, at least learn to be nice to people. Bullying people and rudeness block your path to your destiny the same way plaque clogs your arteries. I am sure you understand what I mean. You need to insert the stent of niceness into yourself to make it. If you fail to heed my advice, you may end up the same way your former wife, Rounds, ended. I'm just telling you. I'm just doing you a favor.

Yours truly,
Donald J. Trump
The 45th President of the United States of America

Donald Trump's Letter to His Father, Fred Trump

Thursday, May 2, 2018

Dear Daddy,

Guess what? I am the president of the United States of America. Yep! Your favorite silent film British actor, Frank Dane, was right after all – "Get all the fools on your side and you can be elected to anything."

I know that I never mentioned it as my ambition. But after I had reached the peak of the business world, I needed a new challenge. The only challenge that I found worthy of my genius was to be the president of the United States. And guess what was even more spectacular? I made it in my first try. As you know, over two-third of US presidents tried again and again before they made it. But your big boy made it at first try. I defeated over two-dozen low-energy competitors.

I stunned the world. The whole media of the world, from Cape Town to Casablanca, from London to Las Vegas, screamed that it was unprecedented. The name Trump has gone from adorning the tallest and biggest buildings in New York City to the greatest White House in the world, the official residence of the US president in Washington, DC. If you were still with us, you could just drive into the White House without anybody flagging you down to search your trunk.

83

You should be very proud, Daddy. Now, whenever your name is mentioned, they have to add "father of the 45th President of the United States of America" Anyone who fails to do that, I can send my FBI to go after them. If I want, I can even sign an executive order saying that anywhere anyone mentions Fred Trump, they must add "Peace be Unto Him" or else... That is how powerful I am.

Remember your first home in Queens? It is now one of the greatest historical buildings in America. In fact, it is considered more important than George Washington's Mount Vernon. My New York City building, Trump Tower, attracts over ten million visitors every year. Imagine that. And I am still the president. When I retire in 2029, I can ask each visitor to pay $100 to look at the building and maybe another $100 to take a picture of the building. You can imagine how much that will bring in a year. Daddy, I can pull in over $1 billion a year just from that alone.

But you know I have my prized possession, my Mar-a-Lago in Florida. That one is already beating Disney World as Florida's destination of choice. People queue to marry in my estate, to have Bat Mitzvahs and numerous conventions. Even some rich amigos are coming to throw sweet sixteen parties for their daughters. I don't care who comes as long as they are paying top dollar.

Daddy, your family is set for the next two hundred generations. From now on, it is winning and winning and winning. As long as the republic exists, nobody will ever mess with the name Trump.

I know you would like to know how I am dealing with the enemies within the deep state. You know those idiots who investigated you for wartime profiteering from military buildings you constructed? Their modern-day evangelists of doom are suing me in court for what they call a violation of the emolument clause for my hotel in Washington, DC. Instead of them thanking me every day for refurbishing the dilapidated Post Office building in DC, they are in court wasting the time of judges that should be handling cases of illegal immigrants. I modified your great saying; "The Trumps are the law wherever they are." When a Trump does something, if it was against the law before, it becomes the law. I told them outright that the law is not meant for a president. Finished!

You know how the US Justice Department in 1973 came after you over how you managed your properties? The same thing is happening again. The way those stupid people wanted to tell you who to let into your own building, saying that you were violating some useless Fair Housing Act and the civil rights of people who had no money to their names – people you extended favors to by allowing them to have a roof over their heads. Well, some people at the Justice Department are foaming at the mouth again. But I will deal with them. And as a Trump, I will put them in their place. You just watch and see.

Some good news—I saved "Merry Christmas." This Muslim man they made president before I came to power to fix things had erased Merry Christmas from our lexicon. He told Americans to say, "Happy Holidays." What a stupid thing to say. Well, I came to America's rescue. I brought Merry Christmas back. In America now, you can once again put up Christmas trees in your living room, and also lights, the way we used to do in Queens long time ago. You are once again allowed to go door-to-door singing Christmas carols. I made it happen. So, tell Angel Gabriel what your son has accomplished. It was a tough war. But as you know, I am a tough guy.

You know, despite your plea that I should follow in the footsteps of my grandfather, I did not go to Karlstadt, Germany, to marry after all. I thank God I went to Slovenia, instead. Our cousins from Germany have not impressed me. There is this one that runs Germany today. She is so stubborn. She won't follow my instructions. And she doesn't look smart no matter how much they say she is. She is the kind of woman that I would have since divorced if I had made the mistake of marrying her.

I know you are worried about my health, as usual. Believe me, I haven't forgotten that Grandpa died in the 1918 flu pandemic. I am very careful about my health. I only eat cheese hamburgers from McDonald's. I'm in very fantastic health. When I was elected president, my doctor said I was the healthiest person ever elected president of the United States. Not an ordinary feat, if you know the line of fat slobs who had held that office. I still wash my hands after any handshake with people who do not look perfect. For instance, I used extra soap after I shook the hands of that sick president of the shithole country in Africa called Nigeria. I still remember your counsel – never take chances with your health.

You know the way you used to tell friends and family that your family was from Sweden, when it was not cool to say that one had anything to do with Germany. I am using alternative facts to escape some tricky situations here. There is this little thing about my lawyer paying some loose woman to keep quiet. I have told them I didn't know about the payment. When it became necessary, I also told them that the money came from the retainer that I paid my lawyer every month. You understand stuff like that. I thank you for preparing me for the kind of things that I encounter here in this godforsaken Washington, DC.

Remember how it took me just three years of joining your company in 1968 to become the president in 1971. In less than two years as the president of the United States of America, I have become the strongest man in the world and the first leader of the free and un-free world. All other presidents before me have only managed to lead the free world. I lead both. For instance, the president of North Korea, that dark and mysterious country that America fought a long time ago, is now my buddy. He calls me when he needs advice. The only problem is that he doesn't understand that we have a time difference. He calls me when I am watching *Fox and Friends*, and that is a no-no.

There was this incident in Charlottesville, Virginia, last year that reminded me of what happened to you in New York City on Memorial Day in 1927, when the Ku Klux Klan marched against assaults by Catholic police. Some native-born people were protesting against the activities of liberals who wanted to remove the statue of our past heroes in Virginia and all over the South. In the encounter, some people were killed. Somehow the liberals wanted me to condemn the natives. They were mad that I said there were some good people on both sides. They don't understand. You were on the KKK side in 1927, and good people like you could be on the other side all the time.

By the way, your friend Benjamin Netanyahu, the former United Nations Ambassador of Israel, is working hand-in-hand with me to solve the other big problem of this world – stopping the rogue nation of Iran from getting a nuclear weapon. He is such a great guy. I am not sure if you know, but Benjamin is the current Prime Minister of Israel. The other day, I sent him to go out there and show the world why we need to destroy Iran and cut them to size.

I must admit, you had an eye for people who had great potential. As you can see, that loan you gave me in 1972 has made all the difference. Like Larry Kudlow said, like an unending stem cell, I have turned it into billions and billions of dollars.

I will keep reporting back to you on the differences I am making in this great nation of ours. But one thing you can be sure of is that I have brought to America the respect that passes all understanding.

I owe it all to your tutelage.

Thank you, Daddy.

Yours truly,
Donald J. Trump
The 45th President of the United States of America

Donald Trump's Letter to Kanye West

Friday, May 3, 2018

Hi Kanye,

Since our meeting in December of 2016, I would have written you before now, but as you know, I have been busy of late. I had to make out time to write the moment I heard that the Pulitzer Prize people gave their prize for music to Kendrick Lamar. What a travesty of genius! It must have been rigged. I'm telling you. Maybe some Mexicans were allowed to vote.

No one deserves that prize more than you. In my world, you have won it again and again. You are the voice of every generation of the last one hundred years and, most likely, the next one hundred years. You deserved it from the first day you came onto the stage with College Dropout. Who else has chronicled the plight of black folks like you? Nobody. Each of your albums is a masterpiece in art.

You see, while Lamar is the Obama of hip-hop, you are the Trump of hip-hop. They will only acknowledge your genius after they have run out of every other option. But people like us who know genius know that you have it. Despite their jealousy and shenanigans, you remain the number one rock star on the planet just as I remain the number one personality on the planet. They cannot take it away from us. Those who have it do not need frontin' (isn't that how all you GED people say it). Those who don't have it, like Obama, go about in Europe fronting.

Like me, you express your genius on and off the stage. You do not strive to be politically correct. You say it the way you see it. That is my kind of man. Not the sissified pussies like Obama who try to please everyone. They shy away from the uncomfortable truth, just to make some weak-minded group feel good about their miserable lives. It has not worked in the last fifty years, and it is not going to work in the next fifty years. Over the years, America has become weak because of people like them.

The future of this country depends on people like you and me. So, I say, be steadfast on your path. It's good that you have a goddess for a wife. My good friend, Howard Stern said that Kim is a piece of ass. Trust me, I believe that. Between you and me, I will join a swing club if you and Kim will join. You know what I mean? Unlike my woman, Kim is comfortable in the limelight. In this business, you need that kind of woman around you. Not the docile sit-at-home ones who know nothing but how to paint their nails and try new clothes and shoes. If I had someone like Kim around me, I would have gotten where I am long before now. I would have made it impossible for someone of Barack Obama's pedigree to be president of the United States of America. (Do you remember his middle name?) That aberration should not have happened in our beloved country. But I am glad that I am quickly wiping away any memory that he was once at the White House.

I'm glad you recognized that Obama did not do any shit for black folks. Of course, like all failures, he has a truckload of excuses. You bravely called out President George W. Bush for not caring about black folks. I think Obama pretended that he cared. He sold a dummy to black Americans that he tried but was held back by Republicans. Now look at what I have accomplished in just one year. The unemployment rate for African Americans is the lowest it has been since recorded history. Any black man who does not have a job now is just too stoned to know where to send his resume. Look at you: you get stoned, but you still perform; you take your psychiatric pills – I heard you take so many? – and you still write great songs. No president in the history of the United States has been able to move black people from the column of poverty to that of prosperity more than I did.

You grew up in Chicago. Just like you, I am concerned about the killing of beautiful young black men on the streets of Chicago. When I am done with this Mueller thing, I will roll out my plan for the inner cities of America. I have Ben Carson working out never before seen strategies – that is, when he is not sleepy. The Democratic plan of constantly taking away guns from black people has failed. In my plan, soon to be announced, I will make it easier for black folks to buy any gun they want. I believe when grandmas in the inner city are known to be packing AR-15s, punks will think twice before they threaten their grandchildren. Just imagine Medea holding an AR-15 or Glock model 19 semi-automatic pistol, 9 mm caliber instead of a tiny handgun. All those street thugs will learn to be polite to grandmas.

Just in case you are wondering, Omarosa told me about Medea. She said it was created by one of your people who is now a billionaire. I told her there could not be an African-American billionaire. She said Oprah is a billionaire. I doubt it. I asked Ben Carson, but he didn't know Medea or her creator. I am not sure if he is trying to burnish his conservative credentials, but he said he never met Oprah.

We need to project you out there beyond one who has accomplished what was once imagined as a fantasy in music, fashion, and business. We need to showcase you as an activist. That is what black folks need more of, your kind of honest true-to-God activism. As you can see, I have restored the fantasy of the white nationalists who were afraid that they had lost their America. I have given them reasons to believe in America again. I think you can be projected the same way, quite the opposite of the hope that the likes of Jesse Jackson, Louis Farrakhan, and Al Sharpton were selling to black people for over four decades now with devastating results.

Obama called his "Audacity of Hope." Since your folks came down from the slave ships, over four hundred years ago, you all have been hooked on hope – hope for a return home, an excursion to heaven, or hitting the lottery jackpot. I think it was your nigga Ice Cube who said that hope and dope are the same. You people have been high on either or both of them at the same time. Muhammad Ali was right to demand manna here on Earth and not wait until you get to heaven to be rewarded.

With a vision of greatness, you started from a basement studio and reached a throne far higher than where the Beatles, Michael Jackson, or even Elvis ever aspired. Twenty-one Grammy Awards are not earned by spending time cutting watermelons and flipping burgers at the barbeque grill, getting high on hope, dope, or both.

By the way, I love the music video of "Bound 2." I can't get Melania to try that with me. She is so boring at times. Sometimes, I envy you. I wish I could rap. It would have attracted lost suburbia white millennials flirting with Nancy Pelosi to my shows. I don't campaign; I put on shows.

My buddy, I love what you said about slavery the other day. That is what I have been trying to tell victimhood-hugging lots like Martin Luther King Jr. Slavery is by choice. We all have the power to choose if we want to be slaves or free people. I'm not a slave to any man or woman. The only person I serve is Donald Trump. I often wonder if I had to teach some of your black folks their own history. Didn't some slaves walk back into the sea at Igbo Landing in St. Simons Island, Georgia, rather than become slaves in America, picking cotton? That is a choice.

You will like this one. I want to work with you to heal the rift between the police and black people across America. You and I agree that the killings of black men by police are at an epidemic level in America, even though I will not acknowledge it in public. Beyond asking black people to obey the police by not running when asked to stop, something has to be done about it. I want you to be the arrowhead in that effort. The way you put Taylor Swift in her place when she stole that MTV Music Award from Beyoncé, that gave you the credibility to lead this effort for black folks. You are tough, and I like that.

While Eric Garner, Michael Brown, Freddie Gray are not really Einsteins in the making, I do not think law enforcement should be killing black men indiscriminately. For good reasons, you should not expect me to blame our police for the killings. That will mess up my PR. And that is where you come in. You can take the shine away from the Black Lives Matter movement and the likes of Jesse Williams by bringing your rational but uncompromising approach to the matter. I will tactically back you up. You have gone through the wire, and I am confident that you will bring that experience to bear.

Kids like Tamir Rice, Laquan McDonald, and Trayvon Martin should not be falling under a barrage of bullets when their age mates in Norway are falling in love on safe and quiet streets. I believe if you champion this, you will overshadow Malcolm X and Martin Luther King Jr. put together. I'm 100 percent sure of this.

I recall you telling me that you used to live in China as a kid. Would you be willing to be my special envoy to China in charge of negotiating intellectual and property rights? Your vision for Tidal has prepared you for such an assignment. If at any time you feel like taking a break from music to do a little diplomacy, just let me know. The job is yours.

All these will help beef up your resume for 2024 when you will run for president to become the truly first black American president – not that phony from Kenya.

Yours truly,
Donald J. Trump
The 45th President of the United States of America

Donald Trump's Letter to His Wife, Melania Trump

Friday, May 4, 2018

Hi Melania,

I will say this just once – stop embarrassing me in public. If you know that you do not want to hold my hand in public, just stay back in the White House. Do not bother to come out. Don't even open the windows or the doors. Turn on the TV and watch classic episodes of *The Jerry Springer Show* while you file your nails. I can get Sarah Sanders to come up with an excuse for you.

If you want sympathy from Americans, I can come up with a story that can make Americans sympathize with you. I can tell Sarah Sanders to announce that you had a miscarriage. You will be adored like Jackie from Camelot, if that is what you want. Only you know that we have not been close to each other in a long time. And try as we can, we cannot deceive Americans on that one. That sucks!

You cannot tell me that it is all these fake stories about what happened in Russia some decades ago that are getting you mad. Or is it that Stormy Daniels's lies? Or is it the Karen McDougal lady? Or it is Summer Zervos? Or is it the crazy Florida woman? Do any of them look like a serious competitor you should worry about? I mean, give me a little credit. Omarosa once told me if I want to eat a toad I should eat a well-endowed one. Do any of them look like a toad that I could eat?

In any case, I am the man. I mean, I know how I rescued you from the slavery of Paris and Milan runways where you were basically selling yourself to the highest bidder. I brought you to this greatest nation on Earth. If you are not dishonest, you should be forever appreciative. It is not as if you were the brightest crayon in the box. What was your IQ again? You dropped out of college after just one year of studying design. And by the way, bimbos like you in Eastern Europe are a dozen a dime.

Tell me, honey, when I met you at Kit Kat Club, what other bright options were there for you? In your family's shithole country of Slovenia, your mother was working in a children's cloth-making company and your dad was a communist selling communist-era cars. What a dazzling future you had ahead of you.

I brought you to the greatest country in the world and gave you a life worthy of princesses like Lady Diana. People like you, from parts of the world you came from, spend a lifetime singing praises of men not worthy of untying my shoes, for just giving then the almighty US green card. Do you know how much women like you pay in dollars and in-kind to get it? Of course, you have zero idea.

I gave you a wedding at Bethesda-by-the-Sea in Palm Beach, Florida, attended by the top two hundred celebrities in America. It was a tremendous *Guinness Book of World Records* event. You wore a $200,000 wedding dress designed by Christian Dior. That is more than the budget of your home country. Not that I expect you to know these things or others of their kind.

Come on, I scooped you off the gutters of Slovenia, and you expect me to tolerate nonsense like frowning your face in public? Let me tell you, don't mess with me. I have billions and billions of dollars at stake in this relationship.

I introduced you to the high society of New York City. You met governors, mayors, Major League players, and great pimps. I'm sure you did not notice that you also met legendary mobsters. I made you the darling of Hollywood. For my grace you were guest in the homes of Hollywood's greatest actors. In Florida, I placed you in a palace better than the Palace of Versailles. What else do you want?

Instead of you waking up each blessed day to worship me, you had the audacity to make faces. You should be kissing every floor my feet touch. Do you know if this was Africa, I would have taken my second and third wives by now? After all, South African Jacob Zuma just married his seventh.

I even brought your parents out of that shithole Slovenia and placed them in a luxury home in the greatest city in the world. I gave them access to the White House. Little woman, what else do you want?

Please, I will say this once. Don't bring out the monster in me. If you like, go and ask my former wives. I'll shake you off at the first sign of any disloyalty. And I don't need to tell you that I have options. After all, now that I am the strongest man in the world, my eyes would not be at beauty queens with their empty heads. I should be looking at princesses of some of the great kingdoms of the world. And all I need to do is point at one and we will have a royal cum presidential wedding at Mar-a-Lago. Wouldn't that be nice?

Whatever you do, remember that you are nothing without me. Don't ever forget that.

Yours truly,
Donald J. Trump
The 45th President of the United States of America

Donald Trump's Letter to Jeff Sessions

Friday, May 4, 2018

Hi Jeff,

What do you think the first line of your obituary will say? "The man whose decision to recuse himself in an investigation being conducted by an agency that he is in charge of led to the destruction of America, which ultimately made America weak again"? Is that what you really want?

I don't want to believe it. You know that you can rewrite this first line so easily. You can turn this narrative around overnight. In just one phone call, you can make it happen. If you do that, we are going to take care of the noble tasks we were elected to accomplish.

I know that you know all these. Why you have refused to choose this noble path in the service of our great country is beyond me. You cannot be tired of winning when we are just starting. What happened to the spirit of the Southern gentleman in you? If anyone had told me that I would have been better off having that Arizonian captured hero cum maverick in my cabinet than you, I would not have believed it.

I have asked Steve Bannon what your problem was. He said that you were protecting the rule of law and zealously guarding your reputation. Big deal! What reputation do you have? You were just an archaic senator from America's shithole of Alabama on your way to the grave when I picked you up from an obvious plunge into oblivion to make you somebody. If I had not done so, you would have died as a borderline racist. I gave you the chance of a lifetime, and this is how you repay me? It sucks so bad!

You know what? Fuck you, Jeff. Fuck out of here. You are a disgrace to the man that you were named after, President Jefferson Davis. You have soiled the nobility of your Confederate roots. I wonder how someone like you, without honor, is allowed to serve in the Army Reserve. Dangerous move, I tell you.

If you think you can bring me down, you do not know where I came from. I am not your sissy Italian mobster who folds up when they hear "Justice Department." Go and ask them in New York City. Go and ask my ancestors in Germany. When we go in, we are all the way in. Nothing scares us. History is full of great Germans who have proved that beyond any reasonable doubt. In your own eyes, I will prove it to you.

I am not Richard Nixon. And you cannot turn me into one. There is German blood flowing in me, not some slimy weak English blood. We are as rugged as the caterpillar. We can withstand heat of up to a thousand degrees. So, fuck you.

If you like, recuse yourself from breathing. Stupid! When I feel it is time to end all this grandstanding, I will step in like a man. With a tweet, I will dump you inside the trashcan of history where you will spend the rest of your life gnashing your teeth. You know I can do it. Totally easy! Or, if I really want to punish you, I will remove Rod Rosenstein, name you a deputy attorney general, and get my ghost personal lawyer, Rudy Giuliani, as the substantive attorney general.

By the way, don't forget those meetings you had with the Russian spook, ambassador Sergey Kislyak. I know some things that you don't think that I know. I know even things about Marion Three that are not yet public. I can force those things that I know down the throat of the dishonest media. You know they love you so much. And trust me, if I want, I can have you spend the rest of your life in prison.

You don't even have the decency to resign your post. So much for Southern charm. You just stand there like an electric pole taking all kinds of embarrassment, dog pee, and flood splashes. I have never seen a man who has no shame like you.

Trust me, you are going straight to hell. I will make sure it happens. Unlike Joe Biden, I will not follow you to the gate. I will have my people bundle you into the bowl of the great American caterpillar and heap you into hell.

…Ungrateful bitch like you.

Yours truly,
Donald J. Trump
The 45th President of the United States of America

Donald Trump's Letter to His Daughter, Ivanka Trump

Friday, May 4, 2018

My beloved Ivanka,

Fine Babe, this is another of Daddy's daily assurances.

I love you.
I love you.
    I love you.
    I love you in ways that pass all understanding.
    Don't mind that Mueller of a guy.
    If he touches you,
    Daddy will start a Third World War.
    I love you.
    I love you.
    I love you.
    I hope you remain amazing for me,
    Always.
    Not for that disposable husband.
    Babe, you are the terrific mirror
    That I'll use

To measure the beauty
Of my next wife.

Yours truly,
Donald J. Trump
The 45th President of the United States of America

Donald Trump's Letter to a Mysterious Woman

Friday, May 4, 2018

Dear Miss Thing,

66 Amongst all those who have loved you, I'm the one who has loved you the longest."

"How do you know? What if my first boyfriend still loves me?"
"Not that kind of love."
    "What kind of love?"
    "I'm talking of active love."
    "As opposed to inactive love or passive love?"
    "In active love."
    "What makes love active?"
    "He doesn't go out on a date with you."
    "Do you go out on a date with me?"
    "Sort of!"
    "How? When was the last time you went on a date with me?"
    "Just last week."
    "In your dream?"
    "On your recommendation, we listen to the same music."
    "And that counts for a date?"
    "Yes."
    "I'll ignore that."

"You mean you will check that good for me?"

"Next."

"On your recommendation, we watch the same movies though on different Tvs."

"And that is a date?"

"But we talk about it afterward. That is what lovers do after a movie date."

"What if one of my former boyfriends was watching the same movies too?"

"But not at the same time as we do, and you don't talk about it with him thereafter."

"You are too presumptuous."

"I take that to mean that I've won."

"Whatever."

"I take it to mean that my thesis is valid. Amongst all those who have loved you, I'm the one who has loved you the most."

"You need one more instance to prove it."

"If I give you one more, will you validate it?"

"Yeah."

"Okay. Say he listens to the same '80s music with you, sings it on the phone when you talk, butchering the lyrics. Say he watches the same movies with you. I bet you that he doesn't write poems for you anymore. That is, if he even did before."

"Alright, you win."

"I win?"

"Yeah."

"Please say it twice; let the heavens hear it."

"You are pushing your luck."

"Okay, now that I've won, what are you going to do about it?"

"Longest is not the same thing as passionest."

"There is no word like that – passionest."

"Now that I've said it, there is now a word like that. Yeah. What about passion?"

"You have never given me the chance to show my passion."

"You don't need my permission to let your passion come out. No man does. Passion defies logic."

"You moderate passion if only it is weak enough to be moderated. Strong passions are beyond subduing. You know why? Because passion is the stubbornest character we humans have."

"There is no word like stubbornest."

"Again, add it to your dictionary, for now there is."

"But wait, am I hearing you well?"

"It depends on what you heard."

"That dinner lasts longer than sex, but it is sex that is thought about the most."

"Yes."

"Weren't you the one who said I was coming on too strong? Remember? Some twenty-something years ago."

"You know what? I've got a proposal for you. Forget about twenty-one years of seduction. I will see you this weekend."

"Seriously?"

"Yes, seriously. I will fly to Washington, DC, and meet you and break this twenty-one-year-old thirst."

"No way."

"Yes."

"But I have an all-day meeting with the joint chiefs this weekend. Something about a dire situation with Iran."

"Oscar Wilde was right. 'I can resist everything except temptation.' Where should I meet you? Your controversial DC Post Office hotel or mine?"

"Maybe I can reschedule the meeting with the joint chiefs."

"Schiller said that, 'Against stupidity the gods are helpless.' Saturday or Sunday?"

"You know, my chief of staff said—"

"When pleasure interferes with business, our elders warn, give up business. So, what's the best time for you, p.m. or a.m.?"

"And how do I slip out of SSS's sight?"

"My most powerful man in the world, the time is ticking."

Yours truly,
Donald J. Trump
The 45th President of the United States of America

Donald Trump's Letter to Rex Tillerson

Saturday, May 5, 2018

Hi Rex,

Y ou called me a moron. I said nothing. You played your own kettle drum and arrogated to yourself the title, "Adult in the Room." I ignored you. You openly yelled that I was driving on the wrong side of the road. I did not step on the brake. Instead, I accelerated more.

At a traffic stop, I slowed down. I expected you to open the door and jump out. But you didn't.

When you went behind me to poop at my parade ground, I had no option but to send out a tweet that was retweeted by billions of people all over the world.

That is your life, Rex.

That is how you ended your career as the secretary of state of the greatest administration in US history. Total disaster. You had the chance to meet the North Korean leader, shake his hand, and watch the picture published on the front page of every newspaper on the face of this earth. But you screwed up out of greed. Vladimir Putin is ashamed of you. He could still rescind that "Order of Friendship" that he gave you.

Your problem is that you spent a lifetime just digging the ground, extracting what you did not put inside the soil. If you were like me, building mansions out of nothing, you would know how challenging life can be. What else did you do with your life, other than bribe your way through some of the most tyrannical governments in the world? And you call yourself a corporate leader? No wonder you could not manage the State Department that Hillary Clinton turned into her fiefdom.

That was why you could not appreciate the revolution that I am leading. I am working to change the stagnant norms of Washington, DC, that has held our country down. I was obviously expecting too much from a dull and uncreative person like you. I should have known that a man with Hillary-like disappearing emails and a Wayne Tracker alias should not be trusted.

As you go home to write your own book, remember to tell the truth. Do not write the kind of fiction that James Comey wrote. In any case, because you will have me on the cover, you are assured that the book will be a bestseller. Take the money and add it to your retirement account from ExxonMobil.

Have a nice life. I mean it. I will never do the kind of things you did to me. Never! If you are an honorable Eagle Scout and you are honest with yourself, you will have the courage to say that I was the greatest thing that happened to your life.

Ungrateful fool.

Yours truly,
Donald J. Trump
The 45th President of the United States of America

Donald Trump's Letter to John McCain

Monday, May 7, 2018

Dear Senator McCain,

I can see that you are still angry. Even at this dying minute? My friend, get over it. Grow up! Are you going to be bitter till the very end? Isn't there a better way for you to round off your life? Shit! Not that I'm bothered.

But if I were you, I would be making peace with my fellow humans to have a better chance of making heaven. Especially with the kind of life that you lived, you don't need anybody to tell you that the odds of making heaven are against you. But I guess you are so fatalistic that you don't care. What a shame!

Many people said your life went downhill the moment you picked that ignorant woman as your running mate. But I think it started long before that. Long before Vietnam. And it has not stopped even at this late hour. Pathetic! Do take your temper with you as you go, because we don't need it.

I'm giving you straight talk, my friend. Nobody knows about your Manchurian candidacy for president in 2000 better than me. The out-of-wedlock black child might have been fake news, but smart people supported some other stories associated with that.

As a smart guy, I very much agreed with them. You made America look bad when you lost to that African. It was a tremendous stain on America, and the blame be yours for eternity.

Just in case you are wondering, I still have no regret for saying that you were captured and that I like my heroes to be those that avoided capture. It is a hard call, but someone had to make it. If one is captured, for him to be a hero, he has to break out of captivity. That is what James Bond does. But sitting in prison for eternity waiting for negotiations and trade-offs and trade-ins is not a mark of a hero in my eyes. That is why courage matters. No apologies for that.

It is funny that we could have gotten along quite well, being that you love beautiful women too and have married more than once. You also share with me that slippery dance that happens when you transition from one marriage to another. It is just that your hothead would never let you see how amazing I am.

For antagonizing me since I came to shake up Washington, DC, and for voting to keep that dreadful Obamacare alive, I say to you what Anthony Scaramucci taught me: *Cagati in mano e prendit a schiaffi* (meaning, "shit in your hand then slap yourself in the face.")

Let me make one thing clear to you. I am not into going to funerals to begin with. So you are wrong – the right to show up at your funeral is not worth fighting for. When a motherfucker is dead, I let the dead bury their dead. How do I say this in a politically correct way – I consider some deaths nature's way of helping me to drain the swamp. So don't think I will miss a thing because I won't be at your funeral.

If you invite me to a wedding, I will be there. I love weddings. That is why I feel bad that Prince Harry did not invite me to his wedding. I heard that it was all because of Obama politics taken too far. Anyway, English food is horrible to begin with.

As for your funeral, you can have Vice President Mike Pence. Frankly, isn't attending funerals of less important people why we have vice presidents? That is the tradition. Excuse me. It is not as if you would know. You haven't smelt the presidency.

When important people die, like queens, kings, and presidents, I will be there.

So, amigo, don't waste the few remaining sleepless nights on me.

Yours truly,
Donald J. Trump
The 45th President of the United States of America

Donald Trump's Letter to President Emmanuel Macron of France

Thursday, May 10, 2018

Bonjour President Macron,

I did it! Yeah, very easy. Did you watch? Did you see how I was hailed from Iowa to Israel for doing it? Nice people. They are on with the program.

Did you see how stupid your fears were? Did I not tell you not to be a crybaby about it?

Forget about those ignorant people's dance of death in Tehran. We have seen it before. They should know by now that rather than fear death, America takes selfies with death and moves on. What is more stupid than buying American flags and setting them on fire? The more they burn, the more flags we make for them to buy and burn. I just hope those flags they were burning were not made in China. Believe me, that is the reason for my textile tariff.

You thought if I announced America's withdrawal from the unfair and terribly bad Iran nuclear deal that Tehran would bust into a fireball that would engulf the old and new walls of Jerusalem? I told you that you sounded unbelievable. See how right I was?

109

Your problem, like I said during that magnificent, never been seen state dinner at the White House was that you were listening too much to those two old and childless women of Europe. Don't say that I did not warn you. They can be very nasty. I know women like those. They are always hysterical over nothing.

I told you that I am an expert on women affairs. Trust me, women make things bigger than they actually are. That is why I like to have them always subdued, if necessary, barely able to speak English. Those women are easier to handle. This type that you have, all around you in Europe, want to be on top of the man. I don't let that happen. We can't let that happen.

For extremely stupid people in your country who would scream that the sky is falling, just let them know that all I did was correct Obama's reckless mistake. Those who said that I fired the first shot of the Third World War, please tell them to stop being ridiculous. You can guarantee them that the only thing that would make me contemplate something as drastic as starting a Third World War is any attempt by Mueller to attack my beloved Ivanka.

You saw her when you visited. You agreed with me that she is extremely beautiful. She is the only person worth putting my country on the line for. As for me, I am the president, and I am the law. Nothing the president did, does, or will do is against the law. It is in the Constitution. If they don't like it, so bad. Let them go and be president.

Now, about what happens next. I know that this is one thing troubling your Europe wannabe Amazon ladies. Just tell them that Bibi and I have them covered. At our time of choosing, we will announce that Iran is restarting its nuclear weapon program. Once Bibi announces it, I will tell my CIA boys to second Bibi.

Then the war starts. At every opportunity that Bibi and I have, we will bomb Iran's nuclear weapon facilities. It will be spectacular. Like Syrian attacks, only one thousand times more brilliant. My generals told me we can overwhelm Tehran with fire and fury until everyone in that country is on their knees begging me for mercy. It is the kind of language that they understand.

The Saudis are thrilled. As a thank you, they are spending some billions of dollars for our fighter jets. These are jets that you and I know are out of fashion. And I doubt if they have pilots that can make them roar in the night sky the way the American pilots they were built for fly them and can make them blaze. You know fighter jets are like women: in the wrong hands they just lie there on the bed, dormant and cold. But in the right hands, they are fired up, hopping up and down the sky like antelopes. Have you seen antelopes making love before?

My Jews are happy about what I plan to do in Iran. It means that my reelection campaign coffers will be buoyant in a few weeks. If Michael Cohen had not screwed up, his LLC would have been getting millions in deposits per hour. There would have been no need to depend on Putin's friends to funnel money to me through Michael.

Just for your information, this is very confidential. Don't even let Brigitte, your teacher wife, hear about this. My bottom line is that I need insurance against impeachment from all of Mueller's shenanigans. The Koreans were trying to be smart asses. They were scared of their countries being used as a theater of war, so they pulled together. The Shia in the Middle East are eternal mortal enemies, so nothing can change that. A president that is at war is a president that has perpetual immunity from everything. He cannot be impeached or even be criticized while the nation is at war. Never happens.

Forget Nixon. That one was a crook. I, Donald J. Trump, I'm not a crook.

About sanctions. I am re-imposing sanctions against Iran. What it means is that any European company caught doing business with Iran will be barred from doing business with the United States. It is that simple. You are either with us, or you are against us. No exceptions. If you need to translate that into French for your old hens of Europe, please do.

John Bolton said that I am the twenty-first century Winston Churchill. He said in our own eyes I am quickly transforming into the man Churchill, with this simple decision on Iran. Once again, I would be the one who saved the West. You have an opportunity to be my Charles de Gaulle. So, I offer you this deal. You will be my Charles de Gaulle. Putin will be my Roosevelt. And I will be Winston Churchill. Together we will remake the world in our own image.

You just need to stick with me and not with those appeasers of Chamberlain-type that I see in Merkel and May. Get on my strong wings and let us ride into the starlight.

This is the only thing that I ask of you. When I am done with Iran and with flushing Muslims out of Europe, because that is coming next, I will want the Eiffel Tower renamed after me. You tell that woman in London to rename Trafalgar Square or Heathrow Airport after me. Anything short of that would be a sign of ungratefulness. As for the Germans, anything short of renaming their capital city after me would be unacceptable. After all, I am their grandson who found success in America. Wouldn't it be great to rename London Trump?

To celebrate Europe's liberation, you should all throw a party for me. Since Europeans don't work on Wednesday, I want a parade from Elyse Palace across the English Channel and ending at Trafalgar Square. I will be in an open-top limousine waving along. You can stand beside me. If you need a befitting woman by your side, I can get you one of the world's best. I own Miss Universe, you know.

The other day, some smart people were so impressed by my strategy in Iran that they offered me a book deal. It's happening already. They want me to write how I arrived at this marvelous decision on Iran and maybe sprinkle other stunning decisions of my young administration. I scribbled a proposal down for them. I tentatively called the book, *The Secrets of President Donald Trump's Genius* or *The Secret Letters of President Trump*, or *Inside President Donald J. Trump's Head*. They were over the roof with excitement about the best-selling prospects of the book. But I don't want to benefit from the services that I am selflessly rendering to America.

As a result, I decided to have the book published under a pseudo name: John Barron, John Miller, Rudolf de Passe, or

David Dennison. You know, one of those names that I use when I speak anonymously to the media or when I need to sign something discreetly. Some of my people prefer Rudolf Hess because it would resonate with my German heritage. The final choice of name and title are of course left for the publisher to choose.

I showed the outline of the book to some book reviewers, writers and friends in the publishing industry, and these are the reviews that I got.

Praises for *The Secrets of President Donald Trump's Genius.*

"Rudolf Hess should be arrested and locked up for breaking into president Donald Trump's brain. How he came out alive is something that I'm sure the Russians are investigating."
—*New York Daily Apple*

"Don't pick this book up unless you are willing to let reason, your reason, crumble as soon as laughter tickles it."
—*Miami Bell*

"Rudolf Hess must have been dropped on a hard floor when he was a toddler. There is no other way to explain his unique madness."
—*Washington Ghostwriters*

"You must not read this fucking book if you do not want to be offended. LOL. I'm not kidding."
—*London Daily Chips*

"If you do not find yourself screaming at some of these letters, then you are a conscientious objector carried away by your chuckles."
—*Publishers' Slush Pile*

"For making me spill my coffee on my pants, sorry, groin, I say fuck eight generations of your ancestors."
—*Moscow Golden Shower Times*

"Be ready for your conscience to lose its virginity before you open this book. You will not come out the same way you went in, even if you are president Donald Trump."
—*European Rags of Paris*

"Rudolf Hess has sprinkled lies into non-fiction the same way Bill Cosby sprinkled drugs into women's drink, with the same effect."
—*Philadelphia Evening Answers*

"This Trump is smarter than the one in the White House."
Grace Upbeat, the author of *My Nuclear Button Is Bigger than Yours*.

"For spending this much time inside Trump's head, I hope Rudolf t.g. Hess is forced to pay rent." – Tony Bacharach, DC Attorney.

"I don't care who you are, this Trump will surprise you in some pleasant ways as you read these letters. Sometimes, against his best interest, he is really really pee your pant funny." - Jasper Bush, Rock Musician.

"Finally, I understood Donald Trump's mind. Thank you, Mr. Hess." – Michael York, Homeless New Yorker.

So, my friend, don't panic. Hang around, and everything will be alright.

Yours truly,
Donald J. Trump
The 45th President of the United States of America

Donald Trump's Letter to Oprah Winfrey

Saturday, May 12, 2018

Dear Oprah,

Congratulations on your speech at the Golden Globe Awards. That was great. Now say, "Not again."

Repeat.

One more time.

That is how I will end your 2020 presidential campaign. I will remind Americans not to make the same mistake for a second time. They allowed themselves to be mesmerized by Barack Obama, the 2000 Democratic Party one-speech wonder, resulting in unmitigated disaster.

Luckily for America, I came around to mitigate the disaster Obama brought on this great nation.

My generation, the greatest generation, did not allow Jesse Jackson to fool them with speeches full of fluff signifying nothing. But this good-for-selfie generation fell for Obama's empty talk from an empty barrel.

Not anymore. So, shove your Golden Globe speech and return to your TV talk show.

Otherwise, if the Democrats are stupid enough to nominate you for president, I will start writing my second inaugural address.

I will beat you so silly that your brand will never survive. If you are their nominee, Melania will start writing her convention speech on time so that she won't plagiarize someone else's speech.

You will recall that as far back as 1999 when I started thinking of running for president to rescue America and make our country great again, I have flirted with the idea of picking you as my vice president. I thought that as someone born in poverty to a single mother in the deep Southern state of Mississippi, that your story of overcoming tremendous obstacles to become one of the richest people on Earth would inspire many disillusioned Americans. I have not given up on that idea.

You are still a terrific woman. Great in the things you do. But politics is not one of your strengths. You are not good at it. And most women that I know are not good at it either. You women are too insecure and too emotional to succeed in politics. Don't look at Theresa May in the UK and Angela Merkel in Germany. Those individuals are not women. They are almost men. And to make matters worse, in those countries, men are no longer men. I don't need to sugarcoat this. European men have reached the end of their feminization. And that disease is what I'm trying to prevent in America with the disinfectant that I'm spreading after the dung that Obama left behind.

Before this noise about you running for president, I had a secret team that I commissioned to work on how to drop Mike Pence as my vice president in 2020 and pick you as his replacement. I felt your inclusion on my team would help heal America. At first, it would break the hearts of American liberals. But the moment they realized that I was handing over to them on a platter of gold the presidency of the United States, they would embrace the idea—and proclaim my genius.

I still want to believe that you were just teasing them on this quest to be president.

In some ways, you remind me of myself. You took a third-rated talk show out of Chicago and made it an international hit of a TV show. It is the same thing that I did with my father's Queens Village company. I took it to number one real estate company in America.

Through your show, you gave an opportunity for the underrepresented to become part of the mainstream. That is exactly what I did with the Trump Organization. All those Mexicans who would otherwise not find jobs in America because they did not speak English or had no education, I gave them jobs and paid them enough to feed their families and have more to send to their relations in Mexico. One day, I will get the accolades that I deserve.

You, however, did something impressive for which I want to bring you closer to me. After swimming in the gutters with the likes of Jerry Springer, Jenny Jones, Ricki Lake, and Phil Donahue, you made a sharp U-turn. You raised the level of talks that you engaged in on your show. You embraced self-help and pseudo-spirituality. It soon transformed you into a guru. That is exactly the kind of transformation that I want in my second term in office.

I want to elevate the discussion and the language. I want the world to know that I am not an idiot. For crying out loud, I went to an Ivy League university. I cannot do it alone. I need someone around me that I respect to be a partner in that healing process. All the people around me now are the "Yes, sir" types. They don't have confidence in their own thoughts. When I push back just a little, they fold up.

It is hard to believe now that you once won the Miss Black Tennessee beauty pageant. Such an accomplishment matters a lot to me. Probably the same way that black life matters to you. I'm sure if you had lived in a decent part of America that my eyes would have caught you long before you became a national figure. Who knows, I would have taken you by my wings and got you to rise to the top faster than it took you. It is exactly what I did for Melania and so many other women, most of whom would not acknowledge it.

How is Steadman doing? I guess that 1992 marriage ceremony is not going to happen after all. I feel it was a right move on your part. You don't need a partner around you who is feeling entitled. It is better to leave the buffoon hanging around without a designated title or legally binding tag. That way the public will lower their expectations of you. If you don't feel like holding hands in public, you don't have a sense of obligation that you should do it because others are doing it. You know what I'm saying?

You know I did not need your Oprah Effect to get my book as the number one best-selling book of the twentieth and twenty-first century, so even if you decline this offer, I will still accomplish all that I set out to accomplish. Though I am on course to reverse all that Obama did at the White House, I have no intention of rescinding the Presidential Medal of Freedom that Obama gave you in 2013. I would have given that to you if Obama did not do so. And if I had given it to you, it would have been more prestigious and more praiseworthy instead of being seen as mere act of nepotism from Obama.

I still love you, Oprah. Despite your touchy-feely style, you are a fantastic woman. When I am done fooling all these poor folks in rural America with their dogs, smell of gunpowder, and dream of manna from heaven, I will rejoin the elite.

Remember December 1, 2005, when you appeared on *The Late Show* with David Letterman, thereby ending your eleven-year feud; I want to invite you to the White House as my reelection campaign approaches. I want you to be the moderator as I host former presidents, all of whom are not talking to me now. It would be like the eightieth birthday party you threw for Maya Angelou at my wonderful Mar-a-Lago club. I could use that opportunity to announce you as my running mate. What do you think? Believe me, it would shake up Washington, DC. Oh, by the way, come with Gayle. Nice lady!

To be quite frank with you, I hope this doesn't count as Oprahfication. I believe you are like me deep down – a hustler with a great sense of timing. There must be something we can do together – you and me. Unlike Obama, I don't need an endorsement from you and the one million primary votes you gave Obama. I fly with my wings. Instead, what I need from you is to have you as my running mate as I predicted in 1999.

Spend a little time and think about this. This is how history will record our partnership. Oprah was the woman who came and tamed Donald Trump. Let the dishonest media celebrate that I have accepted the gospel according to Oprah. I don't give a hoot. After Donald Trump, then comes Oprah, the first female president of the United States of America. That would be the icing on the cake of your great achievements.

Yours truly,
Donald J. Trump
The 45th President of the United States of America

President Donald Trump's Secret Letter to Prince Harry

Thursday, May 24, 2018

Dear Prince Harry,

Congratulations on your wedding. I watched a little bit of it. I wish I could say that it was terrific. But I can't. In fact, it was horrendous. Believe me, it was too painful to watch. I'm sure the ratings were in the gutters.

What was that cheap thing that your bride was wearing in the name of a wedding gown? Awful! I know that your father is unemployed, but if your grandparents had fallen on hard times, you should have reached out to me for help. I could have asked some shell companies to wire some money to your shell account. It was such a disgrace of a wedding gown. For crying out loud, you are a prince. Or are you not? I now regret more that I did not get the chance to date your mother. I would have had the chance to impart on you a little bit of my marvelous taste in style and women.

Didn't you and Meghan take a look at what my Melania was wearing during my wedding? That picture is beautiful people's first stop for inspiration as they plan for their wedding. *All Styles Magazine* called it the "gold standard." And what is up with

120

Meghan not putting on makeup? The cake may be sweet on its own, but it still needs the icing. You see, I pleaded with you to consult me, but out of fear of your grandparents, who were playing fake diplomatic politics, you didn't. You missed a wonderful opportunity to make Britain great again. You messed up bigly.

Oh, where did you dig up Rev. Jeremiah Wright? I thought Obama kept him in a witness protection program? I'm talking of that pastor that preached at your wedding. Disgusting! How could you subject your grandparents to that torture? You make America look bad. If you had told me that you needed an American preacher, I would have given you one of our very fine preachers, like Pastor John Hagee. He is a great guy. He would have spoken in good English that your grandparents would have understood, and not Ebonics.

And that nasty black woman conductor for the "Stand by Me" singers... how did she get into that church? Through which door? She was not good for your reputation. It totally sucked. You know what? I will give you and Meghan a great deal. Come over to Mar-a-Lago for your honeymoon, and I will help you repair the damage your whole wedding debacle did to your reputation. Don't worry about the dishonest media. I will keep them off my property for the period that you are there.

I have a lot of things to discuss with you, including how to handle the upcoming election for the next King of England. I have some friends who could help you beat the establishment candidates. In the meantime, I have to run. I will write you at another time. General Kelly has this North Korean thing that he wants me to look at.

Yours truly,
President Donald J. Trump
The 45th President of the United States of America

Donald Trump's Letter to Kim Jong-un

Sunday, May 27, 2018

Dear Chairman Kim,

I write to ask you to ignore the public letter I just sent you. I was just trying to distract the dishonest media. Lucky you, you don't have to deal with such irritation. The first task of your media is to dress you up in your Sunday best. Anyone who goes out of line goes out of circulation. That is how presidents should be treated all over the world. Damn it, I admire the respect that you are accorded by your countrymen. I bet no late-night comic makes fun of you at night. These are some of the indignations that I have to deal with. Totally unacceptable.

The second reason I canceled the meeting was to reestablish that I am the boss. Everything happens because I want it to happen. There is no other way things happen in the era of Donald Trump. Some retarded people are beginning to suggest that you and I should share the Nobel Prize with the low-energy South Korean leader and the cunny poker-faced chairman Xi Jinping of China. I don't think so. Now that you and I have done the heavy lifting, taken all the risks, they are loitering around to take part in the glory. I won't let them.

The third reason I canceled the meeting was to give the Russians time to take care of something for me. In this chess game that we play, time makes all the difference.

The fourth reason I canceled the summit was because of my vice president. He was hurt by the name your people called him. I had promised him that I would do something about the name-calling shit. My canceling of the meeting was my way of making him happy. He is a sensitive man, but my bitch still. His Christianity is phony though, but nobody is ready to tell him that. He clings to prayers the way some old bitches cling to phony tits to get ahead.

Despite what the fake news media is blabbing, I am sending my people to come and meet your people. Not only are we still looking forward to Singapore, but also we still hope to have it take place on June 12. I have checked every other day in June and July in a history book. The twelfth is the only day that nothing important has happened in history. I want the day of our meeting not to share historical pages with any other event.

After my people meet your people at the DMZ, you can send your best man to New York City for a meeting. Your man will definitely be given America's unbeatable hospitality. Whatever he wants in New York City, we shall make it available to him. If he wants to stay at the Trump Tower, we will make the penthouse available to him. What is important is that we hold this historic summit and stun the world of doubters.

I'm sure you understand my strategy.

Yours truly,
Donald J. Trump
The 45th President of the United States of America

Donald Trump's Letter to a Kid Separated from Parents at the US Border

Tuesday, June 19, 2018

Hello lil' amigo,

Once upon a time, there was a little mermaid lost on the Pacific Sea, trying to make its way to the Atlantic. She has one lifeline left—popping onto the great American ship named Donald Trump.

Forget it! Why am I wasting time with a folktale? It is not as if you have the cognitive skills needed to understand what I am saying.

Let me cut to the chase. How are you? I hope you are enjoying the United States. Isn't this the greatest country that you have ever seen? I'm sure it is. You must have been enjoying our wonderful meals—hamburgers and hot dogs. I bet you have never tasted anything like those. Did you eat our watermelon? I heard you people like that.

I'm fully aware of the sad condition of the shithole country where you were born. It is unfortunate. But it is not my own making. By that I mean, it is not America's making. It is a matter that you need to discuss with your God when you see him. He chose to put you there. Ask him why.

A friend of mine here at the White House, who believes in Eastern religion, says that your lot in life is a result of what you did in your last life. If he is right, it means that you were naughty in your last life. As a result, you were condemned to be born in Guatemala, El Salvador, or Honduras. In your last life, you were probably a rapist or you were bringing drugs into the United States. It has to be one of those. Just accept your punishment.

If you live a better life this time, maybe in your next life, you will be born in the United States. That way, you don't need to sneak into our country with your mother – that is, if she is really your actual mother. Believe me, we know there is nothing you guys will not do to get into God's own country—the United States.

I am building the wall to keep little pricks like you out. It looks harsh right now, but at the end, it will be good for you. You pay your dues, your debt to your society, and in your next life, you will have a better life. But if I allow you to sneak in here, claiming political asylum, you miss an opportunity to repent. Without repentance, your sin will follow you along.

Another way to look at it is that if you all leave your damned countries, who is going to fix them? The United States of America is not interested in nation building abroad. We want to build up our own nation first. Do you catch my drift?

Come to think of it, your parents complain that they were running away because of gang violence and all that. I laugh in German when I hear that. What kind of violence is in Guatemala, Honduras, or El Salvador? Is it anything compared to what we have in Chicago where Obama's thugs are openly and happily destroying the city? Do you see kids and their mothers leaving Chicago for Mexico, Cuba, or the Dominican Republic? No. Chicago parents and their kids are not even packing up to climb into a Greyhound bus for a few hours' trip to Canada, Iowa, or Madison. They are not buying the Eldorado tales about life in Canada, Iowa, or Madison. They are staying put to fight for their hometown. That is what I expect your folks to do.

For those mothers who say that domestic violence is the reason they are running away, have they bothered to look at the statistics about domestic violence in America? There are twelve million victims of domestic violence in the United States every year. That is more than three percent of the US population. In the White House here, the percentage is even more.

Imagine if those twelve million men and women with their kids headed south of our border. Where would they settle? Mexico would not contain them. Who would provide for them? Are there cages in Haiti for Americans running away from domestic violence? Would the UN nonsense asylum expectations cater to the twelve million Americans each year?

I heard that your parents are telling you that the man stopping you from enjoying a good life in America is the Nebuchadnezzar of our time. I know Jeff Sessions. He is not a Nebuchadnezzar. He is a glorified sissy. He does not have what it takes to be a great king like Nebuchadnezzar. So when you hear that fairy tale, don't pay any mind to it.

I'm sure some of you have listened to those talking heads on TV who compare your living situation to cages. You and I know that it is 100 percent better than where you came from. That you enjoy running water and modern toilet facilities in the housing we provided you is something to be appreciative of. Some Americans in Alabama do not have such amenities. Even in New York City housing authority buildings, water tanks have Legionnaires' disease while tenants endure winter without heat in their homes. So be thankful. Don't think for a moment that we don't know that you came from where you drink untreated well water and water from polluted streams and that you defecate inside the bushes or in pit latrines. We know, amigo. We know.

So I advise you to just tell your parents to calm down. Let them enjoy it while it lasts because we are determined to send you back to where you came from. For you, consider this visit as a camp, summer camp in America. When you get back home tell those still planning to make the trip that America is closed.

Yours truly,
Donald J. Trump
The 45th President of the United States of America

Donald Trump's Letter to Roseanne Barr

Sunday, July 1, 2018

Dear Roseanne,

I'm sorry to read that the liberals who run television networks in America have gotten rid of you. I can talk to my people at Fox television to get you a spot at that brilliant network. My only concern is that you often operate like a lone ranger. You are incapable of taking instructions from anybody. There has to be someone out there that you listen to. You cannot operate on your own whims. Who do you think you are? Donald Trump?

See, let me tell you a secret. You can do anything you want to black men. But black women are a protected species. Before you attack them, you have to make sure they are damaged goods like Maxine Walters. Trust me, just like you, I didn't know that bitch was black. I thought she was Arab. That was what scared me the most about her. That she might, just like that Crooked Hillary's Arab assistant, be sending information to Israel's enemies. You never can tell with those people.

If I were to compare her to an animal, I would not have gone for an ape. I would have said a ram. You know, those stinking, angry-looking animals with oversized balls. But, yeah, I'm a nice guy, so I will leave it at that.

People in Washington do not understand my genius. It may look as if I attack people indiscriminately. But, no, I don't. Believe me, there are hours of calculations put into any tweet that I send out. Even the typographical errors are planned in advance. As for the grammatical errors, they are put in there to obstruct and distract the little-minded ones who do not see the big picture.

What baffled me was your reaction to being fired. Why did you beg those knuckleheads at ABC not to cancel your show? It made you look weak. People who voted for me do not fold like that. They attack. When they go high, we drag them down. When they go low, we get a shovel and dig up dirt all around them until they sink deeper.

Why did you blame Ambien for the tweet you sent? I like Ambien. I get it all the time on Air Force One when I am going to important meetings abroad. Let me tell you, once they see that you sound weak, they bounce and pounce even more. Instead of reasoning with them, reminding them that the advertisers were not bailing out and that you were ready to go on TV and explain yourself, you should have been threatening to send a truckload of lawyers to sue them into oblivion.

If you had called me before speaking with them, I would have told you to wear your Hitler mustache and swastika armband, grab your crotch, and spit at them once again. The joke is not on you. It is on them. But if you really wanted to explain, you should have told them that the stress of being the number one show on American TV reactivated the traumatic injury you had when you were a kid, following that accident. You could have said that the numerous psychiatric drugs your doctor prescribed for you were making you lose touch with reality. Liberals love to sympathize with people like that.

When I called you to celebrate the success of your reboot show, I told you I could connect you to a great talent agency far better than ICM. You may have to do a deeper tummy tuck, tighter breast reduction, wider gastric bypass, and a precision nose job to fit in. But I'm not worried. You are used to those adjustments that come with being a major TV star. There is nothing anyone can do about your ugly face. But those who say you are unattractive are not seeing your inside. Once I am done with this presidency thing, I'm signing up with the agency, and that is when I will become much more than the greatest star in the world.

Did I just hear that ABC is moving ahead without you? How could you allow them to do that? It is your show, after all. When I left NBC, on my own terms, I only allowed them to carry on with *The Apprentice* because even though I wasn't there, I was still getting paid for every episode they made. That is smart thinking on my part. As it showed, the failures of the shows made after I left proved that I was the main attraction of the show. That big mouth of a failed actor, Arnold Schwarzenegger, was a total disaster. What is he doing with his life now besides being the babysitter of the amigo child he had with his house cleaner?

Do you still take marijuana for glaucoma? I don't want you to despair. Junior is working on starting a TV network, Donald Trump Network, DTN. If you keep your brain sharp, we can get you a spot on the network. Mind you, it won't be the tear-jerking kind of thing that Oprah is doing at OWN. In the meantime, let John Goodman and co. keep fooling themselves thinking that they are making a spin-off. Their fate will be the same as the fate of all those Republicans who think they can win elections without me. They have started to see that they are nothing without me. Democrats will devour them without my muscles. That is the same with you.

Until then, keep spending the money you have already made. And prepare to run for political office again in 2020, though I advise you not to go straight to a run for president. Winning the presidency in the first try without any political experience happens once in a century. It takes a special legend to accomplish that. I'm not saying this because I did it. It is just the plain truth.

Yours truly,
Donald J. Trump
The 45th President of the United States of America.

Donald Trump's Letter to Queen Elizabeth

Sunday, July 15, 2018

Dear Queen Elizabeth,

I thank you for your warm welcome when Melania and I visited Windsor Castle. We appreciate all the efforts your majesty government made to make sure we were comfortable.

Despite not curtsying to you, which was a minor oversight, I have no doubt that we greatly impressed you. You only got a glimpse of why I loom larger than life wherever I go. It is a humongous gift that I have. Unbelievable! Isn't it?

I understand that I was the twelfth US president you have hosted. I don't need to be told, but I know you consider me one of a kind. You are not alone. I dazzle people everywhere I go. I remind them of a long-gone era when men were men and politicians were what the people wanted them to be.

Before I came, I took a crash course in your country. I was quite impressed by the things I learned. I had thought before then that you all were women, just sissies, with the exception of Winston Churchill. I was surprised that you joined the Second World War and were trained as a mechanic.

If another Vietnam War were to start, you bet I would be first to go to the war front. I missed the last one because I had bad feet. It has since been resolved when I stood on my own.

Did Churchill really say that at age two you had an air of authority and reflectiveness astonishing in an infant? Did he? It is historic that you have met five popes. You are now the longest-lived, longest-reigning British Monarch, but that is not enough. To what end? That is the question. In less than two years, I have accomplished more than Obama could do in eight years.

Since I am the last US president that you will ever meet, I think you should consider renaming one big institution in London after me. Stick it to the face of those ignorant protesters wasting their miserable lives on the streets of London while I was with you in Windsor. Do it as a reminder to that sleeper cell Muslim punk in London city hall, of who truly owns the land. Trust me, it would be the most lasting legacy of your sixty years on the throne. I can reciprocate by renaming the old lady of the White House, the West Wing, the Queen Elizabeth Wing. I know you will like that.

As a smart leader and former host of *The Apprentice* I have assessed your son Charles. I don't think he has the backbone needed to return the failing United Kingdom to its coveted place in the world. He looks weak, like a man that Camilla orders around. Without telling you how to run the affairs of your Kingdom, I think you should state in your will that the crown should skip Charles and go to Prince William. That is the only hope the monarchy has to rejuvenate itself after you. Charles will do to the United Kingdom what Obama did to the United States—turn it into a feminine nation of welfare-dependent bleeding-heart liberals.

I don't need to warn you about that Obama-lit American that Harry brought into your distinguished family. Bad choice! She may look harmless but going by the damage that Obama brought on the United States, I can tell you that she has the potential of ruining the great tradition of your noble family. I know she and her generation will never come near the line of succession, but they can pollute the Windsor family tree. Before they scream "racist," you and I know that I am not a racist, but I personally think it is contaminated as it is. If Harry had told me that he wanted an American woman, there are a lot of fine, smart, and clean

American girls I could have hooked him up with. Not that eh... what again did Omarosa say Peter Tosh called such girls? Yeah, "brand-new second-hand girls." He could well have married Stormy Daniels.

That was one reason why I did not date your late daughter-in-law, Diana. I fancied her a lot, at one point. I even made moves. I sent some bouquet of the finest flowers money could buy. But as I found out now, she had this thing that most of your subjects have about gum-chewing ugly Americans. Since your uncle, Edward VIII's abdication, after marrying divorced American socialite Wallis Simpson, your people have looked at our people with suspicion. It shouldn't be so. We may be cowboys, but we have our hearts in the right place.

How could you even feel that way about us, the beautiful Americans? Your husband's sister married a Nazi. And your husband was foreign-born, from Europe's shithole country of Greece. He wasn't even Anglican. So, what are we saying here?

Since my visit, a thought has remained with me. As far back as 1929, you were born by cesarean section. Great feat, then. So, whatever happened to the Great Britain that I read about in the history books? Your kingdom is losing so badly in ways that matter. Did all your smart and courageous men and women leave for the United States? An extremely credible source told me that you failed to build a great wall, allowing the Irish to flood your country and neutralize your strength. Seriously, how was it that you were left with men with crooked teeth and weak spines, like Theresa May? Oh, I forgot, he is a woman. Lol.

Now let me say the most amazing thing you ever heard. I hope you remember it for the rest of your life. I find you very hot, grandma. It was a surprise to me. I hope you don't take any offense. Consciously or unconsciously, I did not expect that. I'm just being me. At one point I was afraid of being left alone with you in the palace. Just saying. Imagine the president of the United States hooking up with the Queen of England in Buckingham Palace or in a Treetop Hotel in a jungle somewhere. Now that would be the greatest movie of all time.

I hope it makes you smile whenever you remember it.

Yours truly,
Donald J. Trump
The 45th President of the United States of America

Donald Trump's Letter to the President of Croatia

Sunday, July 15, 2018

Dear President of Croatia,

Just like prime minister Theresa May of Britain, you failed to take my advice on the best formulae your team were to use in their game against France. I told you that the fate of the White race was resting on your country's team. I told you that as a real estate developer in New York City, I knew a lot about those people from those shithole countries. I know how to scare the shit out of them. But you, a mere daughter of a butcher shop owner, ignored me. Look at the result now.

You did not just fail your country, you failed the great white race. Do you know how emboldened those godforsaken multiculturalists/globalists will be now? They will hold up the picture of France's team with the World Cup and try to sell it as the ideal. You are such a disgrace.

The good thing is that you and your country will go back to remain inconspicuous in world affairs. Who knows, your country may never get back to the World Cup final in fifty years. You squandered a rare opportunity because you didn't want to listen to Donald Trump. See your life now!

I blame myself for stooping so low to talk to you. You aren't even the most powerful person in your country. I should have been talking to your prime minister. You know what? I think in my speech at the UN this year, I should demand that all countries in the world should abandon the stupid parliamentary system and adopt the great American presidential system. When someone says he or she is president, we really know he or she is one. Not a president who travels at her own expense, flying economy class and watching World Cup soccer from the non-VIP stand. If any country opposes my idea, I will ban them from coming to New York City for the UN General Assembly.

Watch out! Before the next World Cup, my father's folks in Germany must get rid of that obnoxious woman at the helm of affairs in their country. And once again, Germany will come up with a pure white team that will thrill the world and restore the pride and the glory of our people.

Because you messed up, I am coming up with a brilliant idea. I am thinking of starting an alternative soccer competition to be called Trump's World Cup (TWC). Only the top twenty-five richest countries in the world will participate, eliminating insignificant countries like your Croatia, Uruguay, Costa Rica, and Iceland. Can you believe that the irrelevant Costa Rica knocked out the Great United States (GUS) from going to Russia for the finals?

Each participating country in the TWC will put up $40 million to be part of it. The winner takes home $1 billion, which is more meaningful than the pocket change FIFA gives now. I will put up the first $1 billion for the winner to take home. That, my friend, will preserve my name for eternity.

So there's no reason to waste more time writing you. Go back to the beach. Keep displaying your awful, disgusting bikini body that some dishonest people have been telling you is appealing. If you show a body like that anywhere near my Mar-a-Lago estate, I will ban you from coming to Florida.

Before I go, my people told me that you have been flirting with Iranian president Hassan Rouhani. You don't want to be in the line of fire and fury that Benjamin Netanyahu and I are planning to unleash on Iran. Some low-life people in your country may be calling you SWAMBO, as in, "she who must be obeyed." I don't need to advertise my capability, do I?

Yours truly,
Donald J. Trump
The 45th President of the United States of America

Donald Trump's 2nd letter to Vladimir Putin

Wednesday, July 18, 2018

Dear Vladimir Putin,

What a great summit we had, my friend. That was a historical one. Whatever happens from now on, we have made history. You and I are now the two greatest historical figures of the twenty-first century. Bar none. We have changed the course of world history for antiquity. The handshake in Helsinki has caused butterflies to blanket the skies of Europe and Asia. We are the new kids on the block determined to rewrite our histories in ways Lenin and George Washington could not have imagined.

We will change the world even more in the next seven years. That is my promise. And my words are my bond. By the time we are done, trust me, our statues will grace the great squares of the world, from Peru to Prague, from Casablanca to Karachi, from Tokyo to Tehran, from Sydney to Shanghai, from Phnon Penh to Pyongyang, and from Johannesburg to Jeddah.

As you can see, the busybodies here on American TV are displaying their moronic views once again. They want to know what we discussed in our private meeting. I trust that you will never let out the contents of the top-secret talks we had no matter the provocation. I hate leakers with the last fiber in me, so you can be sure that it won't leak from my side. I bet that you will take care of your interpreter the best Putinistic way you do those things. Mine has been taken care of the way the Trumps do things—which is in a sophisticated style.

Let me alert you that in days to come, we may have the need to use harsh words on Russia. These obsolete people around Washington, DC, may even force me to say some uncomplimentary stupid things about you. But you know they are just for the TV. You know that I hold you in the highest esteem. You are a great guy, and there is no other leader with your understanding of power, its use and essence, anywhere in the world—100 percent true. I have said to myself time and time again, if only they knew you, how wonderful you are, they would stop listening to the alarmists in Washington.

If need be, the Congress of the United States and the low IQ people who run some of the arms of my government may impose sanctions on Russia. You and I know they are meaningless gestures. Billions and billions of dollars will continue to flow between our two countries through the dark web located at the backyard of our great financial institutions. You are welcome to retaliate. You should make great noise about the danger of returning the Russia–US relationship to its antagonistic past to the detriment of our people. As usual, it will end there. Our communion in Helsinki is deep and eternal.

Melania sent her greetings. You know her parents' first choice of country to live in was Russia. Maybe when I come to Moscow later in the year, I will bring them with me.

Yours truly,
Donald J. Trump
The 45th President of the United States of America

Donald Trump's Letter to LeBron James

Saturday, August 4, 2018

Dear LeBron James,

My aides have pleaded with me to ignore you and your stupid antics. I have done so for a long time. My tongue rolls up spit, ready to volley it your way, but I restrain myself. Continuing to do so at this point would be an injustice to me. It will make me appear weak. And you know how I hate being seen as weak.

They said you are beloved in Ohio, a state I must win to be reelected. They also said that if our life stories were compared, there would be a contrast. I got the strategy outline they prepared. You were born dirt poor, while I was born super rich. You pulled yourself up by the bootstraps, while I got a one million-dollar head start. I heard them. They said you married your high school sweetheart, while I have dated and dumped more beauty queens than any other man in the world. All your three children were from one woman. On my part, I have married thrice, divorced twice, and had children with more than three different women.

Guess what! I don't give a damn! I need to take care of your ingratitude once and for all. You were born a loser. It was my fellow billionaire that gave you a chance to be somebody. Somehow, you seem to have horribly forgotten that. You should be eternally grateful to billionaires like me who make it possible for at-risk kids like you to be able to put food on your table. It is clear that if your life depends on your intellect, you will be spending time in a penitentiary somewhere in Ohio like your fellow inner-city travelers. At least, show some respect to us, your benefactors.

You built a little wacky school and childishly called it I Promise. And it got into your head. Ever heard of Trump University? Never mind. It is beyond your intellectual level. Do you know all the wonderful things my father and I have done for poor people from New York to Florida and from Florida to Virginia and from Virginia to Las Vegas? Tremendous acts of kindness. If you have any doubt, count the houses in New York alone that have Trump written on them. Do I brag about that? No. Do I get those TV vultures to come each time I cut a ribbon to open another house? No.

And about that talent thing... It is crazy how you people misuse the word *talent*. When we talk about people with talent, don't get it confused with people with muscles. Talent is what the founder of Facebook has. Muscles are what Mike Tyson has. Sorry, had. Talent is what Albert Einstein has. Muscles for laughter are what Chris Rock has. Those who can, do things. Those who can't, entertain those who do things.

Next time you feel you have something important to say, find a better TV channel. If you have no contacts at FOX News, let me know, and I will connect you to some fine and brilliant guys at FOX. Don't go near that fake news CNN. You can do better than that. And even if you must appear on CNN, stay away from stupid Don Lemon. Nothing will revamp Don Lemon's failing career. Not even if he gets an exclusive interview with Elvis, the King. Mr. Lemon is scum. He is not just obnoxious (if you know what the word means), but he is also so dumb, the morons at CNN just keep him there to fulfill affirmative action requirements. Something I hope Justice Brett Kavanaugh will get rid of as soon as he is confirmed to the US Supreme Court.

One last bit of advice. Forget what the dishonest media is telling you, listen to Laura Ingraham – shut up and dribble. You don't have another decade to do the only thing you were equipped to do. Oh, I forgot. You were also equipped to have babies, and I bet you are just getting started. Remember that they need to be fed. Don't count on food stamps. By the time I'm done with my second term, that benefit will be history. So if I were you, I would shut up and dribble.

I don't know the last time you read any book. Very likely not since you left high school. So, let me not trouble you with a long letter.

All the best,
Donald J. Trump
The 45th President of the United States of America

Donald Trump's Letter to Omarosa

Wednesday, August 22, 2018

Dear Omarosa,

Your book could not even crack the number one spot on Amazon's list of bestsellers despite the help I gave you? You lost so big. Shame on you!

Did you write it in Ebonics? Or were you so intoxicated by an evil desire to make me look bad that you lost the plot of your tale?

How could Rachel Hollis's *Girl, Wash Your Face* beat you on the bestseller list? Maybe she was saying to you, "Girl, wash your mouth and let some wise surgeon remove the cobwebs blanketing your tiny brain."

It is very sad that all my efforts to make you somebody were wasted attempts. Like all your people, you desired instant gratification instead of building on something that would last. You sold a couple of books, a few thousand at most, made enough money to visit your neighborhood salon and change your hairstyle. And then what?

Mark my words, this is exactly why you people can never be successful business people. In your own case, I have had reasons to question your mental stability. You were not really smart, but I had thought you had a bit of native intelligence that I could work with to turn you into something. But I guess when stupidity is deeply buried in someone, no amount of exposure can neutralize it. Somehow, it finds a way to surface to the top.

It was a huge mistake investing in you. Sad. Like John said, I just have to accept that some were not just born in the slum, but the slum was also born in them.

Yours truly,
Donald J. Trump
The 45th President of the United States of America

Donald Trump's Letter to Paul Manafort

Thursday, August 23, 2018

Dear Paul Manafort,

You are a man's man, the pride of your Italian ancestors. You have given me hope to keep my faith in humanity. Despite the provocations by overzealous prosecutors, you took it like a man. At sixty-nine, you were a lot braver than that fifty-nine-year-old marine general Michael Flynn, who fell helplessly on his sword. What is eighty years in jail when you have, at most, another twenty years to live? They won't make you come back to the world to finish your sentence. Will they?

Beyond that, you know that I got your back. I do. With a stroke of the pen, I will make you a free man. And you bet that I will do it. When to do so and how is up to me. I'm still watching as things unfold. I'm letting them put up their best attack. When they are done, I will hit back. And you know how powerful my hit-backs are.

There is no need pardoning you for one conviction when other trials and convictions are coming. I feel that the best thing is for them to do their worst. Let them heap it all on you. One hundred years in prison, one thousand years in prison, it does not matter. Let the federal trial run its course. Let the state trial run its course.

And then, with a stroke of my pen, I will correct all the wrongs they have done on a good man like you and make you a free man again.

As a lawyer, you know that by wiping your slate clean, you can go on and enjoy the rest of your life as if nothing happened. Meanwhile, that traitor, Michael Cohen, will spend the rest of his life in squalor. I single-handedly took that motherfucker out of the Jewish squalor where I found him. And this is the thanks that I get?

We shall see how it ends. Believe me, it won't end like your father's. In your father's political profile as mayor of New Britain, it says, "Indicted but not convicted." I, Donald J. Trump, will leave your slate spotlessly clean. Nobody will mention in your biography that you even visited Ukraine, not to mention being tried and being convicted of a crime.

You worked for great historical individuals like Victor Yanukovych of Ukraine, Ferdinand Marcos of Philippines, Mobutu Sese Seko of Zaire and even guerrilla leader Jonas Savimbi of Angola. They are all great guys who live on in history books. You led my guerrilla campaign, slaying the so-called goliaths of the Republican Party. You are a nice man whose life is being ruined by that evil man Mueller.

Trust me, good will ultimately defeat evil. I defeated Crooked Hillary, and so will a good man like you ultimately defeat Evil Mueller.

As long as I am president, you don't have anything to worry about. For a loyal man like you who worked for Presidents Ford, Reagan, and Bush Sr., you will be taken care of. And so, will your family. I am sure that you still have some money left from the $1 million a year Mobutu Sese Seko paid you in 1989 or the $950,000 a year that Ferdinand Marcos paid or the $1 million that the Nigerians paid you in 1991. Use it to keep your family going until I find an offshore account to send some money to your wife, Kathleen, and your two beautiful daughters.

Bill Clinton cheated like a dog, yet they did nothing to him – not even a slap on the wrist. I cannot allow them to destroy a business that you built with your sweat.

Yours truly,
Donald J. Trump
The 45th President of the United States of America

Donald Trump's 2nd Letter to Michael Cohen

Thursday, August 24, 2018

Dear Michael Cohen,

L ook at you. Loser. Look at how little you have become. I lifted you up, but you have no good brain to keep yourself there. You have no clue how massive my goodness was to you.

So, you recorded my conversations with you? I'm bigly disappointed. You are the worst form of scum on the earth! You are a lawyer from hell.

As Omarosa used to say, when I finish with you, you will know that hot water kills the tortoise.

Good riddance. And may you spend eternity in hell.

Yours truly,
Donald J. Trump
The 45th President of the United States of America

Donald Trump's Letter to Secretary of State Mike Pompeo

Friday, September 14, 2018

Dear Secretary of State Mike Pompeo,

This is just a draft.

I, Donald J. Trump, the 45th president of the United States of America, having done my best to make America great, and having resolved that America has failed to utilize my genius, do hereby resign the office of President of Make America Great Again.

Let America continue in its gradual decline until it is fully a subservient nation to the resurgent Russia and the rising state of China. And who knows, in another one hundred years, America may be taking orders from shithole countries like Nigeria. That would be a total disgrace.

I sort of hope that happens so that I will tell you all, "I told you so."

It is on record that I have warned America. My people are under the influence of criminals and rapists from Mexico and the Southern Hemisphere and from the voodoo of people from the shithole countries of Africa.

I have ordered an exorcist to come and remove the evil spirits left by that African that was last in the White House. I'm recommending a thorough disinfectant of the buildings before another American president goes in there. Otherwise, it would be the same outcome of putting in maximum effort for a meager result.

I will pray for the United States of America. The beautiful thing about my life is that I am very rich. Whatever happens, I will continue to live a fantastic life. I am going to have an unbelievable retirement. And when I die, I don't want any former president to come there and shed crocodile tears.

My enemies can smash my star on the Hollywood Walk of Fame. They can take anything away from me, my private jet, my Washington, DC, Hotel, my beloved Melania, but they can never take away the fact that I am, or should I say, was, the 45th president of the United States.

Yours truly,
Donald J. Trump
The 45th President of the United States of America

Donald Trump's Letter to His Son, Barron Trump

Sunday, September 16, 2018

My dear son, Barron,

I must apologize that I often forget that I have a 12-year-old son in the White House. For some strange reasons, not for a moment do I forget that I'm the president of these United States. I'm being 100% honest with you.

I know that Ivanka, Eric, Tiffney and Don Jr. will be alright. They are all grownups. Even when the whole world is going crazy, there is nothing that I do that they cannot make sense of. Don Jr., especially, has mastered my attitude and, even, my lingo.

Barron, you still have seven years to go before you will begin to understand the deeper meaning of everything that is happening around you today.

Despite what historians will write about me, just remember these undisputable facts. Your father is a great man. That is me, being modest. Naturally, I would have said that I'm the greatest president that ever lived, which is not far from the truth.

Contrary to what the liberal left is making of me, your father has unlimited human emotions. Yeah, I have emotions. I only show one on TV and when I tweet. I have fears, though you will never see it on my face – not even when the name Mueller is mentioned. Behind my public defiance, I'm just a kid like you who wants to belong and to be liked not just by the ignorant masses but also by those in high society.

I'm navigating with grace the headache of being president in the age of trolls. It is a peculiar challenge that Obama and Bush did not have to deal with. Despite my tough public exterior, you can attest to the fact that I am compassionate. I show kindness even to my most ardent opponent. Yes, I do. I don't obsess about them the way my tweets suggest.

I surrender to those who least expected me to. I conquer with ease those who are most steadfast against me. Beyond the insults, I'm just a teddy bear scrambling for a loving and lasting hug. I may not be the most humorous president but nobody will say that I don't try to keep America entertained.

My son, you know I am rich. But I'm not just rich in billions and billions of dollars; I also have a rich soul. I make sacrifices for the benefit of posterity. It will surprise those looking from outside that I am a reflective individual. Those who are introspectively impoverished make themselves feel good by thinking that I am superficial. I'm deep.

Barron, your father is deep. Your dad is smart. Don't forget that I graduated from Wharton Business School of University of Pennsylvania. It doesn't get better than that.

Beyond the ugliness of today's politics, history will record it on everlasting marble that I devoted my time as president to things that are more than myself. If people are patient enough, if they flip those things they think make me look small, they will see wisdom that they didn't know that I have.

My dear Barron, the world that you were born in is more complicated than the one I was born in. My job is to keep hope alive in America. When others are losing their heads, I stay strong and push ahead to that glorious future for you and our beloved country. Like a brave soul that I am, I do so without counting the loss to my reputation. It is only my temporary reputation that is hurt. My eternal reputation is sealed and secured far away from the reach of the wretched of this country.

One hundred years from now, my courage under this crushing pressure will be celebrated. Your dad would be identified as the hero who used bursts of energy, rage and genius, in that order, to quench what was once accepted as the inevitable decline of the American empire.

Keep this letter, my son. You may have reasons in the future to show it to the world to prove that you dad was a good man who did his very best for his country. That is all that our citizenship demands of us.

Despite all that I have said in this letter, being president of the United States of America is the best thing that can happen to any man. Eh, women, maybe not. If not for anything else, for the mere fact that as long as you are the president, behind your back, people can call you an idiot, a moron or complete narcissist but nobody can tell you to shut the fuck up.

My dear son, I have made my contributions to America. When you come of age, make yours. As for the verdict, if history gives me less than stellar report card, that history is bunker. It won't matter in the scale of things because the folks at Fox news will always get my back.

When they ask you what drove your dad, please tell them this. I'm driven by the fear of being nobody after all the efforts that I have put in the pursuit of happiness. It is for that reason that I am in constant pursuit of something, anything, that will secure a place for me here on earth, even when I'm gone. I'll not stop until I'm sure that 1000 years after the end of America, that I, Donald J. Trump, will remain somebody.

Yours truly,
Donald J. Trump
The 45th President of the United States of America

THE SECRET LETTERS OF
PRESIDENT DONALD J. TRUMP, AGED 73

VOLUME TWO

Introduction

I thought the concept of a series of secret letters from US President Donald Trump to key figures in America and the world would be an instant bestseller. Who wouldn't want to get into the head of Donald Trump? Right?

Wrong.

When I arranged the letters and I wanted to approach agents, I took my time to choose agents that had represented similar high-concept humorous books. I thought the moment they got my query letter, they would get the concept, drop all they were doing, and rush to represent me. But they didn't. In fact, my top four chosen agents all ignored me.

Actually, none of them responded to my query.

I expanded my search for agents. But after weeks and weeks of emailing query letters and sample chapters, none bought the idea. I threw a wider net. At some point, I lost count of the number of agents I sent queries to. I even tried agents in Canada and Britain thinking the Americans must have been cowed. Less than one in ten even bothered to send a rejection letter.

I was not deterred. I told myself they were either afraid of the high concept or afraid of President Trump. I said maybe they didn't want to appear in his tweets and be tagged peddlers of fake news.

I moved on to the few publishers that still accept unsolicited manuscripts. Again, there was no response—not even one. I even tried European publishers. The few that responded politely said thanks but no thanks. I asked myself, was the writing so bad or the concept so horrible? I didn't sit around to figure it out. I couldn't because President Trump continued to rock Washington, DC, and America, and the world. So, I moved on to the next step, which was to go ahead and publish the book myself.

In the middle of everything, as my effort to promote the book appeared to be fluttering, instead of panicking, I found myself fascinated by the new things President Trump was doing to make America great again. So while I await the official publication of the book, I cannot resist moving ahead with volume two.

As I write this, it has been weeks since the book was published in digital form. Not even a copy has been sold. I got advance readers copies sent out to reviewers. I also handed it to some friends. As reviews started to trickle in, I was encouraged that it deserved to be on bookshelves around the world.

I even took an advance review copy to the library, put it on a shelf beside works by Al Franklin, Ellen DeGeneres, Woody Allen, Dave Barry, Ambrose Bierce, Lewis Black, Andy Borwitz, Chelsea Handler, Dorothy Parker, P.J. O'Rourke, Andy Rooney, Will Rogers, Peter Sahgal, and so many others. The book fit well. I even took a picture of my book on the shelf and shared it on Instagram. People seemed to be okay with it. I know this because I got twenty-seven likes in one week.

While I dream of having millions of people read my book, I'm the first person that is in love with it. So I wasted no time in starting volume two—this volume two that you now hold in your hands. To show you how confident I was, I had not sold a copy of volume one when I was two-thirds done with volume two.

You know what? Forget all the lies you read above.

The truth is that the Russians reached out to me as the publication of the first volume approached. They said I shouldn't worry that volume one didn't have any buzz yet. They assured me that they would collude with *New York Times* and Amazon and make my book a bestseller.

They said I should just give them my Gmail password and they would take care of the rest. All they asked of me is that I prepare volume two. As soon as I said yes, the letters started to roll in again.

Enjoy!

Rudolf t. g. Hess

March 2019

Donald Trump's Letter to His Brother, Fred Jr.

Tuesday, October 10, 2018

Hi Fred,

Yesterday, Maryanne sent me a book called *Things Fall Apart*. It was written by one of those authors with unpronounceable names. Inside it, she enclosed an old picture of when we were all kids. You probably were eleven years old. You were shirtless and had this wry smile on your face as you patted me on the back. Maryanne had her back turned to the camera. It reminded me of the days when I looked up to you to manage our parents' business. Unfortunately, you chose to be a commercial pilot rather than run our parents' business. Which was alright with me. Someone had to do it, so I stepped up and did it. And did it very well. To be honest with you, I hit a home run.

I am now doing the same thing for America. For so long, the management of this country was placed in the hands of suckers. They did a terrible job, especially the last one, called Barack Obama. He was unbelievably bad. In 2016, I came in to rescue the country, just like I rescued our parents' business. Like I placed our parents' business at the pinnacle where it is now, I plan to leave America at a similar height when I am done in 2024. That I can tell you.

Yeah. It is still the same me, Donald, who in 1976 was classified as "I-Y, unqualified for duty except in case of natural emergency." I am now the person saddled with the solemn duty of rescuing America from the moochers and parasites that have been sucking us dry. In a way, it is a national emergency. I'm doing it diligently. I'm accomplishing things never thought possible some months ago. These are things never seen before.

I remember you laughing that I never made honor roll at school. Guess what? I'm now the epitome of honor. World leaders roll honors out for me. I have stopped counting how many of such honors I have received in my first two years in office. I may not have graduated first in my class, but it is not a myth that I am first amongst world leaders. If you grade world leaders today, I will get the highest grade possible. People think I am going to win the Nobel Prize within the next two years.

Do you know how I did it? I did it by pushing my agenda without listening to naysayers. When they said it could not be done, that is when I insisted that it must be done. As a very smart person, I know how to avoid the kind of pandemic that destroyed other leaders. Did I just call those jokes leaders? They are people who have no clue. I'm a winner because my smart memory remembers the lesson from grandpa's death from influenza in 1918. Avoid the crowd. If you don't want to remain a maid to the world, like mum was before she met dad, look good and marry up. I want America to look good and marry up. I don't support all those old family-arranged marriages to major losers.

Anyway, I write you today to clear a misconception that has been troubling me for a while. I do my job so efficiently that I have the executive time to reflect on some of these things. Now that I have reached the summit of American life, I want to get my house in order for history's inevitable canonization. That is how people in the big leagues look at life.

You see, the issue of our father's will, I want to explain it to you. As dad reached his eighties, his memory started to fail him. In his nineties, it got worse. So when it was time to update his will, I had to help him draft it. He decided to take your name out of the will because you had died. It was simple. You did not really contribute substantially to the business to begin with. But the fact was you had died. And to be honest with you, dead people are not placed in a will. A will is for the living, especially the living that are willing. So we completely and totally divided your inheritance.

Now, for your son to come out and sue the estate claiming that he deserved $100 million to $300 million was infuriating. In fact, it was dopey. My plan was to take care of him and his sister, Mary, but not under the gun. His disgusting threat of a lawsuit made me cut off his medical insurance from the family insurance. It appeared mean at the time, considering he had a son that was critically ill with cerebral palsy. But, heck, the guy was out of control. If you look at it dispassionately, there are certain lines you must not allow anyone to cross. Anyone. Wife. Girlfriend. Child.

If I had been soft like you, I wouldn't have managed our parents' business in the excellent way I did. I was brilliant and tough. And that made all the difference. As you know, I was a self-made millionaire at the age of eight. So it wasn't about me or about money. It was about principles. It was about the need to be disciplined and build on what our father and grandfather before us started. It was about legacy, the vast Trump legacy.

You might say that I borrowed over $413 million in today's money from our father in my lifetime. I might not have paid him back, but see what I have been able to do with the money? Forget what *Forbes* magazine is reporting, I have built an incredible $10 billion fortune. You should be proud of me. I must tell you that I kept the faith. I held on to our father's flag. I kept it flying high.

I say all this just to acknowledge that I made tough decisions for the sake of the family. Your son, Fred III, used to say that we were not warm and that we were the *fun* in dys*fun*ctional family. Pathetic. In all fairness though, he has learned to be strong and brave and daring, like a Trump. He basically has stayed off your path of an easy, leisurely life where you don't hurt a fly. I'm very proud of the man he has become.

Like I told the fake news media, I am not sure that I have ever asked God for forgiveness. If I do something wrong, which is not very often, I just try to make it right. To be perfectly honest, I may not express regret or go to confession. I just don't see the need to bring God into stuff like that.

So, my writing this letter is an honest effort to make things right.

I don't remember the last time I went to receive Holy Communion. Since my confirmation, I can count the number of times I have partaken in that ritual of "do this in remembrance of me." It used to make me feel cleansed when we had Norman Vincent Peale as our pastor and mentor at Marble Collegiate Church. I don't feel the same with the new-age pastors we have now. I see through their hypocrisy. It is frankly very disgusting.

What am I trying to say? I'm saying that even though you were a failure, your life left me with a lasting lesson. I stayed away from alcohol and drugs because they killed you. I have no interest in pleasing people, because it did not save you. But more importantly, I learned to be tough, for that is the only way to withstand the inevitable obstacles life throws at us.

In some weird ways, you are my hero, bro. Your mistakes were the engine of my detours. Frankly, your bad choices were the signals that kept my antenna alert.

Of course, I have not read the book Maryanne sent with the picture. And you know your sister, she did not want to summarize the book for me or explain why she thought I should read it. I googled the book and read the Cliffs Notes. It is about a man trying to avoid the fate of his father, but who ends up encountering a worse fate in a changing world that he refuses to acknowledge. As if something like that could ever happen. Absolute nonsense.

Anyway, thanks for the good times.

Yours truly,
Donald J. Trump
The 45th president of the United States of America

Donald Trump's Letter to the Migrant Caravanians

Tuesday, October 24, 2018

Dear Caravanians,

I want to thank you all for setting out on this two-thousand-mile journey at the precious time you did. You all were God sent. It was as if you all colluded with my Republicans to set out at this time. But just like the Russian witch hunt, we`all know wealthy liberals interested in diluting America's purity and adding to Democratic votes sponsored your caravan. What a total disaster for America that would be.

What weapon would I have been using to illustrate my greatest talking point for the midterm election graphically? What would I have used to wipe up and fuel the hidden anger in my long-silenced majority of Americans if not for your dead-end journey to America? I certainly thank you all. You helped me become the hero of conversations that happened at millions of dinner tables across America—with Republicans, Democrats, and Independents alike. I love it. I love you all for that.

For the avoidance of doubt, deep down, I am all for nice, clean, and beautiful people migrating to America. After all, that is how I get my wives. I like those who cannot speak English very well. When they work for me, I have leverage on them. I can always remind them that it would not be a good thing for ICE to know they are at my work site or my hotel or my golf club. It makes them quickly understand what my foremen are saying and work hard for the benefit of those they left behind in whatever shithole country they came from.

When the migrants are my wives, unlike American women, they know their boundaries. They sign all the papers I want them to sign without questions. They understand that a man has to be a man to operate at his peak. Those are the men that become kings. But most importantly, they know there are rooms in my house they should not go into and some questions they must not ask. I love immigrants. I love my immigrants.

You may ask, what has changed? Well, what changed is that during the campaign, I saw that the only way for me to stand out is to put cards on the table that no one wants to get close to. And the moment I placed the immigration cards on that table, I had to carry the people on the table along. It is unfortunate that you all were caught up in it. I called for action, and I have no option but to follow through. If you all were nice, clean, and beautiful, I could have found a way to make an exemption, but unfortunately, you are not. Don't argue with that. Argue with your ancestors.

Thanks to you, though, whatever that witch-hunt headhunter Robert Mueller says in the end, my great American people will be afraid that if I am not around, nobody will save them from the invasion you people are leading. So like I said, if Mueller comes out to say that I shared a bed with Vladimir Putin in Moscow, all my American people would hear is that the MS-13 gangs are amassing at the Mexican border and it is only Trump that can save them—to hell with Mueller. As far as they know, it is only Trump that can save them. Not the docile Mike Pence. So, I thank you.

Let's not be foolish. I understand that it is hunger and poverty that is chasing you out of your shithole countries to America. It is the same hunger and poverty that chased the Irish out in the early nineteenth century. But times have changed. The Irish did not come with diseases. They were not joined in their ship by terrorists from the Middle East. They did not come with drugs. They were not crooked. They did not darken America with their presence. And more importantly, they did not bring down the average height of Americans. They were nice, clean, and beautiful.

In the early nineteenth century, we did not have the means to stop the over one million Irish who were arriving by sea. Remember that we were still trying to finish off the tribal Native Americans who were still kicking and punching the air about their so-called land and their so-called country. It would have looked hypocritical for us to be using tear gas to chase the Irish back into the sea while we were still claiming we had the rights to this land. You understand? Privately, though, at that point, we still needed people like us to come and help us dominate the land and subdue the Natives and the Negros who were already showing signs that they would be a problem. Right now, the opposite is the case. We don't need more people. By more people, I mean more people like you all.

Believe it or not, we love people who come here and work their butts off to build America and make it great. But after the debacle the Negros turned into, we really do not want to make that mistake again. They were the last set of laborers we brought in, and four-hundred years after, we are still dealing with their stupid crap. Now they don't work anymore. They have become parasites—just sitting in luxury homes the government gave them to collect food stamps, smoke weed, watch pornography, make babies, and complain that the heat in their government homes is not high enough. They are getting away with murder.

I must tell you, I can be sympathetic when it is necessary. But history is on my side on this matter of your caravan. At the end of the day, I will build my wall that will not just protect America from your kind, but also inspire you to go back to your country and develop it. That, to me, is the ultimate solution. You all will thank me later.

Or settle in Tijuana.

Let me be clear: your folks have not impressed me even to reconsider. I don't get any sign that if I let you in, you will vote for Republicans in US elections. Some soft-on-immigration

Republicans told me you are conservatives at heart with entrepreneurial spirits. If so, why are your people voting for Democrats? I don't see any sign that you are telling your countrymen and women already in America to vote for Republicans. They still vote for Democrats. So why would I want more of you to come in? Can any of you give me one reason?

I was told that your representatives in Mexico were asking for a $50,000 payment for each of you to return to Guatemala and Honduras. $50,000 dollars? Go ask the former slaves if they received the forty acres and a mule Honest Abraham Lincoln promised them. You know that if I dangle $50,000 before African Americans in Chicago for them to leave the United States and move to Haiti or any shithole country in Africa that even Michelle Obama would jump at it and leave the South Side of Chicago.

To tell you all that I am a nice guy, I have left the border open. I can close it and tell all our border agents there to come back home. I will then have our military there until the Army Corps of Engineers completes the wall for me. Will that be humane? Because I keep hearing your advocates say that my immigration policy is inhumane. And how dare you throw stones at my agents? Next time that happens, I will make sure you all are stopped at the Guatemalan border. You won't even get the chance to enter Mexico and seek asylum in Mexico. So if I were you, I would stay in Mexico and seek asylum. After all, if you are in Mexico, you can perceive the aroma of hamburgers cooking at the nearest McDonalds in the United States.

We all know that the Japanese attack on Pearl Harbor was not televised, but yours was. And like the great leader I am, I took care of it. I have vowed not to let you turn Americans against themselves. As long as I am president, I will not allow you to bring fear to my people. Because I am kind-hearted, I will still leave the door open for those of you who are nice, clean, and beautiful to come into America. The ones like Jennifer Lopez and Rosie Perez.

For that, you all should be thankful.

Yours truly,
Donald J. Trump
The 45th President of the United States

Donald Trump's Letter to Crown Prince MbS

Tuesday, October 30, 2018

Dear MbS,

You are in what we call in New York City mega bullshit. But you are lucky you know Trump. I will help you get out of this shit.

As you know, I grew up in New York City, so I know one or two things about gangsta paradise. Your neighborhood, the Middle East, is a desert version of a gangsta paradise. What that means is that sometimes we need to cross a man. And as Coolio sings, we never cross a man that didn't deserve it.

I'm sure that son of a bitch you crossed deserved it. They all deserve it. Their whole profession deserves to be lined in chalk. I have never understood why self-professed enemies of the state are allowed to hang out at the White House and even claim the right to question the supreme leader of the state. I don't get it. I think our so-called Founding Fathers screwed up on that one. Probably the media of their time were not as vicious as the power-drunk soldier ants of today. Whoever told them they were the fourth estate got their brains extremely messed. Lowlifes.

Someone should tell those folks that nobody elected them. Nobody confirmed them to any position. And as such, their claim of relevance has no basis in facts. Fourth estate, my foot.

I don't get that Khashoggi of a guy. The man is from your country. He saw how you cut off people's heads with a sword every Friday on every street for ordinary day-to-day acts—things like adultery, fornication, and stealing candy in the store. Yet he had the audacity to join that fake news bozo Bezos' gang in Washington, DC. He must be as dumb as the trash he was writing.

By the way, I envy you. While we have happy hour on Fridays, you host beheading shows for your citizens to see. Marvelous. You get to show them every Friday what will happen to those who are not loyal. You essentially tell those who have ears, let them hear. Those who do not have ears, like Khashoggi and the houseflies, they follow the coffin into the grave.

I don't have that opportunity here to demonstrate how brutal we could be. I wish we could impose the death penalty as punishment for carrying fake news. I would love public executions for those found guilty. By the time I get Jim Acosta executed in Washington, DC, and Don Lemon executed in Central Park in New York City, everyone at CNN, MSNBC, NBC, and *Washington Post* will behave. But we have this stupid thing called the Second Amendment. Sad Amendment, I call it. Don't worry, by the time I leave office, we will amend the amendment, trust me.

By the way, why did your boys horribly screw things up that bad? Why? You sent in fifteen of them with a medical forensics expert to take care of just one man? Is he King Kong? And to know they were doing the job right inside your consulate makes it even worse. What is so hard in making someone disappear without a trace? I heard your people were using bone saws and acid. That is so 1960s. Why do you send incompetent little boys to do the job of men? If those were your bodyguards, man, you have no security around you. My homeboys in Harlem could have done a cleaner job. A laser could have been used to turn every cell in his body into fine atoms. Next time, if you need something done efficiently without leaving any trace, let me know. Forget your Tiger Squad, I will hook you up with some security contractors already in your neighborhood.

Now, about damage control, I will ask my wonder-boy-in-law, Jared, to reach out to you. If you follow his instructions to the letter, you will come out of it unscathed. Our noisemakers in the Senate will make noise as usual, but they cannot bite. I have told them all I needed to say. Maybe you did, maybe you didn't. That is enough response from me. It is brief and ambiguous for a reason. I have sent a message to my pal, Putin. He is solidly behind you. My friend Bibi has more important things to deal with than what happened to one useless man. The strongman of Turkey, I know how to deal with him. I know what he wants. I will trade a few things with him. If he gives me what I want, I will give him what he wants, okay?

Obviously, I am doing all this chess playing for you. You know what that means. When Don Jr. calls, I expect you to answer and answer positively. The Trump Empire must not be allowed to suffer because I volunteered to save America from itself. Right? I'm sure you understand. You did not let your $3.9 billion in assets suffer because you volunteered to modernize Saudi Arabia, did you? Also, you need to buy more big guns from America and give American businesses a cut from the sixteen nuclear facilities you plan to build. Jared will give you the names of some businesses I have approved. Like Caesar, I need to have some things to show them as my conquests and as tributaries that I brought home.

I don't need to tell you that there are so many people who are doing everything possible to stop you from ascending the throne of your father. I'm talking of powerful people in the world. This includes powerful organizations like my own CIA. They have convicted you, and if it is up to them, you will be in jail somewhere in the Hague. Unfortunately for them, I have veto power. As long as you make Putin and me happy, their evil plan is not gonna happen. Your ascension to the throne is assured. Stephen said I should remind you that the whole House of Saud is under assault by the Wahhabis on the right and ISIS on the left. The only reason you do not feel it is because the almighty America is hanging above the House of Saud with a powerful hose that is blowing both sides away.

If you follow my directions to the letter, ten years from now, nobody will be calling you toxic, tainted, or flawed. You will be described this way: Abraham Lincoln freed the slaves while Muhammed bin Salman freed the women of Saudi Arabia. All other uncomplimentary things ever said about you would have been washed away and forgotten. It is the same thing with me. When I am done building a wall around America, I will be elevated above Lincoln. The US military will name fort after fort after me, for I will have finally done for America what the Great Wall did for China. Two thousand years from now, people will be going to the great wall that I built to take selfies.

Having said that, Yemen and the horrific things going on there, what are you going to do about it? Melania showed me a picture of a starving child with his lungs all showing. I warned her never to show such a disgusting picture to me again. I didn't listen to the CIA's audio of Khashoggi crying like a baby, so why do I need to see the pictures of the children of Yemen? It is not as if the Jews were the ones killing Muslims in Yemen. This is a Muslim-on-Muslim crime, so why should I be bothered? The more they kill those potential terrorists, the better for us.

Still, what are you going to do about a war I was told led to the death of fifty-thousand children in 2017 alone? You can be reckless in Riyadh, but don't take that outside. Don't take that to Yemen, Lebanon, or Canada, else they will call you a crackpot. You don't want to get the kind of reputation that mad man in the Philippines has. I have forgotten his name. Be like Trump. Be like Putin. Be like Erdogan. That stunt you played with the Prime Minister of Lebanon made you look like a beginner. Take your time and learn from the best. If Trump University had not folded up, I would have said you should take an online class on leadership and the art of dealmaking.

If I were you, I would send my kids to come and study in America. In the world to come, you need American education to operate smoothly. Even if you want to do something a little criminal, we are the original smooth criminals. King Saud University is alright, but you need to come to Wharton Business

School at the University of Pennsylvania in order to learn how to beat Qatar and the United Arab Emirates in their quest for modernization. Otherwise, thirty years from now, you will still be sending people with chain saws and gallons of acid to go abroad and kill your enemies. Don't you see how smoothly Putin and Kim Jong Un do their thing? I want you to be like them.

If you play ball well, we can isolate your so-called triangle of evil. You know, if you make Israel happy, I can throw Iran, Turkey, and other sponsors of Muslim Brotherhoods under the bus. I look forward to visiting your kingdom again. This time, I want to hang out in your half-billion-dollar yacht, *Serene*. Together we can sail to the Louvre Museum in Abu Dhabi to see the $450.3 million *Salvator Mundi*. $450 million. I tell you, you Arab guys are nuts.

Yours truly,
Donald J. Trump
The 45th President of the United States

Donald Trump's Letter to General Jim Mattis

Friday, December 21, 2018

Dear General Mattis,

Unlike you, I want to be polite and courteous and still knock sense into your big, ugly head. I'm very sad to see you go from being a mad dog to a wimpy, goofy dog. You were sold to me as a reformed Democrat. I should have known that once a Democrat, always a Democrat. It does not matter how long you pretended to have seen the light. Eventually, the lamb in a wolf's clothing will bleat.

I had wanted an honorable exit for you, but apparently, you preferred to take a nasty path. Still, I have been urged not to oblige you. And out of the respect I have for your uniform, I am holding my fire.

For the first time in my life, I agree with Obama. He fired you when you went rogue. I shouldn't have given you a second chance if not that you helped me clean up the mess my pal, the Saudi crown prince, made of what should have been a minor Khashoggi silencing.

Something in me tells me that you were simply misguided by leftover Obama actors in the Pentagon. Instead of sticking it to you, I will use this opportunity to educate your weak mind. Let me do something with you that I have not done with others. I will give you a glimpse of my superior tactical thinking.

I heard that you come from a bookish household. I was told that you carry around a copy of *Meditations* by Marcus Aurelius. That does not prove intelligence. I carry about classic copies of *Playboy* magazine, and I am still smarter than you. I was also told that your personal library has over seven thousand volumes. Trust me, a man who has been with over seven thousand women is more informed about life than one who has read seven thousand books. Got it?

I have faith in my superb intelligence. The resignation of a million General Mattises cannot dampen that faith. It is laziness and lack of intellectual curiosity that stops people like you from seeing the beauty in the new world order that I am working hard to create. We were looking out from the same window. While I was seeing the age of greatness coming, you were seeing the dawn of doom descending. Let me tell you how you became a victim of that: you allowed absolute fear and ignorance to get a hold of you. Those two human flaws are so powerful that they can sweep away enthusiasm and replace it with cynicism.

The one who gets it, Stephen Miller, gave me this essay I have been reading. The article is called, "The President as Statesman." I believe that one Dr. Joseph Google wrote it. Stephen knows that I have no patience to read books. I believe that no matter how important a book may be, its contents can always be summarized in less than half a dozen pages. If you cannot summarize it, then it must be a terrible book. Even the Bible can be summarized in a sentence: love your neighbor as yourself. So Stephen gets it. Every now and then, he slips nice concise articles on my desk in the Oval Office. He knows not to overdo it, too.

While reading this Dr. Joseph Google of a guy, I saw a paragraph that spoke to my essence. It goes like a prayer that I told Stephen I plan to say at next year's Prayer Breakfast. It says: "Lord, you see, we have changed. America is no longer the nation of dishonor, of shame, of self-laceration, of timidity and little faith. No, Lord, America has once more grown strong in spirit, strong in will, strong in persistence, strong in enduring all sacrifices. Lord, we will not sever from You. Now bless our struggle."

I'm a believer. Don't think for once that I forgot that you were one of those who said that I think like a fifth grader. You carried yourself as the adults in the house, sneaking around writing anonymous editorials in the *New York Times*. Your type is the worst of friends and the best of enemies.

Dr. Joseph Google was obviously talking about me in his 1936 essay when he wrote: "The genius behaves and operates out of childlike simplicity, and stands up to things with a self-assurance and a lack of self-consciousness that are customarily the prerogatives of children."

Let us see what happens now that all you adults are heading to the door.

I made you a big shot. I really did. Your military career was over. You were going to be sent out there to pasture in the service of one military-industrial complex. I thought you had talent and virtue. I brought you in, gave you almost a trillion dollar a year budget to play with. And the thanks I got was disrespect. I say, fuck you.

If you were smart, you should have been repeating the liturgy below day after day to yourself and the men and women under your tutelage.

"All our thanks to you, our love for you, and our glowing trust in you, my president, shines forth today from hundreds of thousands of eyes . . . you there have arisen for these people of America not only a president but also a savior."

I am an elected president. And there is only one elected president at a time in these United States. For the next two years, at least, I am America. Everyone in America is subordinate to the elected president. Which means, that everyone in America is subordinate to me. Do you understand?

I want you to sit back in your rocking chair and watch as I actualize my "fantasies." I heard that is what you call my excellent ideas to make America great again. I don't need weak people like you around me—people who are afraid to use the power God gave them to advance the American agenda. I am not afraid to do the opposite of what history expects of me.

I knew I should have trusted my instincts when they were telling me you were ruthless. One establishment type vouched that there was nobody better than you. They said you understood the principles of attaining power and glory. I didn't know you were such a sissy that you would buckle under a small crisis. And they made you a marine general. I wonder what they have turned the once great American military into. General George Patton would have fallen on his sword rather than end up a disgrace like you are now.

If the marine authorities had been on top of their game, your career would have ended after the 2004 Mukaradeeb wedding incident in Iraq. You think I didn't know? It was a crime scene where you ordered airstrikes that killed forty-two civilians attending a wedding just because your little provisional brain could not imagine that some people could be attending a wedding at 3:00 a.m. At Urozgan Province in Afghanistan, you refused to dispatch a rescue helicopter from Camp Rhino that would have saved the lives of our service men and women. If you could not wrap your mind around these ordinary incidents, how could you understand the genius in my Syrian or Afghanistan policies?

Those little men of Iraq who slap women around for not wearing a veil, those men you said had no manhood, actually have a stronger and much more useful manhood than you have displayed in the last two years. If you had assassinated President Assad when I gave you the order, we would have installed our puppet in that country, and we would have been pumping their oil straight to New Jersey.

I understand that the only woman you brought close to the altar abandoned you a few days before your wedding. You never got married or had any children. So I should probably be nice to you because you have no way of understanding the fight that I am absolutely waging for my children, the American children.

I hope God gives you a long life so you will live to see the completion of my resurrection of America. You can bet that historians to come, not current degenerated historians, will declare my presidency as the greatest political miracle of the twenty-first century. Frankly, I'm like stem cell therapy. When I am done, I will have given America a new lease on life. I will have added one hundred years to America's life. The often-parroted "America's decline" will have been postponed indefinitely.

Pardon me as I end this with another of Dr. Joseph Google's quotes about me: "The ingenious statesman dares the impossible in order to make the possible. His essential strength is in the simplification of seemingly insoluble complications. Before the average intellect has seen or known a solution to impatiently anticipate a problem, our great president is already involved in solving them."

As you probably go home to write your memoir, remember to tell that to your gang of average intellects.

Here is the summary of what guys like you do not get about me: I am predestined—my genius and my greatness. I know what I want and I want what I know. I am great enough to be simple, and I am simple enough to be great. I speak to the American people as people and not as dummies, and they appreciate me for that. I say unpopular things because neither the flattery of history nor the history of flattery seduces me. And more importantly, I don't deploy flattery on the American people. I am not a product of my time; I am a legend in my lifetime.

Since you will be the last of the adults to leave the room, help cowards like you who will die of hysteria by turning off the light . . . and then sit down and relax, for the real show of the real Donald Trump is about to begin in earnest.

Yours truly,
Donald J. Trump
The 45th President of the United States

Donald Trump's Letter to Michelle Obama

Saturday, December 29, 2019

Hi Michelle,

I was in the middle of a top-security briefing where my generals were telling me about Russia's new weapon, the Avangard hypersonic glide vehicle, that can travel twenty-seven times faster than the speed of sound, when a news flash on my phone showed that Gallup had named you the most admired woman in the world. Another unbelievable disrespect for Melania by your friendly liberal organization! You, most admired? That is phenomenally sad. Must they cheapen everything in this country?

As the CIA showed me their secret satellite images of the Russian Dombarovskiy missile base in the Southern Ural Mountains from where the Avangard test was done, my mind wandered to who rigged the polls for you to win. Was it because of that useless book you wrote? The unbecoming of a book? When I am done with you, the last book you will write is *The Unrevealing of the House of Obama*. Trust me.

Let me tell you, when you were promoting the useless book, saying that you would never forgive me for putting the lives of your family in danger when I stated the fact that your husband was born in Kenya, I ignored you. I found you totally insignificant to waste a tweet on. But now that you have erroneously been named the most admired woman in the world, it is a call to bring it on.

I'm from Queens, New York. An ugly little black girl from the South Side of Chicago should not disrespect me. Ever! Letting that rudeness slide is totally unacceptable to me.

While my security people were trying to explain that the Avangard had eroded our missile defense system, which is our ultimate nuclear deterrent, I was seeing a parallel with my wall on the Mexican border. The wall is my ultimate deterrent against illegal immigrants. Why your dope husband and your fellow Democrats cannot get it is beyond me.

Guess what? I'm like Avangard. I'm constantly changing my course and my altitude as I fly through the political atmosphere of today's America. It baffles my idiotic enemies. For my awesome supporters, they struggle to catch up. When I make a move, when I strike my target, they do not know what hit them. If you like, ask Jeb Bush, Chris Christie, John Kasich, Ted Cruz, and their likes. Chokers! The same thing will happen to Jeff Flake if he dares to challenge me.

Those disgusting US attorneys at the Southern District of New York have closed my foundation. But your husband's foundation is still raking in millions and millions of dollars. You think I do not know? Wait until I get an attorney general that will be loyal to me. I will make sure he scrutinizes your husband's foundation. I was duly informed the other day that donations to your husband's foundation grew from $13,175,732 in 2016 to $231,993,748 in 2017. All those left-wing celebrities, business executives, and unnamed donors who pump money into the foundation will have to explain to the IRS and to me how they made their money and how much they have paid in taxes in the last twenty-five years. Phonies.

Believe me, I am aware that for you to accomplish your sinister, corrupt goals, you changed the charitable mission of your foundation from building a $500 million presidential library to some deceptive talk about inspiring the world to bring about change. Why don't you first inspire your South Side Chicago gangs that are killing young black boys and girls? Didn't they say charity begins at home? You should learn something from my America First mantra and start with South Side Chicago first.

Keep collecting money from Oprah Winfrey, George Lucas, Mark Benioff, and Bill and Melinda Gates. When my people finish with this Mueller investigation, we may get a special investigation to look at your foundation and all those who gave it a million dollars or more. What did they get from Obama and Hillary Clinton that made them give out such money? And how is the money being used? I understand that the foundation now covers your first-class travel around the world. US attorneys won't see that and do something about it. It is only when the Trump Foundation pays for services that the Trump organization delivered that everyone wakes up to cry fraud.

I heard that both of you are worth $135 million. All thanks to Uncle Sam. A little while ago, you were living paycheck to paycheck trying to pay off your student loans. Now you want to join Jay-Z and Beyoncé on the list of billionaire black folks? What an audacity for you to aim to be billionaires. I was told that is what you two are up to. You signed a $65 million book deal and another $50 million deal with Netflix, all benefits of the fraud you and your husband perpetrated on America by claiming he was born in Hawaii. Trust me, I will open those things up as soon as this Mueller witch hunt is over. The world must know the staggering fraud that happened here in Washington, DC, from 2009 to 2017.

Is it true that some people pay you as much as $225,000 to speak to them? What BS do you tell them? What do you know? It is not as if you are as beautiful as Melania. Is it your affirmative action education at Princeton and Harvard that is deceiving people into thinking you know what is up? Oh, someone mentioned to me that you were gifted in school. Excuse me, but showing off your muscles is not a gift. And your husband makes $400,000 a speech? That must be a crime having him benefit from fraud that he perpetrated against America. I will look into stopping his $207,800 pension as former president immediately. I'm 100 percent a better speaker than him. Unlike him, I connect with people. I don't lecture them. That is rude.

My new attorney general will also look at companies like Cantor Fitzgerald, Northern Trust Corp, and Carlyle Group that dole out $400,000 each to your husband for a goofy speech. For what? And they say that my buildings rip off tenants. That right there is your husband ripping off stockholders. It must be illegal for company executives who are friends of a former president to decide to dole out such amounts of money without consulting stockholders. Now, that is a Wall Street reform I will fight for. You bet. We must close all the loopholes where you and your husband are fleecing America. I was not surprised that you conceived your two daughters by in vitro fertilization. Just looking at your husband, I knew he was not a real man.

Men like me score per play. It is good you had couples counseling before because by the time I finish closing all the avenues from which both of you are raking in millions, you may return to counseling. From what my friends at the *National Enquirer* are telling me, it is the money that is keeping you two together. Take away the money, and he will follow some white woman back to his old Columbia University world of drinking and smoking weed.

Oprah chose your book as her Book Club's choice, so? I bet she did not read it. It must be one of those favors that have consistently taken wretched people like you two to respectability in America. By the time I finish exposing the both of you, you will wish you had remained in your South Side Chicago doing community grassroots work.

Remember Rev. Jeremiah Wright? The way he disappeared from the limelight is the same way I will make sure the two of you disappear. You can take that to the bank.

Yours truly,
Donald J. Trump
The 45th President of the United States

Donald Trump's Letter to John Kelly

Monday, December 31, 2018

Dear John,

After I fired your weak white ass, I chose to ignore you. I have good reasons for doing that. There was no need writing you. I wanted you to slide quietly into the night. You had joined the list of overrated generals who disappointed me, and I wanted to put you behind me. Then, you opened your cowardly mouth to the *Los Angeles Times*.

It's sadly only because you knew a lot, that you were there when certain things went down. I would have put you in your place, but I did not want more exposure than I already had. Frankly, after Michael Cohen, I do not want another insider to go and betray me by frothing at the mouth.

What is wrong with all you generals? I love our soldiers, but I hate our generals. The problem with the generals is that when they become generals, they exchange their Purple Heart for a Democrat's heart. You saying that the job of chief of staff was the most difficult job you ever did, makes me wonder if any of you generals can be great presidents like me. I can now confirm that I would have been a general or even a field marshal, if not for my spur heel. Easy! Anybody who knew me at the military academy can tell you that.

Though I don't remember if it was the right or the left leg that had that painful spur heel, I still remember being eager to join you all in Vietnam. On my own, I was parading and marching with a toy gun, in readiness. The whole world would have marveled at my exploits. It would have been combat moves that had never been seen before. If I knew what I know now, I would not have brought weak and compromised generals like you into my government. Absolutely not. Despite the pumping up of your reputation, you ain't shit. Neither is your brother-in-arms Tim Mattis. You are all hype but no substance.

You showed off in Hanoi, in Baghdad, in Kabul, but in Washington, DC, you folded up. Those who sold you to me quoted a statement you made about immigration that I loved. Remember it? "If lawmakers do not like the laws they've passed and we are charged to enforce, then they should have the courage and skill to change the laws. Otherwise they should shut up and support the men and women on the front lines."

I loved it. It had gut and gusto.

What I didn't do was to read the rest of the memo they passed on to me. If I had done so, I would have seen you ranting about your desire for never-ending war.

"If you think this war against our way of life is over because some of the self-appointed opinion makers and chattering class grow 'war-weary,' because they want to be out of Iraq or Afghanistan, you are mistaken. This enemy is dedicated to our destruction. He will fight us for generations, and the conflict will move through various phases as it has since 9/11."

How could I have brought anyone with this kind of opinion around me? I guess I was so determined to remove the simpleton, Reince Priebus, that I overlooked many things about you. At Homeland Security, you said the right things. You came in and I thought you had it all together. I even allowed you to fire my buddies—Steve Bannon and Anthony Scaramucci. Little did I know that you didn't want smarter people than you around. You wanted a boring and uninspiring bunch. Little by little, I watched you crumble. Such a sad sight to behold. You appeared on Laura

Ingraham's show and in less than one hour committed massive atrocities with your mouth. This is a show that I appear on for hours, mesmerizing the whole country.

How could you not have known that Robert E. Lee was a bad guy? You called him an honorable man. You might as well have called Nancy Pelosi an honorable woman while you were at it. You might even call Barack Obama an honorable man one day, to my embarrassment. And then, you said it was the lack of ability to compromise that led to the Civil War. How could you be a general and still be that ignorant? You don't have to attend the University of Pennsylvania to know that the Civil War was caused by Negroes demanding forty acres and a mule.

Didn't the media catch you lying about your boy Rob Porter? You knew the kid abused his two wives and you still protected him. Not good. What kind of a man with morals does something like that? If you call such a woman abuser "a man of true integrity and honor," what are you going to call me? I wanted to make you a friend, a confidant, and a trusted professional but you were too timid to ride with me. How could you allow a little congresswoman from Florida to embarrass you? You could not get right what congresswoman Frederica Wilson said about the FBI building in her constituency. When it was pointed out to you, you didn't have the decency to apologize. What kind of leader does something like that?

If the White House were such a miserable place for you to work, I would have thought you would be glad to leave. But your interview with the *Los Angeles Times* showed a horrible and bitter man. In the last days before I kicked you to the curb, I stopped talking to you. I showed you that I could run the country perfectly without you. A real man would have gotten the hint and walked away, but not you. You must have been enjoying the perks of the exalted office.

Don't worry, I am rounding up the wars around the globe. I am bringing our soldiers home, including your son in the marines. The military industrial complex will have to produce new things. I have pointed them to a sample of new things they could be doing by ordering them to begin building my special wall. So if you need a job, being a foreman isn't a bad option for you. Maybe when you work on the construction site you will know that when I say wall, I really mean a wall.

For someone like you who understood that terrorism is everywhere, constant and non-stop, to misunderstand the essence of the wall is a huge failure of imagination. If you want to know the whole truth, to me and friends at Fox News, the wall is highly sacrosanct.

Yours truly,
Donald J. Trump
The 45th President of the United States of America

Donald Trump's Letter to Tucker Carlson

Saturday, January 5, 2019

Hello Tucker,

I have just arrived at a staggering conclusion. You are the last remaining true giant of journalism in America. There is no contest here. After watching you lament on the decline of men in America, I had no doubt about it. You captured what was going on in my mind. What Steve Bannon called the "feminization of American men" is almost complete. Scary! It is left for you and me to force a reversal.

It is the unspoken reason why I am in the White House today. Real American men, not sissies like Obama, are fed up with the relegation of men in America. The women lobby, like the gay lobby and the Israeli lobby (yes, I said it), are on track to take over completely if we let them. I have done the heavy lifting by stopping Hillary Clinton. And you can be sure that come 2020, I will stop the Pocahontas, Elizabeth Warren.

What the women are planning to do to us is exactly what we did to African American men in this society. They want to squeeze us out using biased child support rulings, wage inequalities, an opioid cum weed cum alcohol crisis, psychiatric medications prescribed by depressed psychologists dominated by feminists, and finally, incarceration. That was how we subdued the once fist-raising, raging, Black Panther-loving African American men.

Tucker, we must never let that happen to us. If it does, we will become major losers.

When you look at my fantastic boys, you can see that I have groomed them to be very conscious of the women's agenda. The Trumps will always be the last bastions of real men in America.

So preach it, my brother. Never let your woman earn more than you do. It gets into her head. Melania can never talk down to me because I picked her up from the Slovenia gutters and made her something. That is the best state in which any man who calls himself a real man should keep his woman. Don't even let them go out there and work, unless they are working for you. The good book was talking about women when it said, "If you give them a yard, they take a mile."

Let your viewers know that I am fighting China's unfair trade practices to bring back manufacturing jobs to America so that men will become men again. Conniving women know that those things with penises that work at Walmart are not men. But those kinds of places are where they want to isolate American men for final domination and destruction.

If we continue on the path we are on, if you and I do not intensify this fight, one hundred years from now, the domestication of men will be so total and complete that we will become substitute dogs. At the snap of their fingers, women will tell us to sit, stand, and run after cars. Tucker, we cannot let that happen. If we have to tear down the modern American family, we must. Forget what people say, the best of the great white men has not been seen.

Women who do not want to marry men who make less should take a look at educated African American women. They have been at that point for a while now. Their men are either in prison or about to go to prison. Those who come out of prison are ruined forever. It forces their women to either marry from other races or have babies out of wedlock. And as you know, no matter how well-to-do a woman is, a single mother is always short. Short in wholesomeness. Short in elegance. Short in the number of children she could have.

Let me make a confession here. I used to think that Sean Hannity is the greatest journalist alive in America. I tell you, when compared to you, he is a beginner. You go deep without clowning around. Maybe it is because, just like me, you don't drink and you don't smoke. Those are the best traits that make fine men.

I was so impressed with your work that I asked Pence the other day if I could send some SSS guys to guard you twenty-four hours a day. I heard that some Antifa motherfuckers came to your house to threaten your family. Such is hate crime. Those anarchists had the audacity to vandalize your home because you were telling the nation the bitter truth about their run-away liberal policies of the last fifty years. Pence said I do not have such authority. See, that is another thing. This presidency thing, being the most powerful man in the world, is highly overrated if I cannot send out my SSS to go guard you, a real fighter for American values and the once-great American white men.

Believe me, when I win my second term, we are going to change some of those obsolete things. What is the use of having a president without real power? Must I declare a state of emergency to get things done? I asked that question about the wall. I'm asking that question about so many other things. Trust me, at the end of my second term, if I feel that we have not completely reversed things, I may have to declare a state of emergency to sidestep whatever amendment there is stopping me from going for a third term. After all, the founding fathers of our nation did not put it in the original constitution, which, to tell you the truth, is the real constitution.

My friend, you are right. We are going to separate the real politicians from the partisans and the parasites. I'm particular about parasites like Nancy Pelosi. If you don't mind me borrowing your brother's expression for Bill de Blasio's spokesperson, Nancy is a whiny little self-righteous bitch. She is not good for America.

I'm proud that despite the fact that your father worked for the Corporation for Public Broadcasting, VOA, and other liberal institutions, and your mother left your family when you were three to enjoy a bohemian lifestyle in France, you have your head in the right place. I'm happy for you. It is the same thing I am telling my African American friends: that they can overcome their particular upbringing.

I should have known that you had your head in the right place when in 2004 you walked away from CNN and declared it "a frustrating place to work." You saw their weak future. You saw something Don Lemon will not see in another fifty years. I'm glad you are now dancing with the true stars of journalism.

Let me state clearly that President Donald J. Trump recognizes you as one of the few people in your profession who is still fighting for the minds of the American children. I have asked my people to pencil your name down as one of my friends to receive the Presidential Medal of Freedom. I am determined to bring to the mainstream all those that Obama's socialist leftists call ethno-nationalists. If they are so pissed off, let them jump off the Golden Gate Bridge. After all, they were supposed to have left the country and moved to Canada when I floored their Crooked Hilary and won the election.

My friend, I agree with you that the demographic changes happening in America due to immigration are more than we are destined to digest in a lifetime. I am doing everything to contain it—the wall, the Muslim ban, and soon, a slowdown of immigration from shithole countries. Those ugly, poor, and dirty immigrants must not be allowed to overwhelm our United States. We must keep our United States white, just like the Founding Fathers wanted it.

If we fail, it is going to be war. What the liberals do not know is that if I had not come to Washington, DC, at the time I did, if lying Hillary Clinton had won, my constituency could have exploded. They were not going to go down without a fight. The pressure was so high that the cooker was beginning to boil over. My coming lowered the pressure. In years to come, they will thank me.

Even the dead would be grateful.

Yours truly,
Donald J. Trump
The 45th President of the United States of America

Donald Trump's Letter to Nancy Pelosi

Sunday, January 6, 2019

Dear Nancy Pelosi,

I just saw a story from the failing CNN that you are more popular than me for the first time since I became president. The story says that your stock is going up. Congratulations!

Congratulations on taking over the gavel at the House of Representatives for a second time. You are now the second person in the presidential line of succession, which means if something happens to Pence and I, a motherfucker like you will become the president of the United States of America.

Okay. Let me calm down. Let me not think about all that. Let me surprise myself and make this a love letter. Yes, I can do it. I can show that I can have a civil discussion with the opposition, no matter how deep our disagreements are. After all, everyone is now saying that we all love America equally.

Moving forward, I won't reduce myself to the level of that new congresswoman. After all, I am the president and she is just a lower animal in the dungeon. You know the one I am talking about—the one who dishonored her family and America by referring to me as a motherfucker. Melania told me that when they go low, I should go high. I will listen to her this time. I will quell my first instinct, which was to add her home country of Pakistan to the

187

list of Muslim countries banned from coming to America.

So, Nancy, since you are the highest elected woman in America ever, I want to strike a deal with you. I don't want to be seen as anti-women. I need women voters in the suburbs to win re-election in 2020. What about we call a ceasefire?

Your second term as speaker is a great accomplishment. You did something that was last done in 1955 by Sam Rayburn. Unlike little men like Newt Gingrich, Dennis Hastert, John Boehner, and Paul Ryan, who feared to step down and take up a smaller office, you didn't mind. Just like me, you didn't let your ego take control of you. I appreciate that in a woman.

I was told that you win your re-election every time with an average of 80 percent of the votes. That is the kind of result I want to have in 2020. And I need to be nice to you in order to get it. Not that I cannot do it without you, but why sweat it when there is an easier path. So, without suggesting any weakness on my part, I am appealing to you that we should get along.

When you start working with me, you will discover that I am a misunderstood genius. I have a very beautiful mind. My only crime is that I question what I know and what others are so sure about concerning our American truths. I am outstanding and original in my thinking, and that is something that is not very common these days. I despair for America, but I am certain about where I want to take our dear country. You will like the place if you spend the time to understand me and understand my genius.

The closer you come to me, the more you will see that I am not traveling back in time but rather using a mirage to advance America and truly make it a more perfect union. Unlike those who give the quest for a more perfect union mere lip service, I am doing something about it. I'm doing the most basic of things to purify America. I'm taking out the impurities. Why people are freaking out is something I do not understand.

You use Botox for your face. I mean, I was told. My assumption is that you do so to enhance your looks and get closer to a perfect you. That is not different from what I'm trying to do. You can consider the wall along Mexico's border as Botox, for the purpose of enhancing America's look and maintaining that pristine look it had when America was still America. Is that so hard to understand?

I want to move America in a new direction. I am offering you a nice front-row seat for the ride. You say you are a master legislator. You say you are a strategic leader. You now have the opportunity of a lifetime to work with the one predestined to make America great again. If you do, your name will be placed in the shining light where mine is heading. If you choose not to, I will still get there on my own power.

You don't need to beat your record of making the longest speech in the House of Representatives for your views to be heard. All you need to do is work with me. Be it on DACA, Social Security reforms, gun control, whatever pet project you liberals want, we can make it happen. Just forget about impeachment. There is no Russian collusion.

Having said that, the least charitable thing anyone can say about me is that I am half genius and half buffoon. Well, that is on purpose. Presenting pure genius scares people and makes them compare me to an evil genius like Adolf Hitler.

Yours truly,
Donald J. Trump
The 45th President of the United States of America

Trump's Letter to Thomas Friedman

Friday, January 11, 2019

Dear Tom,

I just got a text from Sean telling me to tune in to Wolf Blitzer on CNN that you were unloading on me. The first thing I said was, "Tom who?" He said, "Remember him—the one from the failing *New York Times*?"

I guess nobody is reading you anymore in the lying *New York Times,* so you immigrated to the fake news CNN to market your wears. You and Wolf are leading a bunch of disgraced Jews in the US media who have refused to go along with the program. That is a real shame.

I know if you were part of David's brethren when he said he was going to take on Goliath with a string and a stone, you would have called him disturbed. If you were part of Solomon's brethren when he built the Temple Mount on the hilltop above the city and asked his Congress for money to expand the walls around Jerusalem to protect the temple, you would have called the wall immoral and a waste of precious dollars.

I find it so disturbing that you and your so-called fellow journalists are said to be writers of the first draft of history when, in actual fact, you all lack a basic understanding of history. Sad! Let me lecture you. For there to be a paradigm shift, especially in matters that have been going on for generations, we need to reposition the bits and pieces of the matter. But as soon as we do so, your likes cry that we are lying. Kellyanne called it "alternative facts." I simply see it as a restating of the long-accepted dogmas to shake the table. There simply is no other way to move things around.

Not that I expect small-minded people like you to get it. Your job is very easy. You open your mouth and repeat the same boring thing you have been saying for decades. Even though you know that it has not moved the needle an inch in all those years, you are sticking by it. Who could blame you? It is not your task to actually do the heavy lifting of changing the situation of things for millions of people across the globe, who have been imprisoned by the products of your archaic thoughts.

Your brain is so programmed that it cannot hold complex thoughts that might be conflicting on the surface but when examined with a wider lens would be seen for what it they are—sophisticated and designed to advance the human race. You argue out of the facts that you got. I proclaim out of the figures I have received. While facts can lie, figures do not lie. And the figures I have are not good. In fact, they are terrible.

Since 1896, you have claimed to have been publishing "all the news that's fit to print." Yet the other day, you went back to publish obituaries of people that you overlooked when they died—Charlotte Bronte, Ida B. Wells, Emily Warren Roebling, and others.   You were so smart that you did not know that in fifty years, some of the people you thought were nobodies will become the real deal when time proves them right and dispassionate historians look at their works. Bad judgment! Those were remarkable people who contributed to humanity. Wink, wink, the same thing will happen to you and your coverage of my presidency fifty years from now. I foresee you screaming on your front pages fifty years from now that Donald Trump was a genius, a president that achieved in two years things that no other president in the history of the United States was able to achieve in eight years.

Did they say that you won the Pulitzer Prize? It must be an affirmative action award. In any case, they have cheapened those things these days. How could it be of value if nobody at Fox News has won it? I checked. They have not given it to Sean Hannity or Tucker Carson.

When you say nobody trusted me, I take it that you have never come to any of my rallies. You know what? I will give you a free ride on Air Force One to any of my rallies. Come there and see real Americans who trust me. All of you pretentious elite sitting in Washington, DC, and New York City should come out every now and then to the real America and feel the pulse of the people. Oh, I forgot, you went to fancy schools and speak high-sounding grammar. Does that make you better than them? Does that make you wiser than the people making a living tilling the soil and hunting for their meat?

Trust! Your *New York Times* has trust? What you guys do over there at the *New York Times* is to look for and publish any story that fits into your preconceived notion of who I am. Anything that does not fit that template you discard. That is why you jumped at your usual faceless sources as soon as they told you the FBI opened an inquiry into whether I was working for Russia. That you could stoop this low is not a surprise to me. Even a fourth grader would have known that firing the lying bad cop named James Comey, a man that everyone wanted fired, was a great thing for America.

You told Wolf Blitzer that if we faced a crisis it would be a disaster because I have a C team and my White House is dysfunctional. Let me tell you, the opposite is the case. If we have a crisis, the country will rally around me for leadership. They will see for the first time that I have been right all this time. People will be on the streets of America chanting, "Trump told us so." If we have a crisis, I won't have to beg Congress for money to build the wall. If we have a crisis, the people will rise up, follow me, and go and build the wall themselves. Oh, you don't know how much I pray for a crisis. You don't know.

It is crisis that makes a president great. I am pumped up. I am primed. I am just waiting for a crisis to unfold—any crisis will do. We can stand on it and solve all the problems this country has. And trust me, it is coming. When it comes, people like you will run away to Europe because with the way you were running your mouth on CNN, this America will not contain you and me.

You bet my millions of admirers will make sure you do not remain in this country to distract us all from the predestined work of rebuilding this nation and fortifying it against terrorists, criminals, and ignorant peddlers of discarded knowledge, like you. Ditto with hacking historians like Jon Meacham who are going from one cable channel to another saying that Trump's White House is like the Titanic steaming toward an iceberg.

I saw that you have embraced the childish talking points of the *Washington Post* about Trump and 7,000 lies. If truly they were 7,000 lies, why is it that they have not become the truth? Didn't your people say that Adolf Hitler enchanted Germans with 1.001 lies? How is it that I have not enchanted Americans with 7,000 lies? Why is it that millions of Americans are not following me to go door-to-door to remove all illegal immigrants in this country, put them on a train, and drive them down the southern border into the Amazon tropical rain forest? Can you explain that if your proposition is true?

The truth is that all you snobbish brats do not understand the language of your forefathers. You are stuck speaking the language of the queen, her dukes, her knights, earls, bishops, and all the upper class of the British society. My people understood what I meant when I said Mexico would pay for the wall. They did not take it literally to mean that Mexico would bring pesos in hundreds of bags to pay for the wall. They know that I meant that one way or the other, Mexico would pay for the wall.

By the way, I like senator Ted Cruz's idea that drug lord El Chapo should pay for the wall. If the attorneys at the Southern District of New York were not busy pursuing shadows in the Russian witch hunt, they could strike a deal with El Chapo. He gives us $5 billion, and we release him back into the wildlife of

Mexico.

Incredible! With a straight face, you told Wolf that I had no shame. Sitting on the stinking CNN chair, you had the nerve to say that Fox News, the most credible news organization in the world, had no integrity. I'm sure the camera crew in the studio was laughing at you. They must have been looking at you like a Nokia 3310 in the age of an iPhone 10 X.

I could see that you were baffled at how I had the Republican Party in my armpit. That is what is called leadership. Unlike your Democratic colleagues, Republicans know that if Trump sneezes, they all sneeze. You know why it is that way? I'm the Republican Party that they are fighting for. Case closed. Those who could not handle it left. And the back door is still wide open for others to follow suit. So your liberal dream of an insurrection or uprising in the Republican Party is not gonna happen. I am the Republican brand.

I suppose it was Thomas Jefferson who said that given the choice to have "a government without newspapers or newspapers without a government," he would choose the latter. I may be the first president who does not have to choose. By the time I am done ignoring, sidestepping, and consequently, strangulating newspapers, I will finally attain that blissful state of having a government without newspapers.

Goodbye Tom. Goodbye failing *New York Times*. Goodbye divorce-splitting *Washington Post*.

Yours truly,
Donald J. Trump
The 45th President of the United States of America

Trump's Letter to Mass Shooting Victims

Monday, January 13, 2019

Dear parents, brother, sister, children,

I am writing this to preempt the next mass shooting in the making. Oh yeah, there is a mass shooting coming up. If you have not yet been a victim of one of those things, you will soon be. That is how it is. That is what it means to be an American. It has always been like that. Remember that our politicians used to settle their differences with gun duels. Wasn't that how Vice President Aaron Burr killed former United States Secretary of the Treasury Alexander Hamilton? How I wish I could have a gun duel with Nancy Pelosi today. I would blast her and Chuck Schumer to outer space and get the funds to build my wall.

If you hate our gun culture, move to Canada or Europe. I heard that only about forty people die from gun violence in an average European country. Pathetic. That is where sissies live. You cannot have the apple pie and reject the lead bullet—they go hand in hand. Just so you know, it is our gun culture that gave us the great $40 billion Hollywood movie industry. They have cameras in Europe and Asia but have no film industry. Do you know why? They have no culture of shooting up a storm. An armed society is not just a polite society. It is also a performing arts society.

But if you want to live in the great United States, prepare yourself to be the first to fire the shot. One woman in Far Side, Chicago, who had a license to carry a concealed weapon, did that the other day. She fired the first shot and killed the worthless teen that was poised to rob her, and who knows, he might have even raped her. Doesn't that make you proud that our eternal right to keep and bear arms is working?

I know the moment that I say this, some of you bleeding-heart liberals will say, "What about Sandy Hook Elementary in Newtown, Connecticut? Should elementary school kids or their teachers also bear arms?" What is wrong with that? At six years old, some of these kids have mastered marksmanship by just playing video games. All they need is some training with the real thing. After all, I have seen ISIS and Al-Qaeda training their own six-year-olds with AK 47s. These are the people that we are contending with. We might as well get our future warriors trained on time for the fight ahead. Another way of looking at it is that training six-year-old kids will guarantee our all-volunteer armed forces a steady supply of soldiers.

I know what some of you liberals are doing now. You are rolling your eyes as you roll out statistics. One person dies from gun violence every seventeen minutes in America. A mass shooting occurs every five days. What else? There are over 350 million guns in America, more than all the people in the US. Okay. But I don't see you panicking over the other statistics that says that five people die in the US every minute. What is killing them and why have you not done anything about it? And if you are someone that looks at the bright side of things, according to the US Census, one baby is born in the US every second—that is sixty babies a minute. So what are you talking about? We have surplus people. Not to add that every minute, two immigrants enter the United States by air or across our porous border with Mexico.

People are still pissed about my plan to seal the border. What they do not know is that coming up next, I will find a way to seal the air too. If you fly in as a visitor, we will put an electronic monitoring device on you to track your movement. On the day your visa expires, if you are still in our country, ICE will come and pick you up. Simple. We have the technology to do it at every point of entrance without increasing the immigration check line at the airports.

As you can see, more people are added every day to the United States than are leaving by death or out of frustration. If we don't want to overpopulate America, we have to make sure people are leaving via deportation, frustration, and, of course, death. There is nothing wrong with that. It is a natural path. We, the white people who own this land, can still have somewhere to run to when colored people move into our neighborhood. But a time will come when we may run out of places to run to. We must not let that happen. So we must leave the loopholes through which people die in these United States of America.

The other day, an anti-gun lobby got a six-year-old kid to write me. The brainwashed kid reminded me that every year, an average of 35,000 people die from gun violence in the United States. She did her elementary mathematics and arrived at the conclusion that it came up to 674 people every week. Then the kid threw in adult logic. She wrote that if planes carrying 674 people crashed every week in America, that I would ground the whole aviation industry until something was done about it. Imagine!

Obviously the kid and her advisers were clever by half. What they did not factor in was that we care about plane clashes more than those who die on the roads or by any other means because the majority of the people who fly are important people. When we roll out statistics about gun violence, we are fully aware that it includes those black people in South Side Chicago and the Oakland gangs. Really, should we be very concerned about them? Really?

That we lost about 5,000 people in over seventeen years of war in Afghanistan or 47,000 people in over twenty years of war in Vietnam is more important in the scheme of things than the 300,000 people that have died in America from gun violence in the last ten years. It may not be politically correct to say it, but the truth is that some people are quality people and some are not. It is also true that our healthcare is one of the best in the world because our doctors get an ample supply of gunshot victims to practice on each day. When we say that 35,000 die each year, we are actually saying that another 100,000 survived. Great job, doctors!

So, I, Donald J. Trump, am not one of those who celebrate a day or a weekend without a murder in New York City or any other city. Unless we have a corresponding deportation, I am not impressed. Or if you tell me that Michael Moore decided to leave America forever.

I have told the anti-gun lobby that the right to bear arms is not the problem. Switzerland is a country in Europe where one out of three of its eight million citizens owns a gun. Yet they don't know how to use the guns. They don't shoot up each other the way we Americans do. Which is established proof that not only do guns not kill people, but also people with guns do not kill people. The people who actually kill people are those who were destined to kill people. As for those they kill, it goes without saying that they were destined to be killed. There is no other possible explanation for what is going on.

So dear parent, sister, brother, child, our founding fathers were infallible. If you are a victim of gun violence, please take it as one of those things that happen. It must have been written for you and your family. There is no pursuit of happiness without the right to bear arms. Have you seen Germans? They do not laugh. Do you know why? They have no guns, and without guns, they do not have the right to pursue happiness.

I don't need to remind you that America's independence as a nation is also at stake. I pulled America from useless treaties like the Climate Treaty and the Iran Deal because they compromise America's independence. I pulled America from UNESCO, and very soon, I may have to kick the UN out of New York, renovate the building, and make it the World Flagship Trump Hotel.

I don't need to tell you that if we continue on the path Obama and other presidents placed America, one day we will wake up and see United Nations troops on the streets of Mississippi, shooting at Americans. We need to arm a strong militia just in case the UN pulls that stunt one day in the future.

In four years of our Civil War, we lost 620,000 Americans. It would take twenty years for that number of Americans to die from gun violence. That is a price that I am willing to pay for our freedom.

Yours truly,
Donald J. Trump
The 45th President of the United States of America

Donald Trump's letter to American Historians

Thursday, January 17, 2019

Dear American historians,

I wish my father were alive today to watch me meet with my smart White House advisers as we narrow down which of you I should pick as my official biographer. I, Donald, the son of Fred, am choosing my presidential historian. What a beautiful thing! Who could have foreseen that just three years ago?

My fellow billionaire Henry Ford said that all history is bunk and that the history that mattered was the one he made. I tell you, that saying is more relevant when looking at the phenomenon I have been in the history of America. The whole history of the United States of America should now be divided into two: BT and AT—Before Trump and After Trump. All the other lines of demarcations have been blurred or mashed up.

Everything before Trump is bunk. Certainly.

I want a historian that will go beyond the biased and abridged stories of the daily news cycle. I want someone who will get unrestricted access to my highly developed thinking faculty. I am looking for someone not yet poisoned by the daily chatter of the talking heads on cable TV. Definitely, I am eliminating anyone who wrote the biography of Obama or Clinton or Carter. They are clowns. They are beneath me and beneath writing my biography. I also do not want anyone who has made an appearance on any of the fake news channels, CNN, NBC, or MSNBC. Having such dopes write my biography would be a disaster.

Which means that David McCullough, Douglas Brinkley, Edna Greene, Edmund Morris, John Meacham, A. Scott Berg, Doris Kearns Goodwin, and Robert Caro are out. Jared said that Ron Chernow did a great job writing on Washington. Stephen thinks H. W. Brands was wonderful in his take on Andrew Jackson. Some are throwing up the names of Robert Dallek and Jean Edward Smith. Some of the names sound like lightweight names.

Whoever I pick, I want to make sure he or she understands the history that we make every day in Washington, DC. It is an unprecedented history delivered consistently on a daily basis. It will never be surpassed in the history of the United States. I'm 100 percent sure of that. At least, not in a billion years.

I have heard some of you say that America is in its last days as a great country. You say it as if it is a foregone conclusion. One news report even suggested that as early as next year, America would cease to be the greatest economy in the world. It says that China would become number one. Those peddling such stories are discounting where I would leave China when I am done with them. I, Donald J. Trump, will push them and tell them where to fall. And they will be there, on the ground, for a very long time.

I see no threat from India in another hundred years. That projection that by 2030 India will inevitably become the number two economy in the world after China is just a stupid exaggeration. Where will they keep their billions of poor people who live amidst dirt and share their meals with flies?

Here is my message to all historians. The false idea that America is following the path of Rome is a misnomer. If Obama had been replaced by Crooked Hillary Clinton, maybe. But I am here now, baby. Big daddy will strengthen things for America. And when I leave six or ten years from now, depending on how I feel, there will be no doubt that the good times will last for another one hundred years, at least. Didn't these same historians tell us that Japan would eat our lunch by the 1990s? But they did not know that Ronald Reagan was coming. It is the same way now. Those who wrote off America in the 2000s, concluding that China would eat our lunch, did not know that Donald J. Trump was coming.

We are the richest, strongest, and smartest nation in the history of mankind, bar none. And as long as we continue to elect smart men like me once every one hundred years, we will reverse any sign of decline. It is quite unfortunate that men like me come once every one hundred years. I wish they made more of us and brought us to America very often. The good thing is that once we arrive, we scrape off the cobwebs and reverse the mistakes of the previous one hundred years of making merry.

So, my dear historians, please stop being extremely hysterical. Let our people know that there is nothing to worry about. Over the years, countries have risen to challenge America, and we have successfully brought them to their knees. We will continue to do so as long as America continues to listen to geniuses like me.

In recent times, some of you have gone on TV to scream that American institutions are in decline. Don't think I don't see you all. You complained that age-old norms were being eroded, making our institution vulnerable. Please! I'm the norm you are talking about. What I say is the norm becomes the norm. And as long as I am behind the steering wheel, you have nothing to worry about. The foundation of America is as strong as my top-notch mental and physical health. The possibility of a collapse does not exist.

Rome failed because the leaders who came after the original Caesars went soft. That I can tell you. They went soft on immigration. They embraced a nanny state that provided everything for the citizens and then wondered why their people lost the edge and the drive to remain at the top and conquer the world. That is why I am reversing all those policies that pamper our people into laziness. I've halted the march to single-payer healthcare. I will be cutting down on the number of people on food stamps and all the welfare goodies. There should not be public housing at all when I am done. For as long as there is public housing, there will be people who will not have a reason to aspire to own their own homes. Right? I'm sure none of you have ever made that connection.

The people who founded this country and made it what it is today were strong people willing to dare. They left Europe to come to America not for a ready-made good life but to dare and build the good life they could only imagine in Europe. But because of our screwed-up psychology, we have created generations and generations of dependent citizens who have no reason to strive. We will make it clear that such a lifestyle is un-American. Those who wish to live that kind of life should go to Europe. I've heard that not even the shithole countries of Africa provide such an innovation-damaging environment.

Those who say America is so big are merely looking at how far we have stretched our tentacles. We have 294 embassies, consulates, and diplomatic missions around the world. That is crazy chaos. As soon as I bring our soldiers back from Syria, Afghanistan, Germany, South Korea, Djibouti, the next thing will be to cut off diplomatic posts around the world by half, or even more. Can anyone tell me why in the world we need American soldiers in Djibouti? The tons of money I will save by closing down these unnecessary outposts will be used to make America forever great. I want to walk away into the sunset when I know that every real American baby born in this country will have over $1,000,000 in a trust fund—right from birth. The only condition is that both parents of the new-born baby must be natural-born American citizens.

I have ended the tyranny of the liberals who look down on the majority of our citizens and wish to force their weird lifestyles on us all. Everybody is talking about it. These hateful liberals tried to criminalize their political opponents for no good reason. Witch hunt! Instead of pushing for personal responsibilities, they were advancing wealth redistribution. They were the ones who were making our society chaotic. Their runaway train of unlimited freedom had to be stopped by someone, and I'm glad I stopped it.

My task is to restore law and order so that those who worked hard for their success will enjoy the fruits of their labors without undue harassment and subsequently inspire those at the bottom to work hard and make something of themselves. A simple idea that is also very fantastic. As you can see, those who used to demagogue the rich have either left the country or have become so disillusioned that they have left the political space. Where is Al Franken, for instance?

The other matter I hear you all talk about is public corruption and the corruption of public institutions. I said somewhere that what the liberals call corruption is just an effort by jealous losers not to let the winners enjoy the perks of their offices. When I said I was a star and could grab any woman I wanted, many liberals went insane. But real men understood what I meant. I know it does not sound politically correct, but it is what it is. Take it or leave it. I did not get this far by being politically correct. If you don't make the people who are the brain behind the greatness of this nation happy, you are essentially telling them not to give their best. If we succeed, America succeeds. When people like us who were successful in private practice come to the public arena to serve, we should be well taken care of. That is how we can give our best and bring the magic of the private space into the inefficient public arena. There is nothing spectacular about public service run by incompetent civil servants. Nothing!

I say all this just to remind you all that there are no parallels between what happened to Rome and the fate of the United States. Unlike you all, I have great faith in the American people. I will always deliver for them in spite of the gigantic distractions thrown in my path. I do not have time for hoaxes. I do not bend to public opinion. I'm going to make decisions that are deeply rooted in principles. As long as I do that, the American people will side with me. I don't even need 51 percent of the people to be with me. I only need 270 electoral votes. The rigging Hillary Clinton and her illegal voters can keep their three million votes.

Let me repeat it. I hear you all cry about weakening institutions. Some of you say people are losing faith in public institutions. Contrary to what some of you historians think, the American people know I am the institution they are fighting for.

There may be other institutions, but I am the only one that matters. They are not fighting for compromise and consensus. They are fighting for results. And I deliver results.

Write that in your books. Let generations yet unborn read it. May it be taught at schools all over this great country that there was a man called Donald J. Trump who came and stopped the American decline into political dysfunction. Along the way, he added a new lease of life to America.

Tell those who are privileged to see me in their lifetime to appreciate me, for they are the lucky generation.

I think that will be enough, for now.

Yours truly,
Donald J. Trump
The 45th President of the United States of America

Trump's Letter to the Me-Too-Movement Groups

Friday, January 18, 2019

Dear Me-Too women and their friends,

I write you today to clear some misconceptions about me as I prepare for my re-election campaign.

As you know, it is around the corner. I already heard the likes of Pocahontas from Boston, and the Afro-Mexican woman who probably crossed the border into California are all itching to run for president and become the commander-in-chief of this great nation. America is so great that everyone is allowed to dream of becoming her president. Sometimes our people make the mistake of electing someone born outside of this country to be president. I'm sure our people have learned from the last mistake. I'm still cleaning up the mess that he left behind.

I am sure these female candidates will try to make the issues of your Me-Too movement an issue in the upcoming presidential campaign. One thing that should be clear to you all is that this campaign will not be an insurgency campaign like that of 2016. This will be a campaign by those trying to dethrone the president of the United States of America. What it means is that I will not dignify irrelevant matters with a comment. There would not be any drama like inviting Bill Clinton's cheap women to the venue of the presidential debate. Been there, done that.

I am approaching this campaign fully aware of the honor and grandeur of the presidency, which I represent. I do not plan to reduce myself to the level of the little people who will try, just for the sake of trying, to challenge me. I will whoop whoever they throw up at me more than President Ronald Reagan whooped Walter Mondale.

Despite that, I think you all deserve to know my philosophy about women. Some of you may find this as a surprise, but I am the child of my mother. I have tremendous respect for women. I grew up respecting women. As a cadet in military school, I was a dashing young man at whom women threw themselves. I'm sure some of you have seen my pictures in those days. I was a heavenly gift to women. I was a one-woman man. I did not just adorn my woman with the luxurious things of life, I also treated her as very expensive jewelry. Believe me, that did not stop this girlfriend of mine from cheating on me.

That incident would have devastated a weak man. But not me. I am a strong man, and I responded in a very strong way. Instead of shedding tears like feeble men do, I became resilient.

Since then, I have come to realize that women cheat, just like men, if not more. While men cheat for the most part just to satisfy their urges, women cheat for more complicated reasons—to meet needs, psychological, emotional, and material. Men go in, go out, and move on with their lives while women leech and drain and drain the man until nothing is left of him.

Because men are often the ones caught cheating, there is the wrong perception out there that men cheat more than women. By the nature of how the sexes relate and the need for men to make the first moves, men are often the ones caught. When women make their moves, they are often subtle and near stealth. It gives them cover as they pursue their erotic desires with ease. Didn't I read somewhere that 25 percent to 40 percent of all children born to married couples belong to a different man than the husband? Who is the cheat now?

As mere mortals, men are generally weak because the circuit connecting their two main sex organs, the brain and the penis, is short. Being weak does not mean that men do not want to have fun. But a weak man who wants to have fun is a disaster waiting to happen. If I had my way, weak men would be barred from having fun. That is how they embarrass strong men like us. They get caught, and people use them to generalize.

As women acquire more power in our society, they advance their various needs. They do so to the detriment of men. Except for billionaires like me, no man can 100 percent satisfy the physical, emotional, and psychological needs of a woman while at the same time providing her material needs. And it has to be 100 percent, or else the woman will seize on that to cheat.

Unlike women, we understand the world better. We understand that when all is said and done, women are like public swimming pools on a hot summer day. In blistering heat, you pay the swimming pool a visit. Once you behold the blue water, you take off your clothes and change into your swimming trunk. You jump in, swim around, breaststroke, backstroke, butterfly, front crawl, sidestroke, and freestyle. Once you release your pent-up energy, you come out, use a clean towel to dry yourself, change back into your street clothes, and off you go. If you like, you drop a tip for the maintenance of the swimming pool.

You don't bother about who has been in the swimming pool before you came in. Sometimes you don't worry about who you are sharing the swimming pool with the moment you are there. Unless there are a bunch of immigrants around, in which case you worry about diseases and the possibility of them releasing farts, pee, or poop while you are in the pool.

In the long term, I worry about the world you all will leave behind if we don't put a stop at where you are pushing men. Other animals in the mammal family are basically maintaining their stock by having free love. They understand the importance of natural selection aimed at preserving the strongest genes in an ever-changing world. It is only humans who are putting restrictions that are threatening the reproduction of the best of humanity, even as the moon and the skies change in a way that only the strongest can survive the strange rays and the violent clouds and the bashing heat and the acid rain coming down on the world. Unless we sacrifice some 21st century fanciful emotional blackmail of women, we are setting mankind on the path of extinction. Forgive the crude language, but scientists all agree that in this ever-changing world, only the species that fuck around will survive. That is why the cockroaches and the rats are doing very well.

I have given this great thought. And I can tell you that it is sheer delusion to think that there is a path that leads to human preservation that does not involve fucking around. We men do not do what we do because we like it. We do it because it is in our DNA. It is nature's way of preserving our species. If we allow you all to crush what makes us men, in as little as one hundred years from now, the rats will take over the world and turn us into their own dolphins, to be exhibited for mere entertainment.

So please get this once and for all. What we do as men has nothing to do with who we are. It has everything to do with how nature has made us. It is the distortions and modifications that you all brought that have led to the mutation of modern men into the alien homosexual beings that we see around. Again, I know this is not politically correct, but as long as I am president, if I cannot speak the truth, who else is morally mandated to speak the truth to the American people? Who?

As men, our emotional language may not be well developed or mature, but I can assure you that when we say we have conquered a woman, we really mean that we have won one, not for the gipper, but for the creator whose intelligent design we have taken a step to preserve.

What should worry you all is that men are becoming more and more selective. When we say, "She is not my type", a time may come when your desirable option may dwindle to a point where we, men, could as well have gone on strike. Imagine if that were to happen, where would that leave your stock?

The American family is on fire. It is not Trump that started the fire. It is the excesses of women and their supporters that started it. The disruption your agenda caused in the system is like the one caused when manufacturing moved away from America. We cannot be good apostles of the American family if we idly sit and watch feminism destroy the head of the American family. The same way that we cannot be good apostles of capitalism if we idly sit and watch as capitalism leaves behind the real operators of its engine—white men. The impact of one or the other is equally devastating. What I am doing is pointing at the blazing fire alarm to say that if we don't do anything about the fire in the house, it will consume us.

Yours truly,
Donald J. Trump
The 45th President of the United States of America

Trump's Letter to Sarah Sanders

Saturday, January 19, 2019

Dear Sarah,

I am all alone in the White House waiting for the Democrats to come and make a deal on the wall. Melania is not around. Which is a good thing because when she is around, it adds to the tension here. You know how she is.

So I have been spending some time thinking if there is anyone on my staff with whose work I am truly satisfied. Anyone! I went from one staff to another. Even those that were my favorites when I brought them in, I found out that I quickly soured on them.

Remember the generals—Kelly and Mattis. They failed me so spectacularly. I know the problem is not me. Ah, I am 100 percent sure of that. They are obviously the problem. There are no two ways about that.

But that does not answer the fundamental problem. Is there anyone in my staff with whose work am truly satisfied? Stephen Miller? Not really. If there is none, what does that mean?

Believe me, I am not one of those bosses who is never satisfied with the job any of my staff is doing. At the Trump Organization, at least I had three staff members in whom I had absolute confidence. Two of them ended up betraying me. I'm talking of Mike Cohen and Allen Weisselberg or is it Weaselberg? Now, I am

211

not sure of the third.

You have not betrayed me, Sarah. You are one of those who have been steadfast in your defense of me against those enemies of the people. I know you have been mocked, hated, and cajoled because of that. I felt sad for you when Red Hen Restaurant refused to serve you because of the work you do for the American people. Sean said I should express my appreciation to you. He said I should not just wait until you screw up and then I would lash out at you.

It is something that I never think about, commending staff for doing the job that I pay them to do. I always feel that the huge and rare opportunity I give the people I hire is enough commendation. For instance, if not for the opportunity I gave you, you would not be featured on *Saturday Night Live*. What is better than that? At least not sex and not money. You are now part of pop culture. Thanks to me.

Anyway, even though it is not in my nature to do so, you know I truly appreciate what you do each day. You eat up those hyenas who call themselves the White House press corps. Since you are not as beautiful as Ivanka, I would not be able to call you my daughter. Otherwise, I would have.

Your bullshitting style is legendary. You swallow them and then spit them out without care. You waste no time in labeling them "fake news." In so many ways, forms, and fashions, your brain works like mine. I think that is why I absolutely enjoy your back-and-forth with them. I watch you lie on that podium, and I say to myself, "Damn, you are good."

You are at your best when I contradict you. Like in the matter of that woman, Stormy Daniels. You refer them to outside counsel for an answer. Marvelous strategy. I love that you do not just follow my suggestions from the media strategy meetings, but that you add your own elements to it. Borrowing from one of your famous lines, I think it is very biblical for me to show my appreciation.

When you called the anonymous *New York Times* op-ed writer a "gutless loser," it was as if I spat those words into your mouth.

Please don't take this the wrong way. In my quiet moments, I often think there is a scrotum somewhere in your groin. Have you checked? I wouldn't be surprised if there was. I imagine a fully developed one with two fully-grown testicles surrounded by a forest of hair.

Please don't tell me I am right. Unbelievable! If you do have a scrotum, baby, you deserve it. Your performance at that podium is always excellent. Not many men can keep a straight face while they lie. That is why I am pleased with you.

Sean Spicer was a total disaster. I should have known that and followed my gut at the beginning by naming you my press secretary. I was just worried that you do not have a TV face. But I think the nation has learned to watch your face. Or maybe they have learned to look away from the TV and listen as you unload on the media. Whatever they do, all I know is that it is working.

I particularly like your style when you are asked a question, but, in your answer, you go beyond providing a defense and also drop an attack. Genius. It is the kind of thing I specialize in.

Here is an example. One of those press irritants asked you if the president was lying, and you answered: "I can definitely say the president is not a liar, and I think it's frankly insulting that question would be asked." That is classic.

Where were you when I was looking for staff at Trump Organization? A woman with your guts and gusto will not crack under FBI pressure like little Michael Cohen did.

I write to commend you today and to tell you that tougher days are ahead. With this Mueller thing coming to a head, I expect you to go deep into your bag of tricks and bring up new ways to shoot down media questions. There will be so many questions, some of which would be very embarrassing if only they were true.

Let me assure you that when this is over, irrespective of how it ends, I will remember you. I won't think twice before I hire you at Trump Organization and reward you for sticking up for me.

You are a general in your own right. You are at the forefront of our fight to end the dangerous and deceptive agenda of the left that has been destroying our country. That you engage in the fight without compromising your ethical core is a tribute to your parents and the fine upbringing they gave you.

Sarah, you can take this to the bank—your sacrifices will never be in vain.

Yours truly,
Donald J. Trump
The 45th President of the United States of America

Trump's Letter to his Russian Interpreter

Sunday, January 20, 2019

Npnbet my friend,

I write you today to alert you that the Democrats are coming after you. You are their next favorite target in their never-ending Russian witch hunt. They want you to tell them what I discussed with Russian President Vladimir Putin. Their moles in my administration have told them that I did not share your notes with them after my meetings with Putin. Hard luck. I am the president of the United States, and they are not.

If they are interested in knowing what the American president discussed with the Russian president, they should work hard to win the next presidential election. Though judging by the nature of the small kids and spent forces jumping in the Democratic ring to take me on in 2020, they have zero chance.

In the next few weeks, they will try to drag you before Congress to say what you know. If that fails, they will try other means, including subpoenas and other forms of intimidation. Their rich friends will try to entice you with money to get you to sing like a bird. They will even offer you vacations in Hawaii just to see if you will lower your guard in the beautiful island and open your mouth. I am sure their friends in Europe will go as far as to offer you a residence and all the good things in life to make you give in.

I don't need to tell you to remember the oath you took when you got that government job. When you raised your right hand and swore to uphold the Constitution of the United States, you were saying, just like I said, that no matter what anyone threw your way, you would never betray the United States of America. And talking to them about what I discussed with Putin is the exact definition of betraying the United States of America.

Quite frankly, because of the sensitive nature of your job, you are more or less the property of the United States. Just like your international passport; even though it is yours, it belongs to the United States of America. The United States can take back your passport at any time and for any reason.

You, my friend, belong to the United States of America. You don't want America to give you back, do you? If anyone approaches you, tell them that I said that every word out of your mouth is classified. And nobody can declassify them except me. "Hi," "Hello," "No," "Yes." All of them. Classified. That is all you need to say. Don't entertain anything anymore.

They have all gone crazy. Could you imagine that unmarried woman at the *New York Times*, Maureen Dowd, comparing me to Nancy Pelosi and calling me the brattiest? If I had wanted, after Michael Douglas dumped her in 1998, I would have gone for her and torn her apart. But I took a close look at the redhead, and I said to myself, "I don't think so. Not my type." As I predicted, she quickly went down from Michael Douglas to Aaron Sorkin. And who knows, the next men she dates could be a bunch of New York City taxi drivers.

I am the one keeping their failing newspapers afloat. Without me, they would have been out of jobs. Yet they treat me without respect. As you know, I am not a run-of-the-mill president. I serve guests at the White House McDonald's, Wendy's, Burger King, and pizza. It baffles them all. It makes them insinuate that I must be working for Russia.

I do not work for Russia. I have never worked for Russia. And I will never work for Russia. It is all a hoax. You know that and I know that. Frankly, Russia does not have enough money to pay me to work for them. I am already a billionaire. I don't need any more billions in my life. I can sell off all my businesses and still live a good life for the remainder of my time on earth.

The FBI probe into whether I was an agent of the Kremlin is a disgrace. Nobody asked Obama if he was an agent of Kenya. Nobody asked Bill Clinton if he worked for the Irish. They are picking on me because I am not a conventional president. Those who perpetuate that hoax do not really understand spying.

In the world of espionage, you cover your tracks. If I really work for Russia, I will disguise it by pretending to be tough on Russia. Only stupid spies try to be friendly with people whose assets they are. It is the very elementary of counterintelligence to go after those agents who are chummy with the enemy. I am not that stupid.

Some even suggested that I might have unknowingly worked for Russia. How do you unknowingly work for somebody? Without knowing? Do I look that stupid? If I work for somebody, I would be paid for the work, wouldn't I? Is it possible to work for someone without receiving payment? What payment have I received from Russia? I have not built a Trump Tower in Russia. Could they be considering the Miss Universe in Russia as a payment?

Russia is like a sexy female teacher. And every American president is like her high school male student. Every able-bodied high school boy is infatuated with his sexy female teacher. The sharp ones go on to sleep with her. Amongst the sharp ones are the smart ones and the stupid ones.

The smart boys do not go about showing their classmates the phone records or texts and sexts they exchanged with their sexy female teacher. The dumb boys do. That is why they catch the dumb boys. I am not just sharp. I am also very smart. So all these charges are not just preposterous, they are quite frankly very insulting for someone of my intelligence.

Sorry to have digressed. Now if they ask, tell them that I asked Mr. Putin tough questions. Tell them that I got him to confess that he had no hand in the outcome of the 2016 election. If they ask you why I took those notes from you, just tell them you said they were too hot for you to keep. No. That would raise more questions because their heads are screwed in the wrong direction. Just tell them you didn't want to be at the center of the drama of the FBI hoax so you decided to hand the notes over to me.

Tell them you did not want to be dragged before Mueller and Congress to explain what was discussed in Helsinki, Finland. Tell them you don't have the money to hire a lawyer for such a time-wasting jamboree. Let me take it from there.

I am beginning to learn Russian. I am using the online software Babble. It is my hope that in my second term, I won't need an interpreter when I meet with Putin.

Yours truly,
Donald J. Trump
The 45th President of the United States of America

Trump's Letter to Tom Brady

Hi Tom,

Your performance today at the AFC Championship game against the Tennessee Chiefs epitomized the very essence of Trumpism—you never stop winning until your fans are tired of winning.

What you did again today was exactly what I set out to do for the United States.

I have already racked up several wins. I have cut taxes and have gotten the economy speeding like a rocket to Mars. Such a thing has never been seen before. That is a touchdown. I loosened crippling regulations and got businesses to return to America and hire more workers such that unemployment is at a fifty-year low. That is another beautiful touchdown. I named ninety-nine Conservative judges to our high courts and two strong Conservatives to the Supreme Court. Those are field goals.

I have given our military more money than they ever asked and more money than they ever needed to keep them as the greatest military force ever assembled by man. At the same time, I am rounding up our never-ending wars and closing down our bases abroad to bring our soldiers back home. I am doing this while bringing peace to the Middle East and the Korean Peninsula. You must have heard that I made Jerusalem the capital of Israel, essentially, and that I brought to an end, with firing a shot, the North Korean nuclear threat to America. These are two important touchdowns all within my first half.

Like you said, everyone thinks America sucks and can't win anymore, but I am showing the world that America can still win and can still be great again.

I did all these things while the Democrats in the Senate were interfering with my ball passes. I would have repealed the obnoxious Obamacare if not for their interference. As a skilled quarterback, I was surgically taking the drive into the end zone. I handed the ball over to Mitch McConnell, my runner, only for him to fumble the ball. He was clobbered at the line of scrimmage. I would have also built the wall at our Mexican border if not for my weak wide receiver, Paul Ryan. I volleyed the ball to him in a perfect trajectory, but he dropped it for an incomplete pass.

Now I have to contend with an old and nasty new Democratic defensive tackle called Nancy Pelosi. Her helmet is made of stem cells from aborted babies. She cherishes stopping me on third downs. You bet that I am not letting them get a sack. They aren't sacking this quarterback. Forget about touchdowns; she wants me to go four and out. But I have refused. I refuse to punt on the great wall. That is why we have the longest government shutdown in US history. At this point I have conceded that I may not get a touchdown on that drive. I will be content with a field goal—a DACA deal for my wall.

Please process this with me. Maxine Waters was caught in an unsportsmanlike conduct. But the referees did not throw the yellow flag. Hillary Clinton was caught clipping. Again, no flag. The FBI let her go. Even before my opening kickoff, long before the snap, the media, like linebackers, came on me with a blitz. Despite their aggressive tackling and helmet hits, I have refused to let my knee and elbow touch the ground. My cornerbacks and safeties all failed to defend me, until I got Rudy Giuliani. Rudy changed our formation. He is good at helping me fake passes and executes a fake handoff to running backs.

While Reince Priebus was a false start, John Kelly was a terrible center. His job was simply to snap the ball, but he could not do it accurately. As you can see, sometimes, I have to run the ball myself. I am still searching for a good running back that is quick on his feet. Mike Mulvaney is just a stop-gap measure.

Did you see how I tried shotgun formation on the Paris Agreement and the Iran nuclear deal and it worked? When I tried it on NATO, my people botched the snap.

You play in a league that does not have foreigners walking in and out. Doesn't it feel all-American? Unlike the mess they have made to baseball and basketball where people who cannot even speak English just walk in and pollute the game. I trust that you understand the importance of the wall.

I will continue to win on the road and win at home. The play calls in my playbook are numerous. I will continue to outwit and outmaneuver my opponents, irrespective of the special team they bring on.

Somehow, just like you, I get the job done. I leave people watching on the sideline and at the booth to worry about how I did it. Can you believe it that over two years after, one Mueller is still at the booth reviewing my first play? My referee recused himself from being there to call the play. Have you experienced anything like that in your nineteen years in the league? I have since fired the referee. When my new referee gets in place, I hope he throws in the flag to stop the reviewing.

My back-up quarterback, Mike Pence, has spent the season on the sideline watching like a spectator. I tried to prepare him to learn how it is done as these Democrats keep talking about impeachment. I tried to push him out there to take a snap or two. You saw how he tried to overdo the Trump thing by declaring that ISIS was defeated the day they killed four Americans in Syria. He was just on autopilot. But I forgave him when he compared me to Martin Luther King Jr. Some jealous people think he is overcompensating. I don't get it. You are the GOAT—the greatest of all time—same with me, the greatest president ever (GPE).

You showed that young-ass quarterback Patrick Mahomes II who the boss is. It is the same way I will teach the young-ass Democrat from Texas, Spanish wannabe Beto O'Rourke and the Spanish newcomer senator Kamala Harris if any of them become the Democratic nominee for president.

On second thought, you advanced the essence of Trumpism by winning more when they said you sucked. You accomplished all these by working hard for your team and insisting that the New England Patriots ceased to be NFL suckers the very day you arrived in Boston.

See you at Super Bowl LII. And I dare say, see you at the White House after the win. God speed.

Come with Gisele. You know I love seeing Brazilian supermodels. Just for you, I will have the White House cooks follow your strict diet, the TB12 Method.

Yours truly,
Donald J. Trump
The 45th President of the United States of America

Trump's Letter to the Supermoon

Monday, January 21, 2019

Hi Supermoon,

As a Gemini, I welcome you this night. I hope you bring me a message from Mercury. I need it now more than ever because Jupiter and all the other bad actors are wreaking havoc on my constellation. I feel so alone.

I need the moon, the earth, and the sun to line up again and eclipse Nancy Pelosi and her Buzzfeed gangs. I need you to announce to America that Trump's era is the closest the United States has come, in its history, to being a more sustainable nation.

Please come closer and hear me out.

Believe me, this is why this country has been lagging behind China and, soon, a shithole country like India: we spent valuable time talking about irrelevant things. Could you believe that former New Jersey Gov. Chris Christie had the time to write in his book that I wore my ties long just to make myself look thinner?

I'm not blustering when I say, what a waste of time. And they wonder why I do not read those so-called memoirs where people who know nothing and people who failed go on an ego trip to justify what they do not know and why they failed. I'd rather spend my time reading how to reduce my handicap in golf.

I'm proud to say that my tie goes down to my fly because I like it that way. Why would I want to look thinner than I am? Do I look like I have low self-esteem? The only man I compare myself with, Winston Churchill, was he not my size? So why would I be as thin as that Kenyan? Real Americans are known to be whole—though not as obese as Christie. I bet he wrote those silly things to draw sympathy to himself. To be frank, Christie is kind of disgusting. He always looks like someone who pleads each night to be allowed to finish the last piece of meat on the dinner table, as in, "Please let me finish it."

Apart from his overweightness, which comes from eating everything on the table, Christie was a nice guy destroyed by his disdain for my son-in-law, Jared. So bad! I would have loved to have him in my administration. He surely knows how to bully the Acostas of this town. Somehow, we moved on without him, but he doesn't seem to have moved on—not an inch, going by what he spewed in his new book. If you can imagine how his vomit looks, you know all you need to about his book.

My childish innocence confuses people a lot. Can you imagine that liberal cable news spent time talking about the length of my tie even though we are on the twenty-seventh day of a partial government shutdown? Preposterous! One talking head said something I have never heard. He said that a psychology professor in Boston said that I use long ties to draw attention to my genitalia and take the focus away from my stomach. Is this what these liberal teachers are paid to study and preach to our young minds in the university? If anyone wants to know how my genitalia is holding up, they should go and ask the women who were privileged to see it in action. It does not need to be advertised. Thank you very much. It is a great product that sells itself. Just like the Trump brand.

Imagine! The media was so obsessed with my tie that they failed to give full coverage to my smackdown of Nancy Pelosi. I grounded her. She thought she was smart by delaying my State of the Union Address. I showed her who's the boss. No going to Egypt, Afghanistan, Iraq, and wherever she was supposed to go with the US Air Force plane. Hell no! And like a good NFL coach, I waited for her to carry her luggage onto the bus and for the bus to head out to the airport before I called a time out. Nice play.

Let her go by commercial airplane and let me see if some terrorists will kidnap her. If she thinks the American government will pay ransom on her small head, she has another thing coming. We will not even entertain exchanging her with Al Qaeda's Zacarias Moussaoui; Richard Reid, the shoe bomber; or even the pitiful Nigerian Umar Farouk Abdulmutallab, the underwear bomber. She would languish in the kidnappers' den until she agreed Donald Trump is her daddy.

Anyway, these are not the reasons I write you. I was just alone in the White House and feeling pissed at how the media is wasting precious time talking about nobodies like Christie when I am here waiting for the Democrats to come with their tails behind their backs, begging me to make a deal. I'm sure the American people will turn against them if I hold on long enough. That is what Ann Coulter said. That babe must have looked hot when she was a lot younger. Now, she is not my type. Kellyanne told me that she is now dating her security guard because she could not find anybody else. Poor Ann. But her conservative credentials are impeachable. If she had not forgotten how to act in a courtroom, I would have made her a judge in DC's appeals court circuit.

Sorry to go back to this matter. The folks at GQ are saying that a man's tie should not go beyond his belt. What is that supposed to mean? Have I ever lived according to other people's specifications? Why would I start now? Even some European tailors think that they are allowed to join this conversation about where the length of Trump's tie should stop. Unbelievable! I don't just dominate politics around the world, but I also am the subject of fashion discussions across the globe.

Don't think this is doubletalk, but I love it when the universe marveles at my intellect. In the last two years, more newspapers in the world talked about Trump than any other living person. What am I saying? My name was on the lips of more people on earth than Jesus, Muhammed, and Buddha put together. I have the distinguished genius of changing the topic constantly and avoiding a situation where things are repeated again and again.

I hope your coming will clear out the impurities in Washington, DC. It is becoming a very toxic environment. And you know that I don't like it. I could roar at those hotheaded noisemakers, but that would give them greater visibility, which I do not want. So I leave it to you, blood moon, to change the elliptic orbit of those wolfs for the good of the United States of America. Make use of earthquakes or volcanic eruptions if you need to. Because if you don't and I have to do it myself, I will use the only option on my desk—the nuclear option.

Yours truly,
Donald J. Trump
The 45th President of the United States of America

Trump's Letter to Rudy Giuliani

Tuesday, January 22, 2019

Hi Rudy,

I thought I was the only one who in my quiet moments wonders where I will be spending time after this life is over. I didn't know that you battle with that too. That is very reassuring. Your mind works exactly like mine. It makes you more endearing to me.

I have a very simple idea. I believe that once this life is over, it is all over. *C'est fini*. The light goes off and everything goes dark. Like the goat, the chicken, the cow, the monkey, we die and nothing else happens. Darkness. Sand goes back to sand and dust goes back to dust—white sand to white sand, black sand to black sand. The same with the dust.

So what matters is what we are able to make out of this life. How many words of Wikipedia profile did we get before we died? How many McDonald's hamburgers did we eat? How many cans of Diet Coke did we drink? And, I must add, how many beautiful women's shoulders did we put our hands over? You know what I mean. I know you do. I hear you are good at those things.

If we are wrong about what happens when this life is over, then we say oops. We will deal with whatever comes after. Hellfire. Deep sea. Outer space. After all, we won't be alone. And no matter where I find myself, I know I will make it to the top of the food chain considering my extraordinary genius.

But if we are right, we will laugh at those who didn't enjoy their lives on earth because of one deity or the other instructing them on how to live their lives. Quite frankly, I consider myself a deity. And I am here to make others dance to my tune, for I have superior knowledge and gifts.

I disagree with you about not caring about memory or what people say or do after it is over for you. That is all we have left. The memories are our only footsteps that will be left behind when we depart. If not for memories, why do we take pictures? If not for memory, why do we strive at all? We may as well sit at home like all those lazy black bums and collect food stamps.

So, I find it pathetic that you were worrying about what should be written on your gravestone. I assume that you were not literally talking about your gravestone. Because if you were, I hope you know that you can make a gravestone of your choice today so what you desire is written on it. In any case, there is no way anyone will write: "Here Lies Rudy Giuliani—the man who lied for Trump." I take that back. The only way it may happen is if one of your ex-wives that you cheated on decides to do you the honor of writing what should be on your gravestone.

I take it that you were talking about a metaphorical gravestone. By that, I mean the gravestone that is in the hearts of millions of people who were witnesses to your contributions to this life.

I am lucky. I write on my buildings while I am still alive. As long as the buildings stand, they will be there to scream my name. Those who do not build and write whatever they like worry about gravestones. What if you write whatever you like on your gravestone and nobody comes to see it? Is it still there? I'm just wondering.

You were right, Rudy. I'm the most unfairly treated historical individual in all of human history. I believe God will ultimately punish those who deliberately mistreated me. I mean, people like Robert Mueller and Barrack Obama. What irks me now is that they have extended the same treatment to anybody associated with me. Look at how they treated those Covington Catholic School students from Kentucky at the steps of Lincoln Memorial in Washington, DC. Because the people at the opposing end were Native Americans and Black Hebrew Israelites, the media immediately assumed they were righteous and those students wearing MAGA hats were despicable racists. Shame on them.

Rudy, you know the ins and outs of the Mafia. Tell me, is Mueller not acting like the Mafia? When did our justice system start to act like a Mafia organization? Someone has to explain this to me. I won't think twice before I declare a state of emergency on our border and our justice department all at once. You know I can do it—I am the president.

Mayor, your reaction following the September 11 attacks transformed your despicable performance as the mayor of New York City. I am looking for a crisis that will transform my performance as the president of the 37 percent of Americans who are willing to die for me no matter what I do. As someone who has an eye on history, I want to finish strong for the majority of Americans.

Your parents, like my parents, were children of immigrants. In just the second generation, you turned out a great American. Just like me. But do you see any sign that these people coming up from Latin America will turn into great Americans in their tenth generation? I don't see it.

I know you once considered being a priest. Ah, the nuns are lucky you changed your mind. You would have ruined so many of them and the creed they believe in. Anyway, I don't believe in St. Peter or St. Paul at the pearly gates waiting for me to come and explain myself. Just the long line at that gate is enough for me to turn around.

Yours truly,
Donald J. Trump
The 45th President of the United States of America

Donald Trump's Letter to Roger Stone

Saturday, February 2, 2019

Dear Roger,

My good friend, I write you today to reassure you that this whole witch hunt is coming to an end. My guy at the Justice Department told me that it would soon be over. So do not despair. Do not bow to their pressure on you to bear false witness against me. When it is all said and done, I will ask Junior to take you to Europe on an all-expense-paid trip to shop for your favorite silver-colored neckties, velvet blazers, English tailored suits, and Italian shoes. You will drink vodka martinis with an olive to your heart's content, plus French wine. Money will not be a problem. Anything you want will be yours.

At this point in time, it is very important that I remind you of my most admired stone rule. Whatever they throw at you, always remember this rule, that says: "Admit nothing, deny everything, and launch counterattacks." It has worked very well for me. And believe me, it will work very well for you in this matter of you and Mr. Mueller. You have no back channel to Wikileaks founder Julian Assange. You have never met him. You have never spoken with him. You have never tried to stop anyone who spoke to him from speaking with Mueller. You sent out a tweet alerting the world of a bombshell that was coming to destroy Hillary Clinton and the Democrats only because you had the premonition. As a seasoned political operative, you could sense political things that are about to happen before they happen. You did not have advance knowledge of the John Podesta or Hillary Clinton emails that Wikileaks was going to put out in the public domain.

Again, remember rule 2: "Attack, attack, attack—never defend."

I have been told that whatever they have on you or me has huge missing dots. These are giant dots as big as donut holes. You are the missing links, my friend. Without you, they cannot connect the dots. And if they cannot connect the dots, they cannot prove collusion. And if they cannot prove collusion, they cannot prove obstruction of justice. And if they cannot prove obstruction of justice, they cannot prove witness tampering. I have it on high authority that if there is no collusion, there will not be any need to obstruct justice. You get my drift? You see how easy it is to floor them?

So, I am counting on you to stay strong. Even if they put you in prison, don't break down or fold like those other sissies, like Flynn, Cohen, and company. Your savior is alert and watching. If need be, I will intervene and stop that raging bull Mueller in his tracks. Trust me. I am weighing my options. While everyone is focusing on my emergency declaration to build the wall, I am thinking of another emergency declaration to end the Mueller probe.

I am seriously thinking of using the first to get the nation ready for the second. If nothing happens after I pull off the first, nothing will happen after I pull off the second. And with those two obstacles taken care of, I will coast to re-election victory. And that is when I will show them who the real Trump is. All those motherfuckers who messed with me will not need to be told that it is time to leave my country.

From Nixon to Trump, Roger, you have had an illustrious career. Your name is written in stone in the annals of Republican politics. You are on the top-ten list of best political strategists ever seen in this country. Your type does not come twice in a lifetime.

The way you have the tattoo of Nixon's face on your back is the same way your name shall be tattooed on the definitive marble celebrating the Trump presidency. Without you, the Republicans would not have won the South. You were the one who warned them in the days of Nixon that the Democrats would not mind electing a black male president.

I was looking at your book on the Clintons the other day and a thought came to me. Could this whole Mueller investigation be another effort by the Clintons to destroy me? You know how diabolic they are. Do you think it is one of their efforts to pay me back for ruining what they thought was a grand master plan—the Hillary Clinton presidency? We both know they will fail. I just want to know if that is what is going on here so I can decide what to do to finish them when I am re-elected.

I have another idea. Do you know how you told me that Lyndon B. Johnson was involved in the conspiracy that led to the killing of John F. Kennedy? I am beginning to think that Mike Pence is secretly involved in something that will result in me being disgraced out of office so he will become the president. The way he sits down quietly beside me while all these things are going on and not wanting his hands dirtied makes me think something is amiss. You once manipulated the ouster of your high school student government president while you were vice president. Do you think there is a parallel here? Should I be concerned?

I hope you will have the time and the research materials in prison to do some opposition research for me on this battalion of Democrats coming out to run for president in 2020. You are the grandmaster of opposition research, and I need your unique skills. I am not worried about the women amongst them. They are like The Supremes without Diana Ross, or Destiny's Child without Beyoncé. I am only concerned about one or two of the men. The rest are wannabe leftists dreaming of turning America into Soviet Union 2.0. The stupid Negro is going nowhere. He thinks he is Obama 2.0. We have not cleaned up all the mess that Obama 1.0 made, and he is aspiring to come in to add to the mess.

Oh, by the way, do you know that Starbucks coffee guy who wants to run for president? Is there a way we can encourage him?

He appears to be getting on the nerves of Democrats. I already like the guy. I'm sure you have his contact. I don't mix with all those bleeding-heart liberals. If you reach him, please tell him that I am rooting for him. If he needs any assistance from me, just connect him to my people and we can support his bid to run as a third-party candidate. It is about time we give our people that important alternative. I'm sure you will agree with me. You have worked with other third-party candidates before like John B. Anderson, Kristen Davis, and Gary Johnson, among others.

Your mother was a small-town newspaper reporter. So I assume that you understand very well those vultures and what they eat. I spoke with the *New York Times* the other day. It was my effort to help them sell newspapers and avoid laying off staff like their friends at *Huffington Post, New York Daily News*, McClatchy newspapers, Vice, Buzzfeed, and others. But guess what? They misquoted me and promoted things which they said I said to make me look bad. Why are they so ugly at heart? Why are their necks and eyes as unappealing as those of vultures? Should I just not care about them and let them all die a natural death? I don't get it. Ungrateful fellows. You do them a favor, but they end up hurting you. As you know, some of them were my friends when I was still operating within their orbit in New York City. I usually do not like to abandon my friends because I have moved on to a higher plane.

Now, about those twenty-nine FBI agents that stormed your house to arrest you— they were just putting on a show as if you were El Chapo. It was part of the deep state's dirty trick to break you. They want to make you feel that they have something earthshaking on you other than mere mendacious concoctions. You will recall that despite your warning that they did not take that kind of force to storm the home of Huma Abedin, that Hillary Clinton's aide whom you correctly identified as a sleeper cell member of the Muslim Brotherhood. If they had searched her home and taken away the number of files they took from your home, they would have discovered that you were right all this time.

Those rat fuckers are out of their minds. When this is all over, I will clean house. All the mischief-makers and their lords on government payroll will be shown the door. Those who live on sleaze shall be left in the sun to dry. We have tolerated this pure bullshit for so long in this country. The final stage of my Make America Great agenda is to detoxify and purify the scumbags that are redeemable, while the rest shall be cast away. No time for crap anymore. The congregation of unbelievers will either convert or be exiled. It is their choice on what should befall them.

As Stephen told me, we have to make sure facts return as the centerpiece of America's moral fabric. No more fiction from the lazy minds of liberals who are too afraid of working hard and competing with other human beings without getting preferential treatments. In the immortal words of Steve, "Those dubious propensities are going to be thrown out the window."

Oh, one more thing. I was looking at one of those lifestyle magazines the other day. I saw the answer to the puzzle you posed to me when you were my Washington, DC, lobbyist during my casino days. Remember? You asked me to guess why you did not wear socks and yet your expensive Italian shoes did not smell. Are you ready for the answer? You sprinkle baking soda inside your shoes before you slide in your feet.

That, my friend, is how I should approach Nancy Pelosi from now on. Before I shake her evil hands, I will sprinkle baking soda on my hands to neutralize the Haitian voodoo she rubs on her hands whenever she comes to the White House. Evil woman. She is not good for America. You have to help me come up with something to tell Americans she is capable of doing if we do not stop her. Remember how you used to tell voters that the opponents of your candidate would make them work on Saturday? Something like that. Maybe a little more graphic or scarier.

I hope you got a kick out of the baking soda reveal. Am I a genius or what?

In case you go to prison, I will avail you with acupuncture services as a treat and as a reminder that better days await you and me when this is all over.

Until then, this is your friend,

Donald J. Trump
The 45th President of the United States

Donald Trump's Letter to Chairman Xi Jinping

Tuesday, February 5, 2019

Dear Chairman Xi,

Xin nian kuai le, happy Chinese New Year. I heard that 2019 is the Year of the Pig. Which essentially means, the year of America. Because I know that America has been the pig to you all. America has been the sucker. Hasn't it?

As you celebrate new beginning, I want to embark on a new beginning with you and the people of the Republic of China. As you have noticed in my meeting with you in Argentina, only two things are important to me. One is building a wall along our border with Mexico as important and historic as the Great Wall of China. The other is bringing manufacturing businesses in China back to America.

There is no compromise on either of the two. And they are connected. If we get manufacturing jobs back in America there will be high-paying jobs for our people, especially our men, my main constituents, who have had the short end of the stick for a long time. But those high-paying manufacturing jobs will not happen unless we stop millions of poor and desperate people from invading America through our porous border in the south.

You guys pray to the gods and to your ancestors. We Americans do not do that. We believe our ancestors have done their part and

235

have gone. It is left to us to do ours and move our society forward. And that is exactly what I have been doing for my beloved country. There is no turning back until we have our stolen wealth returned to us in your traditional red envelopes. We cannot be distracted by the offer of dumplings, egg rolls, nian gao, or tangyuan as Greek gifts.

You know your cherished story of the monster Nian. You remember how it came every New Year's Eve to terrorize people. And it used to make people hide at home. It was the case until one brave boy used firecrackers to fight off the monster and the bad luck it brought. And the next day, people celebrated their survival by setting up more firecrackers. Remember?

That is what I am doing for America. I am the brave boy who is using firecrackers to fight off America's monsters. And guess who one of the monsters is? Your China. The China that steals our intellectual properties. The China that steals our manufacturing jobs. The China that makes fake versions of iconic American products. The China that uses money to lure our friends in Africa and around the world and gets them to vote against America's interests. That is one of the monsters I am determined to defeat with firecrackers.

Unlike you all, I do not plan to burn fake paper money and printed gold bars in honor of deceased loved ones. As you must have noticed, I don't like fake things. Fake news, fake watches, and fake friends. I don't like them. I like real things. I am a very practical person. For the life of me, I cannot imagine the culture of your single citizens hiring fake boyfriends or girlfriends to take home during the Spring Festival to make it look as if they are in a relationship. I say things the way I feel them. There is no fake bone in me.

I was told that you folks do not shower or throw out garbage on New Year's Day out of fear that you may throw away good luck. What kind of garbage superstition is that? And I thought Africa and Haiti were the only shithole countries crippled by their beliefs in superstitions. What does cutting your hair or holding scissors, knives, and other sharp objects during New Year have to do with getting ahead? I can understand not swearing and arguing, breaking things, or talking about death or sickness during that period. I wish we could put those restrictions during American Thanksgiving. But then again, our dinner table would be boring. It would amount to silencing big uncles, sassy aunts, and witty grandmothers and grandfathers.

While your people decorate your homes with everything red to scare the monster Nian, when I look at America's balance sheet, I see a lot of reds. Our deficit with your country is a scary red that stretches from New York to Los Angeles. It scares the hell out of me about the future of my grandchildren. I mean, my own grandchildren will be alright, but I am worried about America's grandchildren. So while you hang red lanterns and red chili papers by the windows and doors, I am bringing out bloodshot red eyes in our negotiation for a trade deal. I won't mind deploying that in the alternative—trade wars. It is all up to you. I cannot allow the future of American children to be eaten up by monsters who think America is a sucker.

As the paramount leader of China, you understand what I mean when I say that America is done being the greatest sucker in the world. China was Japan's sucker for centuries until the Cultural Revolution, so you will understand.

You once lived in the cave in the village of Liangjiahe. So you know what it feels like to live under a restrictive tunnel vision. That was how America lived all these years, until I arrived on the scene.

We can make a deal that will preserve your pet project—the Chinese dream—without burying our divine mission for our people, making space for them to achieve the American dream. I withdrew from the foolish Trans-Pacific Strategic Economic Partnership Agreement (TPP), so I have no problem with your One Belt One Road Initiative or even you taking over Taiwan, eventually. I am even considering withdrawing America from NATO and all the other alliances that essentially cost us money without doing anything to preserve America's divine mission.

Chairman Xi, remember that you were born on June 15 while I was born on June 14. So we share the same star, and I know you more than you know yourself. When in 1985 you spent two weeks with an American family in Iowa as part of the Chinese delegation, you did not just study agricultural practices in America, but you got a glimpse of what America is all about. America is about achieving greatness while still remaining authentic. That is my eternal mission that I must fulfill. You know the way your mother was forced to denounce your father as he was paraded before a crowd as an enemy of the revolution; that is how my MAGA people will denounce me if I do not bring back manufacturing jobs to America. So I am sure we can strike a beneficial deal for our peoples.

Finally, last year, *Forbes* named you the most powerful person in the world. You took over the title from my good friend, Russian president Vladimir Putin. My goal is to retake that title from you when I am done re-establishing a fair-trade deal with your country. You can take that to the bank.

Anyway, I have to go now. It is time to read through my State of the Union address again. I think you should watch it. It is a very good speech.

As my ambassador to China taught me, I should end this by saying, *gong xi fa cai*, congratulations on the fortune. Now, return the ones that belong to America back to America.

Yours truly,
Donald J. Trump
The 45th President of the United States of America

Donald Trump's Letter to Jeff Bezos

Monday, February 4, 2019

Dear Jeff,

I almost puked when I saw the *Washington Post*'s advert during the Super Bowl. I thought you were at least an average businessman. Haven't you heard about not throwing good money at bad business ventures? Irrespective of how much you advertise and promote the typewriter, do you have any illusions that it could be in vogue again? That is exactly what you are doing with *Washington Post*. The newspaper is dead. And the good book said, "Let the dead bury their dead."

Don't get me wrong, I got your unstated mission with the purchase of the dying newspaper. For you, it was not really about breaking even or turning a profit. After all, you only paid a penny for a dollar of its worth. For you, it is just about providing you with political cover as you destroy mom-and-pop businesses across America with your price-busting, warehouse-to-homes delivery service. Because that is essentially what you do—nothing ingenious in it—just upgraded buying and selling that mankind has done for centuries and will continue to do long after we are gone. So don't kid yourself that you are anything special.

I am also aware of your dependence on cheap products manufactured abroad at the expense of American manufacturers. Past presidents have allowed you simply to flood America with these products, killing our industries. You and I know that you cannot do what you do in America in Germany or China. They won't let you. It doesn't matter if you adopt children from each of those countries. Presidents before me have been so stupid that they watched you ruin our manufacturers and the Main Street businesses that sell their products, without raising a finger of protest. Do I need to remind you that I am not like those presidents? I am your worst nightmare. And I haven't even started. I, obviously haven't had the time to take a deep look at your activities.

Let me not go into your abuse of our US Postal Service by paying them peanuts for the prime services they provide for your company. All the years of building distribution infrastructure for the post offices, only to have them serve your company for virtually nothing? Trust me, I will look into all that when I am done with this Russian thing. I cannot be squeezing China to do right by our manufacturers and farmers while I close my eyes to an American-owned business ripping off Americans and contributing to the killing of our industrial base. Hell no.

The quicker you come to the negotiating table with me, the better for you and your business model. A little while ago, I was advised that the solution to your threatening business was to split your company up. My economic team felt it could be done under the anti-trust laws we have in the book. Little did we know that it would not be necessary, as your wife is on course to split your wealth.

Isn't it ironic that the so-called richest man in the world is so dumb he didn't know that in the baseball game called marriage, the first thing that you, the catcher, should protect is your balls? You don't go out into the bullpen without using a plate to protect the zone. Women are like designated hitters. They are always aiming for that soft spot. They know that no matter how secretive and masterful a man might be, he will slip every now and then.

That is when they strike. And you went to Princeton and graduated with a 4.2 grade point.

Jeff, as a high school student, you once worked as a line cook at McDonald's restaurant in Miami. You were paid shitty money. Don't you have any shame? Apparently you didn't learn anything from that experience. When you started your Amazon, you had no problem paying your workers shitty wages. One-third of your workers were on food stamps until that naughty socialist Bernie Sanders embarrassed you so much that you added a few dollars to their pay.

To note that you once got a $600 million cloud-computing contract from the CIA and yet they closed their eyes as you paid your workers cheap. By the way, how is your face recognition software, Rekognition, doing? I understand that our Immigration and Customs Enforcement agency is set to pay a huge amount of money to you to deploy your software in recognizing illegal immigrants as they approach churches, mosques, and even malls. You better not disappoint us. I'm sure it was our CIA money that you transferred to your pet project of running a commercial taxi to space. For someone who declined to join my Defense Innovation Advisory Board, it says a lot. Thanks to my Space Force, the American space is no longer going to be a playground for bored billionaires. My Space Force will put an end to that. You will soon know that a new sheriff is in town.

I noticed that I have made you much wealthier. When that Kenyan impostor was in the White House, you were not anywhere as wealthy as you are now. My people said that I have added $66.3 billion to your wealth in less than two years in office. Only five people in the world have more money than what I added to your wealth in just two years. Did I get any thanks from you? No. Instead what I have is your *Washington Post* tabulating what they called my thousands of little lies.

If you don't start showing gratitude soon, I may have no option but to ask the Pentagon to consider your rivals for the $10 billion cloud-computing contract. You know I can do it with just one phone call. You may be cold-blooded, but I can be coldhearted. If you like, keep hanging your clothes on a rack in your office and keep driving a 1999 Honda Accord; it doesn't move me. You are now a big boy, and whether you like it or not, you have to play by the rules that we set decades ago in New York City.

It doesn't matter if you hide your wealth in the cloud. If you do not recognize that I am the one who decides for America, we may soon have a duel. After the duel, you will be able to answer the question, "Who is your daddy?"

If you play ball, we really can be friends. I could meet you for dinner one day and even join you in eating your favorite food, octopus and roasted iguana. Yucky! Didn't I see you during the Super Bowl with my friend Bob Kraft, the owner of my favorite Patriots? I'm sure that deep down you are as driven to be great, just like me. And like me you have this regret minimization stuff going. If you are nice to me, I can make the crown prince of Saudi Arabia, Mohammad bin Salman, give you a big pie of the Saudi Vision 2030 deals.

If you don't want to play nice, I am also ready. I don't want to add to your Lauren Sanchez thing, but I must remind you of this truth: businesses die of ingratitude. Knowing keeps you free to pursue happiness without interruptions. A word is enough for the wise.

Yours truly,
Donald J. Trump
The 45th President of the United States

Trump's Letter to the Africans

Friday, February 8, 2019

Dear Africans,

I have been told that there are several letters floating around on the Internet purportedly written by me to Africans. I wish to state that until this day, I never wrote any letter to you Africans. In fact, I have never spared a thought for Africa—not even when my wife, Melania, was traveling across Africa last year. It is not the kind of thing I do. Frankly, I have more important things to do with my time.

I write you today because one of my staff brought in my undersecretary for Africa to brief me on the upcoming election in Nigeria and the man my government has decided to support. They have been telling me that Nigeria is an important country, even though they have not provided enough proof to convince me. We don't even buy their oil anymore.

Anyway, they said that Obama messed the country up when he installed his fellow Muslim, who is as lifeless as him. And since then, the country has been essentially without a leader. They convinced me that the guy we want is someone like me—a businessman who knows how to create jobs and grow the economy. The security people told me he had a checkered past, but it is not something we cannot overlook.

So we let him come into America last week. Based on the assessment that I received, he is the man on whom I can anchor my African outreach. And trust me, I do have an African agenda. My people said there is one. They said it would transform Africa and set it on a path of standing on its own—no more a slave of Europe or prisoner of China.

Believe me, lately, I have heard a lot about Africa. There is even a plan for me to visit Africa if the Democrats continue to talk about impeachment. My people said I am very popular in some parts of Africa. I was told those parts are places where Muslims are oppressing Christians. You know that I like Christians, even though I don't go to church and hardly believe in all those stories of Moses and his cousins.

This is all the knowledge of Africa I have. When I was informed that four US soldiers were ambushed and killed in an African country called Niger, I had never heard of the country in my life. All I remembered from my world history class was that Niger was a river in Africa. So I asked the most important question, "What are our young men and women doing in that shithole country?"

Okay, I know what you are thinking now. You are wondering, didn't I call African countries shithole countries while I was discussing US immigration policy in the White House? Well, I did. I did it for your own good. Omarosa, when she was still working for me, told me an African proverb that says, "He who kicks a toad helps it to travel farther." That was all I did. And you all should be thanking me and naming streets and towns and airports after me. Nothing had brought the discussion of Africa into American conversation more in the last one hundred years or even since slavery, than my simple phrase, "shithole countries."

I have since come to learn a few more things about Africa. You all know that I am a quick learner and I am full of superb natural intelligence. The first thing I learned is that Africa is a lot larger than the United States and a lot richer. If I had known that, I would have invested in Africa rather than wasting resources pursuing investments in Russia.

The only problem is that Africa does not know that it is larger and richer than the United States. And that stems from Africa's structure. You are broken down into 54 countries. And if each country has four borders, it mean 54 plus 54 plus 54 plus 54 borders to cross with scores of conflicts raging. You have 54 flags and 54 national anthems. And if there is an average of 54 languages in each country, then you have 54 plus 54 plus 54 plus 54 plus 54 languages. Because of the boundaries, a young man in Tanzania who built a power-generation machine out of a river by his backyard does not get the privilege of having his idea shared across the continent.

A carmaker in the town of Nnewi in Eastern Nigeria has no access to the market in Casablanca, Morocco. Imagine for a moment that the Reed Dance in Botswana is open to all Africans who wish to participate. It would be a tourism boom to the tiny South African country. Ok. I don't know any of these things I just wrote here. I lifted it from a brief I was given this morning. And some people will tell you that I don't read intelligence briefs.

Africa's potential is unlimited. And that is why it baffles those of us outside that you all have not realized it. You all are still stretching your hands toward us for aid and to China for exploitative investments and loans. I will get to China later.

Let me clear one mis conception before I continue. Every country pursues its own interests. It is not my job to fix Africa. And it is not the job of the Europeans or the Asians. I believe most of you have gotten that recently. When the stakes are high and the chips are down, every country does what benefits its people, not necessarily what is right. It is the way of the world.

Some of you will say you asked for no help from us. Some even say you don't even want strategic partnerships, whatever that means. I was told that some radicals amongst you say that you want us to disengage totally. You don't want us to interfere in your affairs. As you all know, that is my mission—to pull the United States away from spreading its tentacles around the world. That is why I will be closing that US military base in Djibouti soon.

Believe me, I cannot find Djibouti on a map of Africa. And if I cannot, two-thirds of Americans cannot either.

The question is not whether we want to leave you alone to run your affairs. It is whether you are capable of running your own affairs without our adult supervision. Remember what happened during just the three months that we left you alone? You killed eight hundred thousand of your own people in Rwanda. In the one hundred days of America staying at home to nurse the wounds of our Black Hawk that your people shot down in Mogadishu, Somalia, in 1993, mutilating our heroic soldiers who had come to help your people to stop killing each other. That was why we left and never looked back.

If you people guarantee me that you will take care of yourselves and not embarrass the world with wanton killings, we will stay away. I will not even stop there. I have a proposal on the ground to give all people of African descents in America $50,000 to leave America forever. I am willing to do so for fifty million of them. Think about it. I can transfer in that single move $2.5 trillion dollars to Africa. What other reparation is better than that? And for those African Americans who wear dashiki and have one leg in America and another in Africa, they will finally have both legs in their so-called motherland without buying air tickets.

Take Oprah, take Cosby, and take Shaq and the all others. Take the two million of your people in our prisons. Take them all back. Those in prisons alone each cost us over $70,000 a year. Those in the inner cities, with their food stamps, Medicaid, and Section 8 housing cost us almost $100,000 a year. So I am willing to make that deal of a one-time payment of $2.5 trillion. Don't ask where we would get the money. We can borrow it from China.

If you like, give them a chunk of Africa and let them build a country that will inspire other African countries. Even though I doubt they can make anything of it going by how they run cities like Detroit and Atlanta and all the black cities in America. Not even their so-called best could run the black historical universities. They run them into the ground and have the effrontery to come to the White House to beg me for money. By the way, didn't we try that experiment in Liberia some two hundred years ago? How did it turn out?

Maybe, instead of giving returning Africans a chunk of Congo or South Africa or the desert, you should just scatter them across every country in Africa. Use ancestry DNA to determine where each individual should go. Those who fail the DNA test use a lottery system to determine where they should go. This immersion plan helps them integrate faster. It also prevents them from defaulting to their propensity to feel that they are different, better, or wiser, which we know they are not. The inner cities where most of them come from are just as shitholey as your countries.

What do you think of this plan?

One more thing: I know that in the past we were involved in regime changes in Africa. I was told of the case of Patrice Lumumba of Congo and Kwame Nkrumah of Ghana, amongst others. One hundred years from now, you will come to appreciate why we did it. We were trying to save you from socialism. It is bad enough that you were poor, but to be poor because you were not allowed to own property and make profit would have been the worst kind of poverty ever.

Which brings me back to China. Your romance with China will end in heartbreak. My experts in Africa told me that China is involved in a sole scramble for Africa. They are not just excavating the last of your minerals and the best of your natural resources, but they are also flying in their citizens in planeloads to do the work your people should be doing. Like locusts, they are replacing and displacing your people with such speed that one hundred years from now, the Africa of today will have ceased to exist. If I were you, I would begin to build a wall around Africa. And I will immediately limit the number of Chinese who fly into Africa each year.

Keep this letter. Two hundred years from now, your great great grandchildren will say that the greatest president of America foresaw what our great great great grandfathers could not see.

Yours truly,
Donald J. Trump
The 45th President of the United States of America

Trump's Letter to Ann Coulter

Saturday, February 16, 2019

Dear Ann,

I did it. After several engagements, I finally did it. I declared the state of emergency that the naysayers said I could not. I am sure you watched that beautiful presentation. In one swoop, I released $8 billion for the wall. I stopped gangs and drugs and rapists and terrorists from coming into America.

Ann, I hope you will now stop haunting me over how many meters of wall I have built since I came into office. I have delivered on my promise. I have set the stage for the reversal of the genocidal reduction of the white population in America which happened through the unchecked invasion of these immigrants. I have squashed the left's plan to turn America into a third-world hellhole.

Are you proud of me now?

The walls will begin to go up by sunrise. No more delays. I could have waited until close to my re-election campaign to start the wall and dramatize it for re-election purposes, but I won't. I am doing the right thing at the right time.

My chief of staff Mick Mulvaney told me that I actually have $600 million from a Treasury Department forfeiture fund I could use without any hassles. He also said that I have another $2.5

billion from a Defense Department counter-drug fund that is wasting away. The only money that actually requires an emergency declaration is the $3.6 billion from Pentagon military-construction money. But as you and I know, the Pentagon budget is full of money that the military does not even know what to do with. I understand that every year we give them more money than they ask.

When Congress passed the executive power law in 1976, it had in mind a situation like what we faced today at our southern border. In a world where successful presidents like Vladimir Putin, Kim Jong Un, and Chairman X do not have to deal with a do-nothing Congress, I need to position America to be competitive.

Tell me that you are you proud of me.

I have said what you and Breitbart and others have always wanted me to—to hell with Congress. Stephen was right. You saw how quickly they folded. Even Mitch McConnell is on record that he supports my emergency declaration move. That guy has no backbone at all.

Ann, I want to assure you that this is just the beginning. In the years to come, I will deploy the same tactic. No more wasting time negotiating with the bunch of losers in Congress, the Paul Ryan type of "squeamish girly-boy" Republicans, and especially, the new delusional Democratic Congress in the House. If the president wants something done, the president ought to have all he needs to get the thing done. That is how it should be.

If the Founding Fathers did not envision it this way, it must be because they did not anticipate the kind of Democrats we now have in America. People who are so lily-hearted that they fear their own shadows.

Like I said yesterday, I know the Democrats will try to get Congress to vote against my emergency declaration, but I am sure they don't have the vote to pass it in the Senate. Even if they succeed in getting some misguided Republicans to join them, they do not have the votes to override my veto.

In the meantime, we will be using the little money in the appropriation bill that I signed to start building the wall while my emergency declaration goes through the court system. I hope the Supreme Court will give us a win when the case finally gets to them. It is my hope that very soon we don't have to guess what the Supreme Court will do.

I expect that old notorious woman to die soon so that I can replace her with a solid and reliable conservative judge. Once that happens, we can finally say goodbye to Congress. We go through the courts to get things done. You can agree with me that I am doing a fine job in packing the lower courts with fine conservatives who will be ruling for us for years to come.

The truth is that I am doing for conservatives in America something no conservative president has done in the history of this country. Not even Ronald Reagan came this close. I may not have been a conservative from kindergarten. I may not have been a member of the Federalist Society in college. In fact, I do not think I have read Barry Goldwater's *The Conscience of a Conservative*. But there is no doubt that history will remember me as the epitome of a modern conservative president.

My father may not have been an FBI agent who idolized John McCarthy, but I am sure that generations to come will be grateful that a great man like me came around to make things right. However, I do expect you to lead the charge of people thanking me today. I need to receive thanks in this lifetime too.

Like your critics did to you at the University of Arizona, you have thrown enough pies at my face. I hope you stop now. I have delivered without being mean-spirited like you. You make $500,000 a year making speeches, but I am the one left to do the heavy lifting needed to get your utterances into policies and laws. You may know how to talk to liberals to stir them up, but I am the one whose job it is to translate your words into actions.

Did you watch me give credit to President Obama for signing a national emergency on cartels? What does that tell you? I am growing. I am busting the hypocrisy of modern liberals at the seam. I believe that was the first time I gave him credit for anything. I even called him "President" as if I meant it. I am definitely growing.

Some of my enemies said that I did all this to save face with folks like you. Does my face look like one that is in need of getting saved? Like I said during the campaign, I can shoot anyone at Central Park in New York without losing a vote. It still remains true today. In fact, like you rightly said, I can now perform a late-term abortion at the White House without anyone raising a finger. When people look at the alternative, the bunch of jokers jostling for my position, they will have no option but to vote for me for the sake of our republic.

The other day, I saw one smart guy on Fox News talking about this emergency move as one that has the potential of creating a Cobra Effect. He said my solution to building the wall could create new problems. He gave an example of future Democratic presidents misusing emergency powers to push their liberal agenda.

Of course, I don't expect the American people to stand for that. American people know that Democrats are screwed up in the head. Like you said in one of your books, if Democrats had any brains, they'd be Republicans.

I am not waiting for that glorious day to come. After my eight years as president, one of the takeaways is not to ever give blanket powers to Democrats. It has been the most devastating thing that happened to this country in the last sixty years. It has been more devastating than 9/11.

Here is my question: now that I have solved the border problem, what else should I use to stir up my people as the 2020 elections near? Maybe I should warn them that if the next president is a Democrat, he or she could tear down the walls the same way I nullified Obama's executive action on DACA.

I warned Congress and the country then that Obama was overstepping his powers by using executive action to craft immigration policies. I cautioned that executive action was not the way to run a country. I wanted him impeached for that violation, but nobody paid me any mind. I probably should warn Americans not to elect the Democratic presidential candidate in 2020 else he or she will nullify my executive action and make a spectacle of tearing down my wall.

I think that will resonate with my people.

As it is now, this president is off to a great start. In this second quarter, I won't mind using extraordinary powers in consequent disputes with Congress. Since I have scaled through this emergency declaration without a scratch, next time it will be a declaration of martial law to scare away liberals, like your friend Bill Maher, who are poisoning the minds of gullible Americans with half-baked bullshit.

I hope we are cool now. I hope you will be on my side pissing out when the crazy Democrats in the House come up with their fictitious list of high crimes and misdemeanors.

If what they say about you is true, we share a German ancestry that has made all the difference.

Yours truly,
Donald J. Trump
The 45th President of the United States of America

Donald Trump's Letter to Robert Kraft

Sunday, February 24, 2019

Dear Robert,

I am sorry that the horrible mainstream media took their hatred of me to your doorstep. They could no longer pick on me, for I give it back to them pound for pound, dose for dose, so they picked a soft target like you.

You know your Patriots' sixth super bowl win in eighteen years is pissing them off. They had to find something to spoil your fun. It is the same way they would be pissed off when I win my re-election, in spite of all their shenanigans and the shenanigans of their accomplices like Robert Mueller, Michael Cohen, and the Democrats in the House of Representatives. The good thing is that I am ready for them. I am ready for whatever they throw at me.

But let me get this right. You, Robert Kraft, a seventy-seven-year-old $6 billion man, the head of the multibillion-dollar group of companies, took a ride to Orchids of Asia Day Spa in Jupiter, Florida, to get a parlor massage with a happy ending. You are unbelievable! When I grow up, I want to be like you.

Whatever happened to buying the spa? Whatever happened to bringing the spa to your house or your hotel room? Even if you did not want all the hassle, you could have simply called me and I would have made the Mar-a-Lago available for your use. For a good friend like you, it comes with whatever services you desire, no questions asked. Discretion is our number one priority.

By the way, did you consider this other option? You gave Vladimir Putin of Russia your Super Bowl ring. Out of respect, he could have provided you with some sweet Russian girls to massage you into a very happy golden shower ending. I know he could make it happen with a snap of his finger. That is why he is the greatest.

To have you charged with soliciting prostitution is a disgrace to our justice system. Don't those knuckleheads know who you are? You are an institution in this country. I have finalized the plan to give you a Medal of Freedom. You can be sure that none of these witch hunts will stop it.

Whatever happened to individual privacy in this country? Why would the police put a surveillance camera at a private business to capture men paying for sex acts? Don't they have better things to do with their time? Are there no trouble-making black men to shoot at?

I remember the last time we spoke. I told you that we have to rein in the media and you were supporting all the nonsense about the Second Amendment and what not. The media that do not respect the privacy rights of individuals do not deserve Second Amendment rights for themselves. That is my stand.

To say that you, the man who owns the most successful football team in America in the last twenty years, are facing a first-degree misdemeanor, is a shame. What are they going to do to you? Will they give you one year in jail or ask you to pay a $5,000 civil penalty? Maybe they will sentence you to one hundred hours of community service and place you in a classroom to teach you the negative effects of prostitution and human trafficking.

Preposterous! What a joke! I know some people in some Florida police departments. I will be making calls to them. I also understand that some of those women were trained in Flushing, Queens, after they arrived from China. That is my old neighborhood. Which means that some of my people may know these women well. We can do something to resolve this little matter without causing you more stress.

Like I have always said, that is exactly the problem with a nanny state. It is only a welfare state like ours that wants to determine what a man should do or not do with his money. Police officers that are paid from the taxes billionaires like us pay do not have any respect for vulnerable men like us in our seventies. I bet they do not know how it feels to know that time is running out to get our last fucks in. As for the hypocritical media, they enjoy nothing like the fall of a successful man.

Again, it is this liberal victimhood culture that wants to tell a woman who is making a good living doing what she likes that she is a victim. They concoct stories of women brought into this country with promises of a better life and then forced into prostitution, to make people feel bad. The real truth is that these women are doing what they love and are well paid. Otherwise, they would be working at MacDonald's. They walk past the restaurants with hiring signs at the door to go work at the spas.

I don't blame you, my buddy. Those Chinese women are something else. Things they can do with their hands, legs, and mouths are unfathomable. They are very professional. Wives and girlfriends are no competitors when it comes to the heaven they can bring down on earth. The way they call you "big boy" melts away every iota of stress in your deepest muscles. I cannot wait to get out of this prison and get back into my own private jet where I can be free to invite anyone on an excursion up in the sky. You know what I mean. Up there, there won't be any media or any police surveillance.

But come on, who goes to a spa in a Bentley? Even if it is your friend's car, that Bentley is worth more than the spa and all the women in it. It was smart of you to have paid in cash. But you probably should have learned one or two things from the lives of rap stars. If you must visit establishments like that, places of disrepute, you do not pay yourself. You get your driver to pay. That way your fingerprints will not be on the money.

What really struck me in the whole story was that you did all this and then flew to Kansas City to watch your Patriots defeat the Chiefs in their divisional game. If I were you, I would be worried that God would see what I did and make my team lose. I know. I still have those Sunday school lessons in me. My preference would have been to do those things after the game and days before another game go to confession and plead for forgiveness of sins. It works all the time.

We are used to reading that you prayed at the Tree of Life synagogue in Pittsburgh after the shooting before going to the Patriots game against the Steelers. Now when we see you before any game, we wonder where you came from and why you have that smile on your face.

Anyway, just remember that the world has changed for the bad: what happens in Jupiter does not stay in Jupiter anymore.

Yours truly,
Donald J. Trump
The 45th President of the United States of America

Trump's Letter to Spike Lee

Wednesday, February 27, 2019

Dear Spike Lee,

This is Agent Orange. Do not get jungle fever because of this letter. I am writing you today to see if there is a way to get you to do the right thing. I am not saying that you are a black klansman, but you are surely speaking like one. How could you go up there at the Academy awards and instead of talking about relevant things waste time on praising your ancestors who were caught? You know I do not like people who get caught. I'll tell you this truth that you are avoiding. Your ancestors were not stolen. They were bought. Your ancestors who were brought to America as slaves were those who were caught and paid for. The strong ones were those who were left behind in Africa. They were the ones who caught your ancestors and sold them off as slaves.

Did I just call those people who reside in those shithole countries strong? But you get my point. Relative to your ancestors, the slaves, they were strong.

I have to correct you because next time you may join those dreamy Democrats to talk about reparation for slavery. If that ever crosses your mind, tell yourself that our forefathers already paid to get your ancestors to Jamestown, Virginia. We paid your brothers and sisters in Africa. We paid for their free ride across the Atlantic sea. We paid to house and feed them in America. We paid for their health. We clothed them. Paying again would be more than quadruple jeopardy. If there is any other payment to be made, go ask your brothers and sisters in Africa who collected the initial payment over four hundred years ago. Ask them to refund it in today's dollars with interest. That is what you should do. The refund should be able to get your folks the Eldorado life that you all dream about. That is how to think of these things. Not the simplistic way that you think now.

About your claim that the slaves built this country, I have addressed this in one of my letters to your people. I have busted that illusion, and I thought it has been discredited for all times. For the sake of dumb people like you, let me repeat it here. If you were the ones who built this country, why haven't you built your inner cities and black neighborhoods across this country? Why have you allowed black universities and black neighborhoods in America to be the most deplorable places for anyone to live? Even the Native American reservations are better kept than the inner cities of New York or Chicago or Oakland. Don't let me talk of Detroit and Baltimore.

What are we talking about? And when the great white people come to fix your dilapidated neighborhood, we hear cries of white invasion or *gentrification*. What is stopping your people from gentrifying these neighborhoods on their own? Must we, the great white people, hold whips and flog your people before you get up and build anything? Because that was what happened when you claimed you built America. We had dogs chasing you around and whips landing on your lazy ass to get you to work. Do you want us to send some white men on horses with guns and whips into Chicago's South Side to get your young men to shape up? Is that what you want?

Spare us this lecture about the genocide of the native population. The natives are not complaining. Do you see them on TV complaining? I don't. Do they make movies lamenting genocide? No. We gave them their own territories inside America; provided them with everything that they needed. What else do they want? They even got the right to build casinos and collect money from real Americans who work hard and keep the country going. Never forget that the land America was just bushes for thousands of years until my forefathers came. If we did not come, New York City would have remained another great Amazon forest. So when you talk all this rubbish they teach you at Morehouse, a historically black college, pause for a moment and think for yourself.

Even if your mama taught you that adulterated history, rewind and use your head to put it in context.

They said that you won your first competitive Oscar, and it got into your big head. The truth is that they have cheapened the Oscar. They have brought in new voters to help push affirmative action on the former prestigious award. That is how you were able to get one. So do not forget that. There should be an asterisk attached to your Oscar to show that it came after the award was diluted to make your people happy. I heard that it is the same with the tenured professorship NYU gave you.

As for the 2020 presidential election, I have seen the people the Democrats are assembling to come after me. They are not capable of lifting up Olympus. Have you seen them? Have you paid attention to the things they care about? Once again, I will floor all you liberal elite. Our great people know where history actually resides. History is on the side of people who are working hard to lift the liberal burden on America and stop America from becoming a failed nation. The only choice is one between quick restoration and stiffer regression.

Sometimes I have pity on your kind. You confuse pampering a wayward kid with love and see using the cane to correct bad behavior as hatred. But history thinks otherwise. The new generations of Americans who are weak and unable to uphold the valor of their forefathers are those their parents pampered. They are the ones who were not challenged. These were kids who were not failed in school when they deserved to fail and those who were told they won when they did not even make it as runners up. I am reversing that trend. I am bringing America back to that envious position when competition was stiff and people who were called the greatest actually were the greatest.

I also recommend that you go beyond racist biopics in your career. Surely there are other stories in America that you can tell. When you dwell so long in racism, you have no option but to be a racist. If you seek some uplifting stories out there, you will find them. I am an example of an uplifting story. Nobody knew I would be where I am today. Nobody believed that I would do well when I got in as the president of the United States of America. But I am living beyond the expectations of you all. Do you know why? Because I believe in myself and in the power of positive thinking.

As a merchant of racism, you believe in the power of negative thinking. It can get you temporary applause or a few minutes of a standing ovation. But what I do, what I believe in, and what I accomplish are things that bring about one hundred years of applause and an ever-lasting standing ovation. As you know, though your hatred of me will not let you acknowledge it, I have done more for your black people than any other president in the history of this country. Abraham Lincoln freed the slaves, but he did not give them a job. He promised them a mule and forty acres, but he did not build the wall to stop others from coming in to grab the land and seize the mule.

I have done more for the image of black people in America with my criminal justice reform. Some of your friends with criminal records can now get a job in the White House. Instead of taking a swipe at me at the Oscars, you should be telling the NAACP to give me a special 2019 Image Award as part of their 50th anniversary on March 30th. I deserve it. I lifted more black people up and through my tax cuts put more money in their pockets than a hundred Barack Obamas could have done in a thousand years.

By any means necessary, get them to honor me, and I will forgive all your youthful exuberances.

Spike, as someone who admired your earlier works, I say stop looking for monsters. Stop trying to infiltrate the beasts. Trust me, we are far from the time when the American government was using Negro men in Tuskegee to study what happens when syphilis is left untreated. And very soon, we will stop using today's Negro men to study what happens when police bullets enter the body of unarmed men running away from police.

If you are looking for a new story to tell, I can introduce you to my friend Kim Jong-un of North Korea. You can come with me on the trip this week, and you will have a front-row seat in history as we strike the greatest deal mankind has ever made that will save the world from nuclear catastrophe. You can capture it and maybe win a real and deserving Oscar for that.

See you at the New York Yankees opening game.

Yours truly,
Donald J. Trump
The 45th President of the United States of America.

Trump's Letter to Michael Cohen

Friday, March 1, 2019

Dear Michael,

Watching you from Hanoi, I thought that when you were done with your testimony in front of the kangaroo US House of Representative Oversight Committee, I would have no option but to tell the world who you think about when you masturbate. But there is no need to go there. There is nothing you said that should worry me. Nothing.

In fact, the first thing I did when I got back to the White House was to pick up the letter I wrote to secretary of state Mike Pompeo and tear it into pieces. It was just a draft of my resignation letter, just in case. But as I can see, there is no need for that—not now and not in the future. You've got nothing, and since you've got nothing, Robert Mueller has nothing either.

I must say that it was sad seeing you at the hearing grappling for any anecdote, any tidbit you could remember to make what you were saying look important. You flashed two checks that I signed as if the checks were indications of my intentions. My friend, those checks had no entries under memo. It was intentional.

Don't ever forget that you were dealing with a thorough-bred New Yorker.

In case you have forgotten, Americans know from pre-historical times that lawyers are liars. So I did not need to say a thing about your testimony for them to know where to dump it. In your case, you have confessed to lying before the same Congress, and you are heading to prison for that offense. Who will believe that you suddenly transformed into an angel fighting to make heaven?

For crying out loud, your job was to fix things. And part of fixing things was to lie for me. You knew it and I knew it. You didn't need my instruction to lie. You were like a zombie. Anything to protect me and make me look good was your stock in trade.

Washington Post is busy counting how many times they think I have lied. As of today, I think they are at about eight thousand times. According to Malcolm Gladwell, by the time they get to the ten thousandth time, I would have become a master. It would become natural to me. As for you, on that stand, you didn't look natural. You looked like a shadow of your former self.

You know what is sad? I brought you out of poverty. I picked you up from the gutters of New York City where you were rolling in dirt in search of nickels and pennies. I made you a rich man and introduced you to important people. You were not particularly a brilliant lawyer. I just picked you because I thought you had guts. But I was wrong. A little shake from the Feds and you started to sing like a canary. Pathetic!

Michael, you have no redeemable quality. I write this letter just to congratulate you for doing your worst. A wise man said that we are as sick as our secrets. I hope you feel better after vomiting what you packaged as Donald J. Trump's secrets. Guess what? It did not make a dent on my pristine reputation.

I bet you have forgotten that the Donald Trump you used to know is not the one in the White House. The one in the White House is the American state. The American state has more need of me than I do of the state. As a result, it is in the interest of the American state to preserve me from scoundrels like you.

Isn't it fascinating that you looked for ways to hurt me and the only things you could come up with are that I am a racist, a conman, and a cheat? That's it? First of all, I have been called these things before. Second of all, there were other horrible things that I have been called too. And you claim that you worked for me for ten years. You must not have been attentive. If you had paid attention, you would have noticed that I was more than those things.

You have been an admirer of the billionaire lifestyle, but you have a tremendous misunderstanding of what it takes to be a billionaire. You have to profile people, products, and processes. You have to out-smart those who are poor at protecting their cards. If that is what you call racist, con, and cheating, I join other wealthy people like me to bear the badge of honor. Abolish the seven deadly sins and watch as mankind disappears and the world is taken over by rats.

The only time you seemed to be having fun was when you were describing how I did everything to stop my academic records from being released. You took delight in explaining how you bullied schools that I attended to stop them from making my academic records public.

Let me make a promise to you. After I win my second term in office, I will make my academic results public, from elementary school all the way to Wharton. Unlike Obama, I have nothing to hide. I paid my tuition and didn't have to claim that I was an indigent foreign student to get grants and scholarships. I may not have been the top of my class because I wasn't particularly interested in the academic tasks of memorizing things and reproducing them during tests, but I was already a successful businessman then, putting into practice things that professors were busy theorizing.

In fact, I may even release my taxes too. It is not as if there is something in my tax returns that you won't find in the tax returns of my fellow billionaires like Warren Buffet, Michael Bloomberg, and Bill Gates. Nothing! We hire the same kind of smart tax lawyers and CPAs and do the same thing to get ahead of the rest. What we all do are legal things. Some cleaners in some high-rise offices or some workers at fast food restaurants may not like it, but that is the way it is. Nobody is stopping anyone from hiring a good tax lawyer to get him or her the best benefits of the law as written.

The American people understand these things. Unlike some of you who are busy complaining of how unfair things are, the American people that I know dream of being like Trump and taking advantage of things that are in the law to make their life better. They adore the flawed Trump. They know sincerely that whatever I did was all part of my pursuit of happiness.

I guess you no longer know what happiness is since you crossed over to the side of the devil. There is still a slight window for you to totally fall off the edge into a bottomless pit. What I mean is that you can still retrieve your soul from the demons in the House before they use you as a spectacle in their useless quest to impeach me. You know the American people would be very angry with them if they tried such. But more importantly, you don't want your already soiled name to be associated with such foolery.

As Omarosa used to say, use your tongue to count your teeth. I do not wish to further kick a toad like you. Doing so will amount to helping you travel farther.

Yours truly,
Donald J. Trump
The 45th President of the United States

Trump's Letter to Kim Jong Un

Tuesday, March 5, 2019

Dear Kim,

As I make my way back to the United States, I was thinking of our meeting in Hanoi, Vietnam. I am so sorry it did not end the way you anticipated. It was not your fault. I want to explain to you the real reason it ended the way it did and not the nonsense the fake news media is spewing around the world.

I was not 100 percent present at our meeting. That is the truth. Most of my concentration was on what was going on in Washington, DC. That fraudster of a man, Michael Cohen, who was my former attorney testifying before the US House of Representatives Oversight Committee totally distracted me. Could you believe that he had the audacity to say that I ordered him to threaten people more than five hundred times? Imagine if anyone is counting how many people disappeared in your country because they did something you did not like.

Think about it. Is it possible for your former lawyer to go public and dish out what happened between you and him? Impossibility. Who would give him such a platform? In any case, you do not have to deal with any stupid oversight committee. Your job is too important for you to be dragged into stuff like that. And if there should be any kind of oversight, it should not be holding a hearing like this while you are away on a very historical summit with another world leader. That is how sensible people in a serious country do things. Not the jokers that I have to contend with at home.

That is why I said it is people like you and Putin, Sisi, Erdogan, Duterte, and Chairman Xi that are real leaders in the world today. Not all these sissies that walk around Western Europe and the Americas. Look at how the Israelis are embarrassing Netanyahu. I thought they had the common sense to know that he is the greatest prime minister of their country ever.

You, my friend, live like a leader, and people follow you, as it should be. What we do in our part of the world is a disgrace. To my people, a leader is someone elected for them to make fun of. But by the time I am done with America, I will have changed it. I may not get it to the perfect structure you have but at least something less comical than what we have today.

I know I walked away amidst this confusion at home. But do not worry, it is all part of the intrigue. The world is watching, including the Nobel Peace Prize people. We do not have to make it look as if it is easy to arrive at a historical agreement. We want to drag it and drag it so when we finally reach an agreement, they will acknowledge that we put a lot of work into it.

I heard what you said about sanctions. Like I told you, I will immediately make provisions for you to get as many Remy Martins as you want. If you want Hennessey, I will tell my people to throw that in too. Next time we get together, I would like you to give up a few nuclear weapons so I can look good. If I come back to America with some of your nuclear arsenal, even it is the oldest models, I will be assured of re-election.

I am sure you know that the Democrats are not your friends. You don't want them to get back into the White House. Not just that they will be nasty to you; they have no respect for a leader of your caliber who is well loved and honored in your country. They are allergic to such adoration. So you need to help me help you. Together we are a team that will change the world for good.

The third time will be the charm. When we meet for the third time, we shall officially end the war between North and South Korea. We will set a date for the reunification of your two countries. You will give me some weapons, and I will give you significant sanction relief. And everyone will go home happy . . . and wait for the Nobel Peace Prize.

Be mindful of what the Chinese and the Russians will be telling you in days and weeks to come. Though they are my friends too, their leaders are envious of the relationship we have established and how we are the hottest political couple the world is fascinated with. I know them. They will want to get a piece of the action.

Don't worry about what my people are saying to the media, especially that big mouth John Bolton. We normally send people like him out there to say those kinds of things just to make our people feel good. The truth is that we are desperate for a deal. We cannot keep going from one summit to another without making deals. That will make me look as weak as Obama. And you know that I hate that more than anything else in this world.

Let me repeat it here: what happened in Hanoi was not a matter of a good deal or bad deal; it was just a matter of bad timing. We had to say that I walked away for me to save face. Fortunately for you, you don't need tricks like that to be the strong leader you are. Anybody in the media or in the political arena that dares say you failed in Hanoi will not live to see tomorrow. I wish I had those powers too.

Anyway, we are going to strike a big deal next time we meet. It will be so huge that it will shake the world. It will be as gigantic as the houses Trump builds. That, I can assure you. And after we strike that deal, I foresee in the nearest future a state visit for you. Imagine yourself in Washington, DC, with all the pomp and pageantry of the American government, addressing the joint session of Congress and sleeping in the famous Lincoln bedroom. I see Trump Tower rising in Pyongyang, and McDonald's dotting all your main streets. I see your country in another ten years becoming an envy of Japan as American businesses transform your landscape. Just stick with me.

For now, let me get home and clean up some of the messes that have been accumulating since I left for Vietnam.

I hope you understand.

Yours truly,
Donald J. Trump
The 45th President of the United States of America

Trump's Letter to Ray Kroc

Wednesday, March 6, 2019

Hi Kroc,

So what do you think? Some said I wouldn't do it again. They said I got away with it the first time because of the government shutdown. But I did it. I served a buffet of McDonald's hamburgers to the North Dakota State Bison football team just weeks after I served the same dishes to the Clemson Tigers. Any other doubts that I am really committed to the spreading of the hamburger and chicken nuggets message?

In the face of sustained liberal attacks that the great meals of McDonald's are full of hormones, bacteria, and antibiotics, I present myself as a counterargument. I have told those who grumble about healthy eating to explain why I am one of the healthiest presidents ever, yet I enjoy my McDonald's hamburgers and Diet Coke.

As you may know, the sole purpose of me running for president was to enhance the Trump brand. I had envisioned that the notoriety that comes with running for president would have me negotiating great deals with governments around the world. I was imagining Trump Tower at every capital city of the world. I was looking forward to having Trump ubiquitous as your McDonald's anywhere in the world.

And then, I won the presidential election and it changed everything.

Since I became president, the Trump brand has replaced McDonald's as the number one American brand. Yours is not even close. My name is in the mouth of more people around the globe each day than Jesus and Mohammed put together. That is how huge I have become. Tremendously huge.

It means that there are wonderful opportunities for me to do big things with my brand. I am already doing your struggling McDonald's a lot of favors by serving it as dinner and lunch to people visiting the White House. In advertisement terms, what I do for you is worth billions and billions of dollars. Just think of what you have paid the likes of Michael Jordan and his likes over the years and multiply it by ten. That is what you owe me.

But I am not asking you to pay up. I am just doing my job of promoting American brands as the president of the United States.

I, however, have a great idea. I think it is the smartest idea to have come out of anyone in the last one hundred years. Looking at how the world is going, I am of the opinion that one hundred years from now, most people will have the meal they eat delivered to their homes morning, afternoon, and night. The way most kids do not know where and how the food they eat today is grown is the same way so many kids will not know where and how the food they eat is cooked in one hundred years from now.

You know the way you were convinced in 1954 that Richard and Maurice McDonald's design of small chains for their San Bernardino restaurant would spread, that is how convinced I am that homes of the future will have no need for kitchen and dining rooms but somewhere chic where people will eat their delivered meals.

I want to join McDonald's as chairman and chief executive after my presidency. I want to position McDonald's to be a leader in this new world that is fast approaching. I don't want you to lose out to Amazon in this quest. I want McDonald's to partner with the Trump Organization to create that world. For it to work, it requires the touch of Trump's luxury. It also requires a buy-in by

McDonald's to the confidence that people around the world have in everything Trump. Trump's brand delivers quality, excellence, and class in a very efficient way.

Of course, you know that the wealth I have already built will serve my children, grandchildren, and great grandchildren if I do nothing to add to it. So it is not about what is in it for me. It is just that, talking from one icon to another, we have a perfect opportunity to create a business that could last for the next thousand years.

I know you squandered an opportunity to move McDonald's to a position of un-matched greatness when you handed the operation to your wife. Knowing women, she messed it all up. She played it safe. You almost lost everything the way your father lost his fortune in the 1920s from land speculation. To make matters worse, when your wife died, she left $250 million of your money to the National Public Radio, NPR. That is one-quarter of a billion dollars. And those socialist/liberal characters pocketed the money and still continued to beg their listeners for donations every three months in exchange for tote bags. It would have been better if she had added the money to the $1.5 billion, she gave to the Salvation Army.

Ann Coulter was right. Without women's right to vote, Democrats have no chance of ever being elected president of this country. We may have to revert back to those golden days again when women spent a bulk of their time in the kitchen and in the garden. Enough of these women's efforts to accomplish what Stephen called the "complete domestication of men in America."

So are you up for the deal?

Just to calm your nerves, we are not very different. Just like you, I believe in self-reliance and oppose the welfare state. You sold paper cups, I sell the Trump brand, which, to be quite frank with you, is a sort of paper cup. You were a real estate agent in Florida, while I am the real estate that people want to sell. You played piano in bands, while I am known to be a very good dancer. You lied to get into World War I, I lied to get out of Vietnam. But just the other day, I was the one who was welcomed to Hanoi as a hero and not the man shut down over their sky.

It would be a glorious thing to work on after my presidency. As the only president who has a real business, I hope to use my post-presidency years to build up American businesses. I have no interest in traveling the world to make speeches for a few bucks. I believe my time will be best used to position American corporations to dominate the world for the next thousand years.

That is how far my vision for this country goes. So please hit me back.

Yours truly,
Donald J. Trump
The 45th President of the United States of America

Trump's Letter to Chairman Nadler

Friday, March 8, 2019

Dear Chairman Jerrold Nadler,

Do you know how tornadoes are formed? You don't come across as a very smart guy who would know. Google it. I will wait for you to Google it.

Did you see that? Tornadoes form when an unusually violent thunderstorm encounters instability and a wind formation that has warm and humid conditions in the lower atmosphere mixing up with cooler conditions in the upper atmosphere. I bet you think that I am as dumb as my Christian rights brothers and sisters who think tornadoes are caused because of what two gay men did in a room in Mobile, Alabama.

Now that I have educated you, are you sensing some unusual violent thunderstorms brewing? From that little office of yours as the chairman of the House of Representatives Judicial Committee, are you beginning to see instability accumulating outside your window? I don't think so. If you are seeing the coming together of those cooler and warm weather conditions, you wouldn't be demanding documents from over eighty people, businesses, and organizations associated with me.

You might also get ready to subpoena them because you are not getting anything from anybody. I am 100 percent sure of that. I cannot allow your kangaroo committee to ground the work of this presidency that is breaking new ground and accumulating wins for Americans. Again, it is an overreach for your committee to think it can harass hardworking Americans who helped to elect me president against your heavily favored candidate, Crooked Hillary Clinton. Isn't that what this is all about? It won't happen under my watch! Sore losers!

You are smart enough to let my Ivanka off your information fishing expedition. I am not letting you intimidate Allen Weisselberg, my chief financial officer at the Trump Organization. That is a no-go area. For your information, I have what is called executive privilege. There is executive time and there is executive privilege. And if need be, I will assert executive massage. They are all in the constitution, if you don't know.

I am sure that you did not pay attention to one pertinent warning Michael Cohen gave the American people during the hearing at your Democratic Party's other kangaroo committee, the US House Oversight and Government Committee. Among all the things Cohen said during those seven-hour circuits, that was the only time he told the truth. He warned that I would not accept the result of the 2020 election if I do not win. You already knew that I was not going to accept the result of the 2016 election if I had not won.

What does that tell you? If I would not accept the result of an election that I did not win, how do you think I would accept an impeachment verdict from the House of Representatives? The easy dismissal I can give to my people is that a bunch of Democrats in the House of Representatives are simply usurping the mandate of the American people. That is all I need to say. The rest is tornadoes.

I went this far just to let you know that you are inviting tornadoes down to Washington, DC, and all across America. Do not say that you were not warned. The twenty-three people tornadoes killed in Alabama two days ago should be a reminder to you of the devastation that will follow if you generate 1,001 such tornadoes across 1,001 cities in America.

How did the good book put it? "He who has ears, let him hear."

I assume that you are a lawyer. Who knows, maybe the Michael Cohen kind of lawyer. So let me remind you of what Article II, Section 4 of the US Constitution says: "The President, Vice President, and all civil Officers of the United States shall be removed from Office on Impeachment for, and conviction of, Treason, Bribery, or other High Crimes and Misdemeanors."

There is no treason, no bribery, and no high crimes and misdemeanors. None whatsoever. All that you and Chairman Cummings, another dull fellow, are doing is turning yourself into an extended arm of the Mueller witch hunt.

I am sure some members of your committee have already drawn up their articles of impeachment. All these shenanigans are a disguise to make it look as if you had a thorough investigation. Everything is pointing at a predetermined outcome. Well, go and ask them in Alabama or Oklahoma if there is a predetermined outcome when tornadoes strike.

My only (and also former) black friend, Omarosa, used to say that, "A handshake that passes the elbow has ceased to be a handshake." This handshake of yours has become something else—something menacing, something aggressive, something insulting.

I have been watching your Democratic House committees' actions. I took you all as jokers. But I think now this handshake has passed the elbow. When the rotating column of air that you are inviting hits you, you will be sucked into the funnel, and when it all dissipates and you see yourself dumped by the roadside, you won't know whether the rotating air was clockwise or counter-clockwise.

A word is enough for the wise.

But seriously, what do you want from me? Do you want me not to run for re-election? Will that satisfy you? Or are you and your bloodthirsty Democrats interested in running me out of town? Which one is it? We can talk about it in private if you want.

You are a New Yorker like me. And you know we New Yorkers are not afraid of a fight. Having said that, we are open to making a deal when it is the best way forward. Whatever happened to fixing Social Security, Infrastructure development, family leave, and even DACA, the comprehensive immigration bill, and all that? We can talk about them all, including your Democratic radical wing's new dream, the Green Deal. Any bill that you want. I am open to negotiations on anything that is meaningful to the lives of my beloved American people. But if you insist on poking the sky and inviting the tornadoes down, be ready for the consequences.

Yours truly,
Donald J. Trump
The 45th President of the United States of America

Trump's Letter to Nixon's Ghost

Saturday, March 9, 2019

Dear Nixon,

In search of a new purpose, I wandered into the White House library. It was my first time there. Unlike you, I wasn't a bookish kind of president. You won't catch me carrying a book in hand as I walk across the West Wing lawn to my Marine One just to pretend that I read.

My aides said such moves make one look presidential. As you may have heard, I am not a pretense kind of guy. But I could be presidential if I wanted to.

I wanted to go to a place in the White House that I had not been to, so I went to the library. I was not looking for a place to blow dry my tears and conceal my fears. I watched my shadow leave my body days before when I made that two-hour fierce speech to CPAC. I was drained like a raisin. (See, I can look presidential by speaking in those high-sounding words.)

Once in the library, I found my way to the non-fiction section. I do not read fiction. Life is too real for that. I immediately went for G, in search of Ginsberg. That was when I saw your ghost on the wall.

You still had your silvery colored hair and the quaintness in your eyes. You appeared on the wall beside the shelf where

Ginsberg's book of poems, *Howl*, was kept. I was going to grab it, when you appeared. I recognized you immediately. But just to confirm that it was you, you slightly opened your mouth like Dick Cheney and said, "I'm not a crook."

I looked away. My eyes blinked. When I looked back, you said, "There is no whitewash in the White House."

I wanted to say, "Are you for real?" But I kept quiet. I watched you hover around. I wanted to pray at that moment, but I did not know how to start and where to begin. Mixed with the smell of oak and ancient books were the spirits of the condemned.

Several people have told me to study your life and learn from what happened to you. Fortunately for me, I do not read books. So I do not have to worry about reading the recommended books some have sent to me. A lot of people seem to be under the impression that my fate and yours are intertwined. It's not just that I reject that supposition; I want to make it clear to you that nothing could be further from the truth. And if you were one of those keeping such wild speculations alive just to keep your soiled name relevant in American affairs, I gently ask you to desist.

Some said you were a smart man. But everyone agrees that I am the smartest president that ever lived in the White House. They said that besides the Watergate scandal, you achieved a lot as president. Whatever accomplishment you had pales in comparison to my gigantic accomplishments in just two years. You opened up China; I brought them to their knees. What else did you achieve? You established OSHA, broadened civil rights protections, and peacefully segregated schools in the South. I bet you are ashamed about the outcomes—The crippling of American businesses, vote rigging, and reverse segregation. So what is it that ties your failed presidency to mine?

I was told that you initiated the Southern strategy, but as you can see, I moved on to reach the forgotten Americans across our country. You appealed to the silent majority, but I appealed to the loud minority. You allowed a female opponent of yours to label you, Tricky Dick. And it stuck. Guess what? I am the one who gives political opponents labels that stick. You must have heard of Lying

Ted, Crooked Hillary, and Rocket Man, among others. I dish them out like the genius that I am.

Just like me, you had problems with leaks of government papers, like the Pentagon Papers. Your answer was to hire White House plumbers to plug the leak. Your mistake was that you went and got amateurs to do the work. When I want something done, I get professionals to do it. I don't look at the cost. Obviously, money has never been a problem for me. Quite unlike you.

The liberal press also gave you a tough time. You did not have the foresight to groom and cultivate a conservative media that could act as your mouthpiece. I did that. I also mastered a plan to distract the world press, especially when bad news is about to drop. With just a tweet, I can hijack the conversation away from any bad news that I do not want to see on the front page for long. I'm that good. I make my army of supporters happy that they go from website to website fighting my battles in the comments sections. We have a way of drowning out the noise from the other side.

More importantly, you were a crook. I am not a crook. You broke the law. I did not break any law. You colluded with others to undermine our justice system. In my case, there is no collusion. You recorded conversations that you had with others in the White House. I did not do a stupid thing like that. And even if I did, I would not be stupid enough to acknowledge it when I know it could be subpoenaed, and if I tried to destroy it, they would call it obstruction of justice. Even though I am not a lawyer, I know more about the law and the constitution than you.

You were paranoid about your enemies. I waste no time making a secret list of my enemies. I call them out on twitter. If they talk back, I curse them out. I have no patience for backroom plots to annihilate them by breaking into their hotels. I simply use words in 244 characters to knock sense into them and let Americans know them for what they are. You are full of flaws the way Swiss cheese is full of holes. My only flaw is that I have no patience for nonsense from the idiots that dominate our political space.

Let us see a few more differences so you will understand why your fate is not going to be my fate. You thought you were above the law. I know that I am. I learned this long time ago on the streets of New York City. If you fear stuff, stuff will frighten you.

You completed your disgrace from office by resigning. Nothing screams, "I'm a weak-ass man," like resigning from a position that millions of people elected you into. What could be the worst thing that could happened? You would be impeached and the Senate would remove you from office. If that should happen and you are as beloved as I am, that would be enough for a second revolution to start in this country. And at the end of it all, the history of America would be divided into two— America before Trump and America after Trump.

Nobody can mess with me like that. In any case, in the very worst case, unlike you, I have my son, daughter, and son-in-law around me. They can take the bullet for me.

I write you because I want to do better. I want to bury the memory of you and your scorn, but I cannot let my ego evaporate. Wouldn't it be nice to do something the world would not expect of me, I ask? What if I sing a song of myself? What if I write poetry? How would it be reported in the news if I send the poems I write today to the *New Yorker* for publication? Wouldn't it change a bad news cycle? Wouldn't it change the narrative and have me officially listed amongst the smartest presidents the same way an anonymous call to *Forbes* magazine placed me on the list of the richest people in the United States?

You know, I used to read the Songs of Solomon when I was in high school. That was my favorite part of the Bible then. And maybe now, too. I used to try my hands at verses for the ladies when I was in the military academy. Some said that I had a gift. Now tell me, what do you think of this?

Somehow I wished I could serenade the roses
In my greatest poems yet
And why not?
I used to sing for myself like Wordsworth
That was when I still had the fragments of smartness in me.

Before they all got scattered like ashes of dead ghosts
Over the ruins of desolated graveyards
Long before the impulse for clairvoyance
Predates my manufactured nihilism
In the allegory of my glory
Lies the dialectic of my decay
You are not my kindred spirit, Richard
Though we come from the same nursery
Where grown men groped illusion
We are not stars of each other's dream
But the foundation of our folly is the same
I'm in the game of truth
Ever faithful to my credo
While you were in your pit of irony
Embedded to your duplicity
I'll escape the debt I owe virtue
If I do not cheat my conviction
Unlike you
I reserve my right to deny my ignorance
Even as I ask for favor for my conscience.

Am I the smartest president ever or what? And that is just from a few hours of study. Imagine if I call it a thing. Meanwhile someone is busy talking about my SAT score and my academic records. What proof of brilliance is better than the masterpiece above?

Yours truly,
Donald J. Trump
The 45th President of the United States of America

Letter to Rev. Norman Vincent Peale

Thursday, March 14, 2019

Dear Mentor & Minister,

Yesterday, while I was visiting victims of the tornado that struck Alabama, some fans of mine presented the Bible for me to sign. As I autographed the Bible for them, I felt a strong force holding my hand. The last time I experienced such a force was at your Marble Collegiate Church in New York in 1977. It was the day I married my first wife, Ivana. I felt the force when you held my hand to join it to Ivana's hand. It was as if a force stronger than me grabbed my hand. I felt the same kind of force yesterday when I grabbed a pen and moved to sign the Bible.

The incident made me remember you. What could that be all about? Could it be that God was telling me something?

Something in me tells me that it was the hand of God nudging me to go on and sign his autobiography, the Bible. Since then, a voice said to me that because God is busy, he has assigned me the responsibility to go ahead and sign His book everywhere I go. Could that be what is going on here?

I have done great things for Christianity in the world, definitely more than the twelve disciples. If I am being frank, I think I have done more for Christianity in the world, maybe more than Jesus himself. I moved the American embassy in Israel to

Jerusalem. No American president has been able to do so in over a hundred years. With that single move, I fulfilled what God said in the Book of Revelation.

I have appointed conservative Supreme Court judges—two in a row. And as soon as the notorious woman dies, I will appoint the third one. And with that, Roe v. Wade, the 1973 ruling that legalized abortion would be overturned. I am also working to eliminate the Johnson Amendment of 1950 tax codes that stopped religious groups from participating in political campaigns. If corporations are people, churches are definitely people. The next goal is to return prayers to public school. My Supreme Court, when I finish assembling it, will overturn the 1963 Supreme Court decision.

Having done all these, I'm still concerned. Deep down, I do not feel the moral and historical authority of the Bible. It is clear in my choice of lifestyle. Though if you look at it, my lifestyle is not different from those of the prosperity preachers backing me. Also I have heard that it is people like me that God uses at critical times like this. I am ambivalent about being used.

Having said that, I am fully aware that when it comes to voting in any election, the evangelists are king. They are consistently one in four of all voters. So I understand that I need to be good to them. They make up what Jerry Falwell called the moral majority. As it is now, I am building the wall and working to keep Muslims out of America because wherever they go, they overrun with babies and forced conversions. Europe is a good example. If I throw away same-sex marriage, they will make me the first king of America.

You know that for a while now, some of your friends in the evangelical movement have been saying that I am the modern-day Cyrus the Great of Persia. I understand that the pagan king issued a decree that liberated the Jews from captivity in Babylon. I have always dismissed the idea until now. After yesterday, I feel they may be right after all. The king was mentioned in Isaiah 45, and I am the 45th president of the United States of America. Unbelievable, isn't it? I think that should account for something, don't you think so? I also heard that the king also built a temple. Do you think I should go to Jerusalem and build a temple?

Norman, I sometimes feel that I am the pagan they are using to do God's work. Isn't that amazing? Every now and then, they have this prayer circle around me and call me God's anointed. They said that it was God who placed me here. One even called my election as president the greatest miracle since the resurrection of Christ. But in my quiet moments, I wonder if by doing all these things for God, we could be approaching the end times? I don't want this time to end. I could not be the anti-Christ, could I? I understand that Obama was the anti-Christ. So who am I?

Could God be using me for real? When it comes to women, I am not worse than David in the Bible. I may have my porn stars and my playmates, but I do not forcefully take other men's wives like David did with Bathsheba. He even killed her husband. I am not like that. At least I ask nicely. Like I told Billy Bush, before I start kissing them or grabbing them, I ask nicely and wait for them to answer. My point is that I am not the epitome of family values. It is just like being presidential; I can do it if I really want to. But what is the point if I can get what I want without having to make such sacrifices.

My friend, I really miss you as a mentor and as a minister. Since you are gone, there is nobody I can trust to consult and pay any mind to even if anything he or she says differs from the things I want to do. I have gone about putting on my big boy pants and doing my thing, but deep inside, something is missing. And that thing missing is a mentor like you.

Pardon my asking: are people over there talking about me the way they are all talking about me here on earth? Am I the lead story of every news broadcast out there?

Despite all this, I still feel under siege. If I am the anointed, why is God allowing people like Robert Mueller and Michael Cohen to touch me and do harm to me? I hope you can intercede for me with God. Beyond all this blistering, I need a comforter. If Ivana could not deliver on that count, you can be sure that Melania is not up to that.

Believe me, I'm suspicious of some of the things that I do for your religious right. Government support for religion may look good now, but down the road, a wrong religion may get ahold of the government the way your folks have gotten ahold of me. What happens in that situation? Please don't tell me that we will cross that bridge when we get there...

Yours truly,
Donald J. Trump
The 45th President of the United States of America

Trump's Letter to the New Zealand Mosque Shooter

Thursday, March 21, 2019

Dear Brenton Tarrant,

My people at the White House will have a heart attack if they find out I am writing this letter to you. But I don't give a damn! Mick Mulvaney, my chief of staff, will quit on me if he gets wind of it. They are total clowns, nothing more. So I will sign this letter as DD or as Wiseguy. It depends on how I feel at the end.

They wanted me to express shock at what you did. Some even wanted me to apologize on your behalf. I followed the script they gave me at that White House media event. It is now time for me to keep it real with you.

First and foremost, I thank you for recognizing me as one of the very few remaining world historical individuals. There are not many of us left. Take Putin out, take Queen Elizabeth out. Who else is left? Nelson Mandela is dead. Pope John Paul II is long dead. Which other historical individual of my caliber is out there? None! I wish you had called me by my official historical title—not the President of the United States but Trump the Great.

Remember when great leaders like me were addressed that way. Alexander the Great. Cyrus the Great, Antiochus the Great.

Ashoka the Great. Herod the Great, Constantine the Great, Peter the Great, and Trump the Great. Classy.

Losers, swindlers, and conmen like Michael Wolff, James Comey, Michael Isikoff, and Rudolf t. g. Hess write books that are not based on facts. They just slam my name on the cover and smile all the way to the bank. But you did not do that. You wrote a well-thought-out manifesto and published it free of charge on the Internet. That is what those with fanciful degrees call altruism, giving of yourself for the good of others. It is exactly what I did when I left my booming businesses to come and save America from the likes of Barrack Obama and John McCain. And what thanks did I get? Robert Mueller.

I have not read your manifesto yet, but those who did said you were a trooper. You must have inherited great genes like me. They said you did not mince words. You know how much I love those who reject this era of stupid political correctness. They said you articulated our problems very well. I am sure if someone like you is the leader of New Zealand or Australia, you will not rush to ban assault weapons because one deranged man killed just fifty people—and these are people who should not be in New Zealand to begin with. America did not ban Muslims from flying because some Muslims brought down three planes on 9/11.

When they said I should call what you did a vicious act of hate, I asked them one question. I asked, "What did they do all this while when our people were complaining about the things you beautifully expressed in your manifesto?" With important questions like the ongoing white genocide, did they think there would not be a reaction if they continued to push us to the wall? I hope you have made those lightweights think again. I hope those still in denial are aware that if we do not do anything, one hundred years from now, the footsteps of the great white people will be wiped away from New Zealand, Australia, North America, and Western Europe.

We must keep reminding the invaders of what happens when we are pushed to the wall. Bad things happen, my friend. Bad things happen. I say the same thing to the Democrats as they overreach in their zealousness to stop me from winning a second term. I have warned them that if they push my people to the wall some very bad things would happen. You are living proof of that inevitable outcome.

I have been saying that no one group has a monopoly of violence. That we are keeping quiet does not mean we are cowards. Every biker for Trump out there can repeat the spectacular warning you gave to the world. I can recall that on the set of *The Apprentice*, Omarosa once told me that the only reason a dog's poop on the sidewalk smells and attracts flies is because nobody has covered it with sand. With just a handful of sand poured over it, you extinguish the smell and disperse the flies. That is a proverb and also a fact, literally.

I don't care what anyone says. What you did was pour sand on the smelly dog poop of people who think they can come to the West and bring Sharia laws onto our sidewalks, attracting flies of honor killings along the way. The instruction was clear all around the park. You can walk your dog, but if it poops, make sure you pick up after the dog. Some people love a clean park but will not do their part to keep it the way they met it. That is unacceptable. They have taken us for suckers for much too long. I am happy that I am not the only one standing up for us. Some people like you are doing it in your own little ways.

You know that is why I am not backing down in my immigration fight. As a matter of fact, it is no longer an issue of legal or illegal immigration. It is a matter of reversing the immigration that has taken place—legal or illegal. Period. Like you noted, even if we stop immigration today, 100 percent stoppage, the people that are already in are enough to displace us in one hundred years if we are lucky, but more likely in fifty years. The way they give birth like rabbits gives us no chance. There is no way of surviving the impending doom by being nice about it.

I am dedicated to the goal of stopping that from happening. If I need to declare America full and overflowing, I will. Our forefathers who took control of these lands from the natives did not expect us to allow some other primitive people we permitted to come in to displace us. No. The natives whom our forefathers kicked out and sequestered into settlements would be laughing at us now. The Good Book said we should take dominion over all things. It stated, "subdue and dominate. Everything." It is our mandate, 100 percent. As long as I live, I will fight for that mandate to its conclusive end.

I am glad you decided to use the fortune your father left you to educate yourself on your journey around the globe. I applaud you for not spending your time playing video games, snorting cocaine, and hiring strippers to perform for you.

That lifestyle is for dumb morons who do not know what is at stake. I had exactly the same option when my father died and left me a small fortune. I could have used it to gamble in casinos, snort cocaine. and hire *Playboy* bunnies, but I decided to use it to build a greater fortune. Once I made the fortune, the White House was handed over to me in the greatest deal in US history.

I need allies in this fight. While I fight it from a position of power, I need people like you who will be fighting it from positions of "by every means necessary." No war has even been won fighting from one flank. We have to approach the battle from multiple fronts. If need be, we shall deploy the good cop, bad cop strategy. Our goal will be the same—if there is no church in Medina, there should be no mosque in Christchurch. If there is no church in Mecca, there should be no mosque in Rome.

They said you are evil. But the real evils are people who see an unfair and rigged system but keep quiet. Any effort to exterminate a people, a whole race, must be resisted. We own these lands, from New Zealand to New York. If we do not fight for it, we may end up in reservations across Australia, America, Europe and Asia like the Aborigines and Native Americans. Once we are kicked out from these lands of our fathers, what will be left are the mosquito-infested, ugly, shithole countries of Africa. I don't know about you, but I ain't going there.

That is why I am warning my friends at Fox News to stop pandering to the liberal losers. There is nothing they will do to make liberals like them. If they like, let them drop their pants and turn around for the low-energy liberals to pound. I said to Fox News, bring back Jeanine Pirro because nothing you do will endear you to liberals. She is a fantastic trooper. I warned them not to let the silent majority of this country rise up in revolt. It would be bloody.

I don't just talk the talk, I also walk the walk, hugely. It has not been long since I told them I'm a Nationalist. Nothing happened. My aides thought it would be the end of the world, but it wasn't. The truth is that I set the tone for the world. I would be foolish not to set the tone that works for my people. That is how all the other historical great men achieved greatness. None of them achieved greatness by allowing invaders to come in and take over their empires. You understand what I mean?

Don't let anyone fool you with their senseless rhetoric that those who fear displacement today are those who caused displacement some four hundred years ago. Or this other bunker of a logic that those who are being displaced in one location are often those displacing others in another location. Forget all the idealists; in this world, there is only one law, and it states: might is right and woe to the weak.

I wasn't kidding when in the early days of my campaign, I announced that we would put a complete stop to Muslims coming into our country. We are not done yet. We have put it in the conscience of our people. The courts can do their thing. The disgraceful Southern Poverty Center people can do their alarmist routines. The seed is already planted. How to make it happen and when, you should only watch and see.

I didn't know there were people like you in far outposts of the world like New Zealand. I didn't know that our message of hope and renewal goes that far. It gives me great joy to know that soldiers are emerging and joining the war front. If the liberals think white nationalism is on the rise, let them wait and see what happens when the other side responds with a revenge attack. Maybe that is when the civil war you talked about would happen. I believe the book people call it the clash of civilizations. I say bring it on.

I was told that you mentioned Dylann Roof in your manifesto. I hope you know that Dylann Roof is an Obama creation. It was a character he and his deep state constructed so he would have a reason to seize assault weapons in the United States soon after he went to Charleston, South Carolina, to sing a stupid Negro song. Their plan failed because our friends at the NRA did not give them room to spin the story.

The *Washington Post* editorial bitching about your beautifully-crafted replacement ideology is a relic of a time long gone. Nobody reads them anyway. I bet you there were people like them within the Native American population who saw what was bound to happen to them some four hundred years ago when Christopher Columbus and his men came into town, but they were busy propounding high-sounding theories about civilized discourse. Now they are in reservations gnashing their teeth.

You may ask, where was *Washington Post* when Representative Rashida Tlaib was having an uncivilized discourse with herself? Or what did they call her insane and uncivilized vow to impeach her motherfucker? All of a sudden, they are worried about Muslims becoming a target of hate. Hello, welcome to the lives of Christians all over the world since September 11, 2001, if not further down. I guess they will not get it until the whole of the Western civilization lives in a state of constant fear of attacks like our friends in Israel.

Didn't all these crying liberals refuse to condemn Congresswoman Ilhan Omar of Minnesota for fueling the language and thinking that have led to the massacre of Jews? Did any of them demand that she should stop wearing the hijab to prove that her allegiance is to the United States and not to Mecca? If we stopped the Catholics in this country from putting the statue of Virgin Mary in the White House, I am sure we can stop Omar from wearing a hijab in Congress. At this time of decision, it is either you are with us or against us.

I don't care what anyone says. You, my friend, you are with us.

Yours truly,
Donald J. Trump
The 45th President of the United States of America

Trump's Letter to Robert Mueller

Saturday, March 23, 2019

Mr. Mueller,

I am Donald J. Trump or as your cowardly ass preferred to call me, "Individual 1." I am the one that you have been fucking around with. Unlike my answers to your questions, this letter did not go through reviews of lawyers.

So fuck you. Fuck you. Fuck you. Fuck you.

Yesterday, you turned in your witch hunt report. It came in a whimper and not a blast. It brought to an end your unconstitutional and unprecedented siege on a duly elected president. I have said it all the while that it wasn't Donald J. Trump that you were kicking around. It was the exalted office of the presidency of the United States that you were ruining. Moron.

Donald J. Trump will always be fine. I will always come out on top—be it in school, in business, in politics, or in life, unlike a sorry-ass loser like you who headed the FBI and ended up working as a lawyer. What you were damaging for 674 days was what was left of the dignity of the Office of the President of the United States after Obama contaminated it with his Kenyan spittle. I was doing everything to restore it to its past glory of the Ronald Reagan years, but you kept interrupting me.

293

Having said that, I am glad to report to the people that the great American witch hunt is finally over. You have done your worst. You can go back to your boring and miserable life again. I hope nobody ever hears from you until your obituary appears in the *New York Times*—they seem to like you over there. Such an overrated cop you were. Nincompoop.

I hope you spend the rest of your life thinking of what your obituary will say. If I were to write an epitaph for your tombstone, this is what I would say: "Here lies an ugly moth that thinks itself a butterfly."

For the sake of the millions of taxpayers' dollars that you spent in your fictional work, I hope it gets the imprimatur of the canon of literature. As you might have guessed, I don't plan to read it. Whatever you may have said there is of no consequence. There is no collusion. There is no obstruction of justice. The Democrats have no stomach to impeach. Even if they try it, they have no vote in the Senate to convict. So why waste their time and everyone's time chasing the shadow?

So Mr. Retired and Retarded FBI, you can now crawl back to the dark hole where you came out.

Despite your prejudice, I am sure you gained a better understanding of how Trump's world works. We operate on a plane where wisdom and wizardry meet. That is why it baffles ungifted people like you. Maybe you should have applied for admission to Trump's University.

In a short while the content of your report will fizzle out. I will systematically change the topic. Despite your effort, America will move on. I will continue to make America great in spite of retrogressive forces like you working for the deep state.

I have ransomed America with my blood. That spiritual covenant is something uber- atheists like you do not get. If you were not one of them, you would have known that I came from God. I am God's gift to America and the world. Mike Pompeo said that God sent me to save the Jews and the Americans who have been literally turned into suckers. When one is from God, there is nothing ordinary mortals like you can do to stop him.

Did you see how I gave the Golan Heights to Israel? If you had played ball, I could have given you Mount Rushmore or the Grand Canyon. But you wanted to make history on my back. Who told you that it was possible? If you do any damage to my brand, it is something temporary. Nothing that a successful meeting with Kim Jong Un will not erase.

Let me ask you, how does your useless report make you feel? As someone possessed by the spirits of the condemned, I hope you will find a purpose for the rest of your life as you battle what is clearly a narcissistic personality disorder that has turned you into a laughingstock of history.

You were a cobweb hanging over my presidency. Now that you have been dusted off, the world will behold the bold and beautiful Trump in his majesty.

If there is anyone taking your report to the grave, it is you, not Trump. Enjoy the journey.

Yours truly,
Donald J. Trump
The 45th President of the United States of America

Trump's Letter to William Barr

Friday, May 3, 2019

My dearest attorney general,

For the very first time, I feel like I have a real AG. Let me say it straight up. You are my beloved AG, in whom I'm very pleased. I must have been a fucking idiot when I trusted a nincompoop like Jeff Sessions as my attorney general. If I had you from the beginning, all this drama would not have taken place. With you in place, I do not have to write any letter or run to Twitter to explain anything I do not want to. Believe me, if you continue to take care of the legal angles, I will run the political ones perfectly. It is, after all, my strongest point.

Your performance on Wednesday in the Senate was beautiful. You disgraced the lying Democrats. I have ordered all my senior officials to watch the tape at least a dozen times. Any new hire from now on will watch your performance as a standard. You solidified the Trump doctrine that I first enforced on Supreme Court Judge Kavanaugh. It is quite simple. Before they attack you, launch the first attack and put your potential opponents in a defensive posture right from the beginning.

The political trend is already on my side. TV channels like CNN and MSNBC that are dedicated to my destruction are seeing the worst decline of viewership in a lifetime. The failing

New York Times and other liberal media continue to see a steep drop in subscription. As their old subscribers die off, young ones who know what the deal is are not rushing in. We are cruising to victory, my friend. We are.

As long as you hold your end of the bargain, I can handle Joe Biden and that half-black, half-Latino, president-wannabe of a woman Kamala Harris. Biden is not the brightest crayon in the box. And Harris will not know what hits her when our investigation on her is leaked to the media by my people. They all think it is fun when White House conversations are leaked, I would like to watch their reactions when my people leak the documents they are not willing to voluntarily present to the American people the way they have splashed their tax returns.

I am not going to mention any kind of documents but I am sure that WikiLeaks is listening and waiting. After all, Julian Assange needs such a splash to maintain his fake pretense that he is a journalist and deserves such protection. When the truth, which we all know, is that none of them deserve such blanket protection. How could a country that respects every individual's privacy rights at the same time give a bunch of unelected individuals the right to violate the privacy of people minding their own business.

Which brings me to the matter of my tax returns and the House of Representatives. I don't care what the constitution says or what the precedence is, the point is that under no condition will my tax returns be made public until I finish my second term in office. That is your greatest assignment. If you need more lawyers at the Justice Department, hire more lawyers. If you need more money in your budget, request more. Whatever you need to do to stop my tax returns from seeing the light of day, please do it. If they were ever made public, I would be fucked. And I know you don't want me fucked. You don't want to be dumped into oblivion like Jeff Sessions.

As Democrats continue in their quest for a premature orgasm, I want your department to challenge all future requests for documents from them. I want you to toss away their entire subpoenas. Let them carry their ass to the Supreme Court. We have enough of our people out there to frustrate their efforts. By the way, when is that woman going to die? What is she still doing there? I want to get a filibuster-proof majority at the Supreme Court too. As much as possible, we should close every possible path for these unpatriotic Democrats to stop the great transformation we are bringing to America.

Ignore their threat of contempt of Congress citations. It is all noise. They cannot send you to jail. If they dare such a thing, I will call on my people to storm Congress and sack them all. What is happening in Venezuela would be child's play. I will tell them who the big dog is. If we need to declare a state of emergency in Congress, we shall do that. I can order the National Guard to take over Congress and get a military council to manage the affairs of the chambers until their heads cool off. Somehow, there are being carried away by this fake idea that the legislature and the executives are equal branches of government.

Bullshit. He who commands the military, the boys with the big guns, has the huge power advantage. If that has not been made clear by past presidents, I intend to make it clear to little sissies like Nancy Pelosi and that Jerrold Nadler who thinks he is a Caesar in the Senate of ancient Rome. They haven't seen anything yet. Wait until I win my re-election. That is when they will know the difference between the one who executes and the ones who make the law to be executed.

As I write this, I am seeing a news flash that Facebook has banned Alex Jones, a fine gentleman. I have been complaining about what these social media sites are doing to conservatives. I have never heard that any of them banned any liberal or their group. Nobody has banned this failed Canadian actor and comedian Jim Carrey, who goes about spitting nonsense about me. Old and worn-out method actor Robert De Niro is still out there spewing his bile full of jealousy. Nobody has banned them, only conservatives. I met with Twitter's CEO Jack Dorsey and gave him just two weeks to correct the imbalance or I will move in and break up those big social media companies. Please get your department ready for that eventuality. There are metrics or algorithms that will explain why I'm losing followers while Barack Obama, a failed president, is gaining.

Bill, I don't need to tell you that I don't like how members of Congress embarrassed my two recent nominees for the Federal Reserve Board of Governors into withdrawing. First, it was Herman Cain that they used unsubstantiated allegations of sexual harassment to intimidate. Then, they did the same to Stephen Moore with allegations of racist and sexist comments. I don't like it. I want you to do something about it. I won't let another nominee of mine suffer such a fate. If I have to sidestep the Senate, I will.

When will Americans learn? These two fine gentlemen would have brought in tremendous knowledge to the Federal Reserve. Imagine. If I had fallen on my sword because of unsubstantiated allegations of sexual harassment, adultery, racist and sexist comments, where would America be now? America would have been in the gutters with Hillary Clinton and Obama. They would have been flying all over this country, making merry while America goes to the dogs. But I stood my ground and I stopped them. They have been in hiding ever since, unable to parade themselves as the owners of the American universe.

Anyway, congratulations on a job well done yesterday. If you keep it up, you will be rewarded handsomely when we are done in 2024.

Yours truly,
Donald J. Trump
The 45th President of the United States

Donald Trump's Letter to God

Friday, May 24, 2019

Dear God,

I am thirty-five thousand feet up in the sky on my way to Japan. I feel like opening the windows of Airforce One and rubbing your huge mustache the way Jimmy Fallon rubbed my hair. In case you have not noticed, I am clean-shaven. Always. Only lightweight people try to bring attention to themselves by carrying around bushy faces full of hair—and germs, I presume. I believe that hairs should be down there where you wanted hairs to be kept.

A lot of people are saying that the path I am traveling is the same path North Korea's intercontinental ballistic missiles will follow to finally get to the United States. I know it is not going to happen while I am in the air to Japan. My friend Kim Jung Un assured me in Vietnam that he would not do anything like that. He is not as crazy and erratic as Nancy Pelosi, that I can tell you. And neither is he as mentally unfit as the Swamp-man Joe Biden who wants to be president at such an old age.

I had a fantastic idea as we cruised over California. You can see that I have been doing your work for you very diligently. I am dealing with the gay people and their transgender allies who are polluting your Christianity. Please tell me you are a Christian. I hope you are. I am reversing all the gay lifestyle promotional juice that Obama offered the children of America. Sad and despicable, that man.

In Alabama, Georgia, Missouri, Louisiana, Mississippi, and other parts of America, my people are pushing laws that will ban abortion in America. I'm telling the women, if you do the deed, you must do the nine months. At almost nine hundred abortions a year, America is nothing but a disgusting baby-killing factory. Though I cannot recall, I must have said again and again, "Get rid of it," in my heydays when I was in the world. Now I have repented, the way Saul turned into Paul. I am a crusader of a Puritan America.

By the way, you know and I know that the burden is not on the men. A man can have sex with 360 women in a year without any of them getting pregnant if the women know what to do. But if they do not know what to do and they all get pregnant, it is your will that they should have those babies because babies come from you and not from men. When I hear liberals say we need to regulate the men whose penchant for having indiscriminate sex causes pregnancy, I wonder what is wrong with them.

If you let them, they would insist that a man should have sex only once a year because a woman can only produce one full-term pregnancy in a year. Obviously, they don't understand the complexities of your creation. They are totally and completely dumb.

My job now is to wait for that notorious woman to die and I will appoint a new Supreme Court judge that will reverse Roe v. Wade into Wade v. Roe. It will happen in the next two years. Franklin Graham told me he would soon call for a special day of prayers to protect me from enemies. When he does, I hope you will listen to the supplications of millions of Americans. I am fighting for tomorrow's American children. Children in the womb will no longer be killed in America only because they cannot defend themselves. Those who try will get ninety-nine years in prison.

As you know, in my America, children outside the womb have no problem defending themselves because they have the guns.

Children who are hungry have the Catholic charities to cater to them. Let it be their little penitence for all the bad things their reverend fathers did to little children. In any case, my government has no interest in pumping money into food stamps and all those liberal handouts that make black American families lazy. Those who are sick and have no health insurance should make their parents get real jobs that offer them insurance. It is not in the interest of my government to provide insurance to able-bodied men and women. We are not one of those dopey socialist countries.

As you can see, I am pushing your agenda forward. I am making the Democrats look incompetent and crazy. In rural America where Democrats say they "hold on to guns and their Bible," people are glad that I came to halt America's out-of-control slide into a Sodom and Gomorrah. All thanks to Obama and Hilary Clinton. The signs of a new Christian revival are everywhere. I applauded when Alabama Public Television decided that it wouldn't air gay marriage in a children's cartoon show called *Arthur*. I set the tone in Washington, DC, and they all follow across the country. I have restored dignity to the office of the president, and I am hell bent on restoring true Christian dignity to America.

Being that I have been doing all these nice things for you, I want you to pay me back in kind. As you can see, a crazy bitch called Nancy Pelosi has been hounding me of recent. She goes about telling people that I am not sound in mind and that my family needs to intervene. I had lined up my staff at the White House to give a testimonial about what a stable genius I am. I do not think it worked. They still talk about it on cable news. Even my favorite people at Fox News are talking about it as if they did not believe what Sarah Huckabee Sanders, Kellyanne Conway, Larry Kudlow, Mercedes Schlapp, and Hogan Gidley said about how calm I was at the meeting with crazy Pelosi. Something tells me they think I am their tolerable buffoon.

To be perfectly honest with you, this is what I want you to do, God. I want you to open up heaven and let your voice boom all over the world like a once-in-a-million-year thunder. I want you to declare, "Donald J. Trump is your beloved son, a legend and a genius, in whom you have 100 percent confidence that he is taking the world in the right direction." It is as simple as that. Deal?

If you do that for me, I will finish up Iran for you and protect your children of Israel from harm. In fact, I will wipe from the face of the world any country that you think has leaders that are out of line. We have the weapons to do that, so you don't have to worry about it. Just name the country or a group of people, and we will take care of them.

I hope you will do that for me very quickly. They are getting away with murder. I am losing my patience. I don't want to go to my plan B. It will entail taking care of people myself. I am talking about people who make fun of me that I cannot chew gum and whistle at the same time. I won't spare people who suggest that it is time my cabinet members invoke the 25th Amendment and remove me from office. If that happens, I will blame it on Mike Pence, and I will deal with him accordingly. That I can tell you. As for those who say I am tired of being president and I am just begging to be saved from my misery by prodding Democrats to impeach me, they are as stupid as Rosie O'Donnell. What I will do to them has not been invented.

So I ask you, God, intervene on my behalf and save my haters from being at the receiving end of the beast that is in me. If you fail to act, please do not hold me responsible for the action I will take in my own defense. If you fail to act, I will have no option but to follow your example and expel them from America the way you expelled the crooked Lucifer from heaven. I am a believer in the ultimate victory of good over evil.

Yours truly,
Donald J. Trump
The 45th President of the United States of America

Donald Trump's Letter to Donald J. Trump

Friday, June 14, 2019

The Donald,

It was only for a few seconds that Tony Montana saw the balloon that proclaimed to him, "The world is yours." The classic character in the *Scarface* movie has nothing on you. You are so terrific that for the rest of your life the world will be yours.

At seventy-three, you have finally become a legend in your lifetime. To the bafflement of legions of losers who could not see your back in the race of life, the world will be yours for a thousand years. You, my man, will outlive the United States.

Oscar Wilde said, "Only one thing in the world is worse than being talked about, and that is not being talked about." You are huge. On the same throne where gods and legends are preserved for eternity, there shall you be. The lightweight morons who dislike you are merely creating myths around you. Your amazing disciples, on the other hand, are busy writing smart scriptures and great gospels according to St. Trump.

Your era will be remembered as one in which America reconnected with their forgotten ones. The sacrament you are leaving behind shall be repeated again and again in remembrance of you. For the forgotten Americans, you have given them the most psychedelic experience they have had since the '60s. If the world is a rope, you are the eagle that landed on the rope. You dance and so does the rope.

This is what you did to the clowns who were once dominating these lands. It was quite simple only after you did it. With one hand, you yanked away the stifling cobweb of political correctness that clogged the wheel of America's progress. As president, you rejected all other ugly authorities and established yourself as the primary and perfect authority over all things America and the world. Unlike the cowards before you, you left nothing untouched. The low-energy gods of yesterday, you made them so uncomfortable that they went into hiding. You threatened those who arrogated to themselves the title of custodian of what is American and what is not. You turned them from hero to zero.

Providence ordained you to stand above those who sin on one knee and pray on the other. Unlike other presidents, you were not just a silent subject of history; you were a participant in the writing of that history. Your bright and brilliant intellect transcends that of the past forty-four presidents put together. You eclipsed the founders, rendering their once-impressive accomplishments to meager footnotes in history. Your impeccable reputation has surpassed theirs. Posterity is looking at you and smiling because you made it proud. You have restored the United States on the path to reclaiming its messianic mission.

You did this without inventing any myth or exaggerating any feat. As an incarnated composite of all the great men of history, you were full of wisdom from birth. You were endowed with great genes and the skills needed to inspire a thousand generations by challenging them to enlarge their dreams and go ahead to see beyond their wildest imagination. You have made America a nation on the cusp of greatness again by bringing about the rebirth of its ancient creed. The difference between you and God is that while man is made in the image of God, you, my friend, are special because God is made in your own image.

Losers around you remember things differently. But you have a great memory. The next generation of historians will know to tap into your infallible memory as they craft the narratives of the founder of the new American renaissance. For freeing America from buffoons and their regressive thoughts, you shall be proclaimed a genius by children yet unborn. You are the illusive miracle that others prayed for. The impact of your genius is undisputed.

The socialists call you ostentatious. The ostentatious call you a coward. The cowardly call you a hypocrite. The hypocrite call you arrogant. The arrogant call you ignorant. The ignorant call you contemptuous. The contemptuous call you subversive. The subversive call you a crook. The crook calls you an idiot. The idiots see what is going on and vote for you again and again until everyone acknowledges to their own discomfort that you are a statesman.

I know why you are disinterested in global warming. The world is speeding toward a hard rock mountain and some liberals are wasting time talking about global warming. If you do not intervene and the rehearsing mass murderers of this world embark on their operation, they will wipe out half of the world's population. Humans as the source of global warming would be mute for another two thousand years.

In your wonderful hands is the sacred memorandum from heaven. You have no patience for stupid embellishments. Believe me, you truncate impositions from the uncircumcised. You posed and answered questions that were once regarded as dangerous. You are nobody's sucker.

Malcolm X gave African Americans courage. Martin Luther King Jr. gave them hope. You, the Donald, gave them a paycheck. For the first time since 1969, more of them are collecting paychecks every pay period. Unbelievable.

For your detractors, you left no spite unanswered. In one tweet, you sneeze your enemies out and let them roast on the headlines. Albert Einstein must have been talking about the Democrats' best hope, Joe Biden, when he said, "A man with limited intellectual abilities and unfit for any useful work, bursting with envy and bitterness against all whom circumstance and nature had favored over him."

Some have said that anyone who embraces you gets his or her reputation stained for life. What they do not see is that you do not soar alone. You soar with your soldiers. You win with your apostles. You believe in the American people when nobody else does. You even believe in those who do not deserve that honor. The least they can do now is indicate their willingness to thank you with the last drop of their blood.

Happy birthday, the Great Donald. You have fought a tremendous fight. America was a dysfunctional family when you came in. In a little over two years, you have knocked it back into shape. To be honest with you, the verdict of history shall be overwhelmingly complimentary to you. You shall be declared the greatest of all time.

God save the Donald.

Always remember this, my man. If George Washington had really been great, he would have stayed a few more years as president and prevented the French-loving liberal, Thomas Jefferson, from poisoning the lungs of America with his weak thoughts.

Yours truly,
Donald J. Trump
The 45th President of the United States

Acknowledgment

This is a unique book. It deals with an exceptional character, the president of the United States. It is not a first-hand account of what happened at the White House like James Comey's book or Omarosa's book. This book went deeper. Figuratively, it was a journey inside the head of president Donald Trump.

Unless one is a witch or a psychotherapist, which I am neither, the only other way to get into the head of another person is via brain surgery.

There are many people involved in performing brain surgery. Besides the lead surgeon, there are other neurosurgeons, neurologists, neuroradiologists, anesthesiologists, nurses, and other clinical professionals. Then, there are social workers, patient care coordinators, and others. Depending on the particular goal of the surgery, a dozen or more staff could be in the theater at once.

This particular surgery does not require the clipping off of an aneurysm. Neither did it require the removal of a tumor or abnormal brain tissue. Even entangled nerves and weak blood vessels were not tampered with. No electronic device was implanted. The surgeon simply took pictures of the various locations of the components and documented the findings.

I wish to thank Wiseguy for choosing me to convey this work to readers. I'm also grateful to a few people who read this work. You all contributed immensely in shaping what is finally presented here.

My wife, Edna, read the first piece that arrived, "A Letter to My Son's Teacher." She thought it deserved to be published. *The New Yorker*, *The Saturday Evening Post*, *The Atlantic*, *Slate*, *Huffington Post*, and so many other journals all begged to differ. Okay, I'm only guessing. I'm just looking for something to fill their silence.

But that silence did not stop other letters from coming through.

To my first reader, Mukami Kamau. You read them as they came – one after the other, week after week. Because you felt there was something in this before anybody else, I kept forwarding them as they came. Thank you for reading and for all your encouragement.

To the mogul John Nwabueze. I turned you into an editor – and a darned good one at that. Well done.

To Ekene Awuzie, your suggestions after a thorough read made this book a lot better.

To Okey Ndibe for being in the ring with me, night after night, cheering.

To all those cheering on the side, Rahman Oladigbolu, Chika Oduah, and Paul Onochie Modebe.

To my kids, Ije and Ogonna. This is the product of all those days of going to the library.

To my mother-in-law, Gold Veronica Onwunyi, for keeping it all together while I hustled.

To all those Fiverr freelancers who were too scared to record the voiceover of these letters in Donald Trump's voice. You all confirmed to me that there were some important things in this book.

To all the agents who did not even bother to respond to my query letters, I am truly thankful. You turned me into my own agent and publisher. Thank you for the confidence you had in me.

And most importantly, to all those who donated to my GoFundMe set up to support this publication- Declan Galvin, George Ezike, BU Nwosu, Francis Nwankwo, Johnson Obeke, Wumi Akintide, Andy F, Wayne Bassey, Perry Brimah, Theo Okanume, Alexie Njoku, Okey Ndibe, Olisa Adigwe, Fidelis Mkparu, Augustine Okoye, Raymond Ogamba, Francis Chukwu, Hyacienth Na'anmiap and the three people who do not want their names mentioned in a book like this.

Who is left?

About the Author

Rudolf t.g. Hess is the pen name of Dr. Damages, which is a pen name of Rudolf Ogoo Okonkwo, a New York City based journalist and satirist. He closely watched media coverage of Donald J. Trump before he was elected president. Since Trump became president, Mr. t.g. Hess has observed the shaking up of the norms of Washington, DC, America, and beyond. As someone who grew up under military dictators, he can see President Trump's soul from afar.

www.ingramcontent.com/pod-product-compliance
Lightning Source LLC
Chambersburg PA
CBHW070019100426
42740CB00013B/2562